To
Promote
Peace

To Promote Peace

U.S. Foreign Policy in the Mid-1980s

Dennis L. Bark, editor

Foreword by W. Glenn Campbell

Hoover Institution Press

Stanford University, Stanford, California

Hoover Press Publication 294
Copyright 1984 by the Board of Trustees of the
  Leland Stanford Junior University
First printing, 1984
Manufactured in the United States of America
88 87 86 85 84   9 8 7 6 5 4 3 2 1

Library of Congress Cataloging in Publication Data
Main entry under title:

To promote peace.

  (Hoover Press Publication; 294)
  1. United States—Foreign relations—1981-
Addresses, essays, lectures. 2. Peace—Addresses, essays,
lectures. I. Bark, Dennis L. II. Title.
JX1417.P73 1984   327.73   83-26394
ISBN 0-8179-7941-7

Design by P. Kelley Baker

Contents

‾‾Foreword‾‾‾‾‾‾‾‾‾‾‾‾‾‾‾‾‾

The title of this book is taken from Herbert Hoover's speech dedicating the Tower building of the Hoover Institution in June 1941. This Foreword, therefore, appropriately begins with a historical note. In the late 1970s, as the United States was approaching the first year of a new decade, it was clear that the year 1980 would be of major importance to the people of the United States. It would be a national election year, and it would mark the beginning of a new decade that would confront the United States with numerous critical domestic and foreign policy problems.

The publication in early 1980 of *The United States in the 1980s* was a direct reflection of this concern. That volume contained 29 essays on domestic and foreign policy problems written by scholars from throughout the United States and abroad. The book drew on the expertise and analytical abilities of individuals on the staff of the Hoover Institution and of scholars outside the Hoover Institution.

In the Foreword written for that volume, I emphasized the following concern:

> As the United States enters the 1980s amid political fragmentation, it is nonetheless clear that confidence can be restored; that a consensus in Congress can and must be rebuilt; that a rediscovery

of a sense of purpose can be achieved; and that there does exist
the national will required to deal effectively with the problems
that confront the country domestically and internationally.

I believe that events since the early 1980s have proved these expectations correct. At the same time one may not enjoy the luxury of taking solace in being right, for much work remains to be done. It was
from this viewpoint that the individual who coordinated The 1980s
Project, of which *The United States in the 1980s* was one result, focused
his attention on the development of foreign affairs during the four
years following that volume's release. As national security and foreign
policy unfolded between 1980 and 1983, it became evident that a measure of the significance of changing foreign relations for the United
States could be found in some of the ideas contained in the essays in
The United States in the 1980s. Because of this development, the coordinator of The 1980s Project concluded that a related undertaking,
four years later, would have considerable merit. That individual, Senior
Fellow Dennis L. Bark, is the editor of this volume.

After lengthy discussion with their colleagues, Dr. Bark, together
with Senior Fellow John H. Moore, concluded that two volumes separately addressing major issues of domestic and foreign policy should be
published in 1984. It would be, once again, a national election year.
Early publication of the essays in these volumes would contribute to
discussion of domestic and foreign policy issues of concern to the
American electorate, especially if both volumes appeared simultaneously and were published by the same press.

Both scholars recognized that the expertise possessed by the individuals associated with the Hoover Institution was extensive, that
many of these individuals enjoyed broad experience in public policy
analysis, and that their views should be presented to the public in a
clear and thoughtful manner. Thus, they have been guided by three
principal considerations. First, two volumes dealing separately with domestic and foreign affairs would appear as companions to one another.
Second, the essays should appeal to the concerned citizen as well as to
the expert; therefore, they must be written in a lucid rather than intellectually turgid style. Third, both editors would draw extensively on
the talents and abilities of the distinguished scholars of the Hoover
Institution and produce two volumes written and edited, for the first
time in the Institution's history, solely by individuals associated with
the Institution Herbert Hoover founded in 1919. The result is *To Promote Peace*, edited by Dennis L. Bark, and *To Promote Prosperity*, edited
by John H. Moore.

As I wrote four years ago in the Foreword to *The United States in the 1980s*, it is imperative to recognize "that the major problems of the coming decade are interrelated, that no problem can be resolved in isolation, and that different perspectives can contribute to a clearer and more balanced understanding of problems that are often viewed as separate from one another." Thus, the major purpose of this volume is to give its distinguished authors the opportunity to express their ideas, their concerns, their hopes, and their expectations as these relate to some of the critical problems facing the United States in this decade. The essays are designed to be challenging, and they are not written with the expectation that readers will necessarily agree with the authors. On the contrary, as Herbert Hoover strongly believed, the only enduring path to peace is to study and learn from "human experience" and for mankind to take inspiration from "human idealism." If this volume can foster that hope, it will serve a purpose of which the founder of the Hoover Institution would be proud. If these essays can stimulate the imagination and the spirit of the reader, the volume will be a success.

W. Glenn Campbell
Director

Hoover Institution
Stanford University

Acknowledgments

Without the assistance of a number of individuals on the staff of the Hoover Institution, this book would never have been produced. Phyllis Cairns and David Fleenor, who direct the operation of the Hoover Institution Press as publications manager and director of marketing, respectively, devoted their attention and expertise to the creation of this book. Ann Covey pursued the details of timetable and correspondence with great care, and Diane McCubbin lent her abilities to the promotion of this volume.

Contributors

Dennis L. Bark is a Senior Fellow of the Hoover Institution and received his Ph.D. degree at the Free University of Berlin. He is the author of two books concerning Berlin and Germany and of articles analyzing relationships between Western Europe and the United States.

Arnold Beichman, a founding member of the Consortium for the Study of Intelligence, is a political scientist who has written extensively on problems of intelligence. He is the author of *The 'Other' State Department* and *Nine Lies About America* and coauthor with Mikhail Bernstam of *Andropov, New Challenge to the West*. In 1982–83, he was a Visiting Scholar at the Hoover Institution.

Visiting Scholar **Alain Besançon,** Professor of History at l'Ecole des Hautes Etudes en Sciences Sociales in Paris, is a historian of Russia and of the history of ideas, with special interests in fields such as education, theology, and psychoanalysis. His books include *Education et société en Russie dans le second tiers du XIXᵉ siècle*, *Les Origines intellectuelles du Léninisme*, *The Rise of the Gulag*, and *The Soviet Syndrome*.

Robert Conquest is a Senior Research Fellow and Scholar-Curator of the Russian and East European Collection at the Hoover Institution. He is the author of numerous books on Soviet and international affairs, including *The Great Terror*, *Power and Policy in the USSR*, and *V I Lenin*.

The research interests of Senior Fellow **Gerald A. Dorfman** include British and West European politics. He is the author of *British Trade Unionism Against the Trades Union Congress*, *Trade Unionism in British Politics Since 1968*, and *Wage Politics in Britain, 1945–1967* and co-editor of *Soldiers in Politics*. He is also cofounder and publisher of two scholarly journals, *Politics and Society* and *Political Methodology*.

Senior Fellow **Milorad M. Drachkovitch** has been affiliated with the Hoover Institution since 1961. A political historian, he has written, coauthored, and edited (in English and French) many books dealing with Leninism, communist theory and practice, and the problems of Eastern Europe.

Peter J. Duignan is a Senior Fellow, Lillick Curator, and Coordinator of International Studies at the Hoover Institution. His research interests cover Africa and the Middle East, international affairs, Hispanics in the United States, and the Western alliance. He is the author/editor of over thirty books, including *Africa South of the Sahara*, *North Africa and the Middle East*, and *Why South Africa Will Survive*.

Senior Fellow **L. H. Gann** holds a doctorate from the University of Oxford and is the author, coauthor, or co-editor of 23 published works on European colonialism in Africa, African history, and related themes. He has also worked extensively on the sociology of the European colonizers. Co-editor of Cambridge University's five-volume series Colonialism in Africa, 1870 to 1960, Dr. Gann is also coauthor of a Rulers of Empire trilogy and author of the two standard works on the history, respectively, of Northern and Southern Rhodesia under British rule.

Senior Fellow **Melvyn Krauss** is Professor of Economics at New York University. In addition to many scientific articles, he has published books on the European Economic Community, economic development, and international trade and economic theory; he is also a regular contributor to the *Wall Street Journal*. Dr. Krauss's recent books include *Development Without Aid*, *The New Protectionism*, and *A Geometric Approach to International Trade*.

George Lenczowski, Professor of Political Science at the University of California, Berkeley, is a Senior Research Fellow of the Hoover Institution and adviser to the Middle Eastern studies program. His books on the region include *The Middle East and World Affairs* (4th ed.), *Iran under the Pahlavis*, and *Middle East Oil in a Revolutionary Age*.

Visiting Scholar **Ronald I. McKinnon,** Eberle Professor of Economics at Stanford University, is now writing a book on foreign exchange fluctuations and U.S. monetary policy to explain worldwide business cycles. Besides numerous articles in professional journals, he is the author of *Money and Capital in Economic Development* and *Money in International Exchange: The Convertible Currency System*.

H. Joachim Maître is Professor of International Relations at Boston University and a former National Fellow at the Hoover Institution. He has written extensively on politics and defense and security issues. For many years, he was associated with the newspaper and publishing industries in West Germany, holding, among other positions, the editorship of the influential German daily, *Die Welt*.

Senior Fellow **Ramon H. Myers,** Curator-Scholar of the Hoover Institution's East Asian Collection, specializes in Chinese and Japanese economic history and contemporary East Asian international relations. His most recent books include *A U.S. Foreign Policy for Asia* (ed.) and *The Japanese Formal Colonial Empire* (co-ed. with Mark Peattie).

James Bond Stockdale is a Senior Research Fellow at the Hoover Institution. Now a philosophy lecturer and writer, he is a retired Vice-Admiral and the holder of eight honorary degrees and the Congressional Medal of Honor. He writes this article as one who has "led and prevailed while under the guns of an extortionist political prison."

Senior Research Fellow **Edward Teller** is a Professor of Physics Emeritus of the University of California, Berkeley, and a consultant at Lawrence Livermore National Laboratory. Among his most recent books are *Energy from Heaven and Earth* and *The Pursuit of Simplicity*. A theoretical physicist, Dr. Teller received the National Medal of Science award from President Reagan in May 1983; he is a member of the White House Science Council and the Advisory Board of the Federal Emergency Management Agency.

Senior Research Fellow **William R. Van Cleave** is Professor of International Relations and Director of the Defense and Strategic Studies Program at the University of Southern California. Dr. Van Cleave has served in various governmental positions involving arms control negotiations, defense, and intelligence. He is the author of numerous publications on strategy, arms control, negotiating, and national defense issues.

Senior Research Fellow **Robert Wesson** is Professor of Political Science at the University of California, Santa Barbara. He has published books on the Soviet Union, foreign policy, and Latin America; he is editor of the Hoover Institution Press copublication series with Praeger Publishers, Politics in Latin America, as well as the series Democracy in the World published by the Center for the Study of Democratic Institutions. His recent books include *The United States and Brazil: Limits of Influence; Democracy in Latin America*; and *U.S. Influence in Latin America in the 1980s.*

Introduction

In 1919 the Hoover Institution at Stanford University was born out of war and revolution and the yearning for peace. It was established by Herbert Hoover while he was attending the Peace Conference in Paris, one year after The Great War. Twenty-two years later, Mr. Hoover dedicated the first building of the Institution. At that time, in June 1941, Europe was already, for the second time in just two decades, suffering the ravages of death and destruction through armed conflict. Only six months later, the United States would face the disaster of Pearl Harbor, and this country, too, would become engulfed in a great war for the second time in less than twenty-five years. Had the Europeans learned nothing from World War I? Or was it that the *few* sought to impose their wishes upon the *many,* whom they considered weaker, ill-prepared, and incapable of fighting another "great war"?

It was this background that provided the setting in which Herbert Hoover dedicated the Tower building of the Hoover Institution. Emphasizing the aim of promoting peace, Mr. Hoover conceived of the purpose of the Institution as opening paths to peaceful development among all the peoples of the world. In his words of dedication in 1941, Mr. Hoover said in reference to the priceless documents contained in the Institution's collections:

Out of these files the world can get great warning of what not to do and what to do when it next assembles around the peace table. True, there must be brought to that table a concept of new human relations, a concept that substitutes peace for war. But if the world is to have long peace, that concept must find its origins in human experience and its inspiration in human idealism.

And here are the documents which record the suffering, the self-denial, the devotion, the heroic deeds of men. Surely from these records there can be help to mankind in its confusions and perplexities, and its yearnings for peace.

The purpose of this institution is to promote peace. Its records stand as a challenge to those who promote war. They should attract those who search for peace.

It would be wise for us to keep these words in the forefront of our minds and to ponder them often. They serve to remind us that the quality of our analysis of the nation's foreign affairs, no less than the actual conduct of those affairs, continues to be vital to the prosperity and security of the United States. Today, more than four decades after the dedication of the Hoover Tower and sixty-five years after the founding of the Hoover Institution, the successful promotion of peace is a matter of vital and uncontestable importance if we are to survive as a free people.

This tribute to peace and to the peacemakers, sincere and wholehearted though it be, still is not enough for the people of a democracy. For them the matter of peace, the search for peace, and the maintenance of peace—in short, the whole problem of peace—is unfortunately not so simple. For the truth is that peace is chameleon-like in nature, taking its character and meaning from its surroundings. Peace is one thing in a democratic society and another, quite different thing in a dictatorship. In a democracy such as the United States, peace is regarded as inseparable from freedom, but in a dictatorship the matter of freedom can be brought up only at the greatest risk to the lives of the "troublemakers" and their families. It follows that when true democracies go to war, they do so primarily in order to preserve liberty, theirs or that of their allies. The sad record of history shows us that wars ostensibly undertaken for noble ends—the war to "make the world safe for democracy," for example—may end up bringing forth dragon broods, as did World Wars I and II, or destroying what little freedom existed beforehand, as did the war in Vietnam. It is quite safe to say that the burden resting on the shoulders of both those who seek to maintain peace and those who believe they have valid reasons for going to war is immense. The preservers of peace may wait too long, hoping for a solution that does not come.

Is any solution open to those who honestly seek both peace and freedom but recoil from war not from fear alone but also from sincere doubts about the possible outcome of any resort to violence? That question must be addressed in all its manifold complexities. We must continue to try to answer it—a task men of good will first assumed long ages ago.

We live in a world in a state of flux. Since the end of World War II in 1945, Europe, the scene of the greatest wars of the past two hundred years, has enjoyed almost four decades of peace. Yet, in both West and East the longer peace has been maintained, the more difficult it has become to summon the will to preserve it. The source of the trouble is to be found in the breakdown of unity within the democracies on the necessity of linking peace and freedom together in a close and unbreakable union. For the democracies, this crucial matter concerns what peace truly means for democratic societies and what is demanded in the world as it is today of those who wish to live in peace. One significant sign of the trouble beneath the surface is the growth of "peace movements," which arise from the assumption that democracies can safely disregard liberty as an essential and coequal partner of peace in the search for a safe and decent world.

This weakening of the will to preserve a peace capable of enduring is, then, a failure to understand what peace is and what it is not, how it can be achieved, and how it can be lost. Peace, like freedom, is not an end in itself. The value of both arises from what is done with them. Furthermore, neither peace nor liberty is to be had simply for the asking. Of all the goals men strive for, these two are among the most costly and the most difficult to attain. It is a mockery of the human condition that only one very human pursuit—one closely related to both peace and freedom—costs more and yet is easiest of all to attain. That pursuit is the one we call war.

It may come as a surprise to many citizens of the United States and of other democratic countries to learn that Herbert Clark Hoover, the thirty-first president of the United States, was one of those who first and most clearly recognized that "human ideals" have their roots in "human experience." When analyzing issues of foreign policy of the kind discussed in this volume, it is important to keep in mind that it is what people believe that determines what they do, and that at the heart of policy are values. Contrary to the impression one might receive in this age of new technology and instant communication, man is not the measure of all things. Man remains man, subject to human weakness and human frailty. The weaknesses, the strengths that have always burdened man are no greater and no smaller than they have ever been. In this century, as in past centuries, man is just as capable of beginning war, of fomenting revolution, and of promoting peace as he has ever been. Today, the question of defense is just as important, and just as paradoxical, as it has ever been. An adequate defense capability can, if controlled by irresponsible individuals, become the machinery for war. An adequate defense, if credible to potential adversaries, can also prevent the machinery of war from being set in motion.

As this volume is published, many countries possess the military capability to wreak great destruction. The one question that will remain central to the foreign affairs of the United States for the remainder of this century is whether it will be successful in its efforts to preserve liberty and to promote peace. There are many different avenues the United States must travel to maintain peace and develop prosperity. None of them, however, can be successfully taken without a defense strong enough to deter aggression. One of the very painful lessons man has learned—and which apparently man must learn again and again—is that those without the military means to defend themselves will sooner or later be attacked.

Over two hundred years ago, the United States was created as an act of will. If the peoples of the world believe that the citizens of the United States still possess the will and the means to defend themselves, the chance of war will be significantly reduced. If the peoples of the world believe that the citizens of the United States want peace and are willing to take the steps necessary to preserve it, they will look to the citizens of the United States for guidance and leadership. Thus encouraged, if the peoples of the world believe a great power seeks to destroy democracy and eliminate individual liberty and has the means to do so, they may nevertheless elect to defend themselves, despite the temptation to seek accommodation with that power. There is no easy way out of this dilemma, but there is an alternative. If we find that we cannot have both liberty and peace, then we may give Patrick Henry's answer of 1775, or we may elect to put a period to the American adventure begun two hundred years ago. We are still free to make this choice.

The issues discussed in the seventeen essays contained in this volume touch upon these considerations in many different ways. The essays do not address all of the questions that concern the promotion of peace. They represent an attempt, however, to discuss ideas and policies in a clear, incisive, and thoughtful manner. They also raise questions—Should the United States withdraw its troops from Berlin,

Germany, or all of Western Europe? What is the meaning of the massive increase in Soviet military strength? Are there significant relationships between the church, the "peace movement," and communism? What does the future hold for the Pacific Basin, or for Eastern Europe? What is the value of the United States' intelligence establishment? What should be the aims of U.S. arms control policy?

The authors of the essays in this volume have been involved with the analysis of such questions for many years. All of them are or have been associated with the Hoover Institution, as National Fellows, as Visiting Scholars, or as Senior or Senior Research Fellows. Their work over the past years has contributed significantly to the purpose to which the Hoover Tower was dedicated in 1941. For this reason, they were invited to present their ideas here and to discuss issues of importance to them. They were aware that the old adage "qui s'excuse, s'accuse" remains just as valid today as in the past. They were not requested to make policy recommendations, but they knew that if they chose to do so, their ideas would be welcome. Their essays were all written during 1983, and therefore, if any of their conclusions seem to be overtaken by subsequent events, I ask the reader to take into consideration that circumstances change rapidly in today's world.

There is no question in my mind that many of the essays in this volume will generate debate and disagreement. That is why they were written. That is the purpose of this book.

At this juncture, it may be helpful to provide a brief overview of the contents of this volume in the order in which the essays appear.

The initial essay deals with aid and development, a subject that will receive increasing attention during the remainder of this decade. Melvyn Krauss, a Senior Fellow of the Hoover Institution, argues that there is "no greater threat to the prosperity of the poorer nations today than the welfare state" and that the transfer of income from "the have to the have-less countries" is no substitute for economic growth. In the long term, it will be economic growth, and the incentives for achievement and economic responsibility that it provides, that will nurture and sustain the development of less developed countries—and not efforts to purchase their obeisance through the mechanism of the "transfer payment" and foreign aid.

During academic year 1982–83, the distinguished French political scientist Alain Besançon was in residence at the Hoover Institution as a Visiting Scholar and joined his colleague Senior Fellow L. H. Gann, in an effort to focus attention on the relationships among religion, the peace movement, and communism. Their essay is a challenging analysis of the role that the advocacy of peace has played in the development of religious and political movements in this century in Europe. They emphasize the irony that while both the Christian church and the communist state support pacifism in the West, the Christian ethic is considered a threat to political stability in communist society. The authors conclude with the obvious but seldom expressed observation that the differences between what totalitarian regimes say and what they do warrant careful attention and that the church must recognize this point if it is to retain its credibility on the issue of peace, which is of such vital importance to the future of mankind.

In times of crisis, the citizens of any country must rely on strong leadership in order to survive. The third essay in this volume, written by a naval officer and scholar, addresses the question of how we as informed citizens can seek to judge our leaders and their abilities. Vice Admiral James Bond Stockdale, a Senior Research Fellow at the Hoover Institution, writes from a perspective that draws in part from lessons he learned as a prisoner of war in Hanoi. In the best of times and in the worst of times, it is character that defines the parameters of leadership. Yet in the free society of the United States, it appears to be increasingly difficult to look beyond the media's packaging of political candidates to a true assessment of their abilities. Thus the author stresses the importance of judging character in a society in which leaders are called on to deal with increasingly complex problems.

The monetary policy of the United States plays a major role in the international financial system. The essay on this subject by Ronald I. McKinnon, a Visiting Scholar at the Hoover Institution during the 1982–83 academic year while on leave as Professor of Economics from Stanford University, originated, in part, from a dinner talk Professor McKinnon presented to the Institution's National Fellows. It recommends a restructured monetary system, with the U.S. Federal Reserve playing a central role in stabilizing prices and the money supply throughout the world. The author stresses that the issues involved are extremely complicated and do not lend themselves to easy solutions. At the same time, he argues that with the agreement of major international financial institutions (for example, major banks in Western Europe, Japan, and North America), new standards could be adopted that would prevent sudden fluctuations in exchange rates and resulting cycles of inflation or deflation. Professor McKinnon provides compelling reasons for his conclusions, and his essay should generate considerable debate.

Energy and peace, the subject of Senior Research Fellow Edward

Teller's essay, has generated volumes of discussion. Dr. Teller argues cogently for increased development of the two major national energy sources, nuclear-generated electricity and coal. Reasonable regulations and technological innovations, in his view, can significantly promote economic development throughout the world and, by increasing the stable supply of reasonably priced energy, decrease the possibility of conflict over Persian Gulf oil. The production and security of energy resources will be of continuing importance, and, the author concludes, "the United States . . . could become an energy exporter by the end of the century—a position that would add considerable strength to the stability of peace."

The essay "Post-Collectivist Politics in Europe and Great Britain" deals with the major role played by union power in European politics. Gerald A. Dorfman, a Senior Fellow at the Hoover Institution, points out that the "long-standing collectivist relationship between labor and government in Europe is changing in significant ways" and that "the most striking feature of this change is the decline of union power." One of the most important consequences of this change is that "political leaders are consciously reducing the frequency and quality of union-government interaction over the terms of public policy." What this means over the long term is that as a new set of relationships between trade unions and governments emerge, policymakers in the United States should remain very much aware of the potentially destabilizing political and economic conflicts that may result. The subject of union activity, well analyzed here by Dr. Dorfman, does not often receive the attention it deserves.

As this volume appears, the "peace movement" in Western Europe, and in the United States, has been a major focus of attention for more than two years. In the name of peace have emerged "demonstrations" involving millions of people. Demonstrating for peace has become fashionable, commands attention, and generates enormous publicity. Yet, as Senior Fellow L. H. Gann of the Hoover Institution observes, "the overwhelming majority" of these demonstrators for peace condemn the West, particularly the United States, for alleged threats to world stability. As the author concludes, "No demonstrations of similar size had ever been launched against the Soviet invasion of Afghanistan, Soviet repression in Hungary and Czechoslovakia, or the horrors of the Gulag archipelago." Although Europe has remained at peace for almost four decades, thanks in large part to the nuclear deterrent provided by the United States, the United States comes under increasing censure as it continues to shoulder the burden of European military defense. Thus, in the author's view, emerges a paradox: the peace movement may very well threaten peace because of its destabilizing effect on the will to maintain a credible defense.

Melvyn Krauss, a Senior Fellow of the Hoover Institution, raises the issue of whether it is time "to change the Atlantic Alliance." The author argues that "defense free-riding" by the West Europeans and Japanese, which is a legacy of World War II, is no longer justifiable. He concludes that "West European military dependence on and subsidization by the United States is no longer warranted or desirable" and has contributed to "the 'new neutralism' and 'new pacifism' in Europe," which is dangerous to the Western Europeans and to the United States. He recommends that the United States revoke its "automatic commitment to come to the aid of any member of NATO in case of war" and in so doing redefine the Atlantic relationship. The author stresses "that is not to say the United States would not or should not come to the defense of Western Europe if it is threatened with military attack." The object is, however, to "restore freedom of action to U.S. foreign policy . . . revitalize the transatlantic relationship, with Western Europe less the junior and the United States less the senior partner."

One of the areas of greatest importance to the United States is the continent of South America. In recent years, however, concludes Senior Research Fellow Robert Wesson, the United States has not given enough political and economic attention to the problems confronting its neighbors. He makes the extremely important point that there is every reason to reforge the community of the Americas. The most powerful potential incentive for Latin American cooperation with the United States, according to the author, is to reduce and eliminate trade barriers to the importation of Latin American products to the United States, and Dr. Wesson supports President Reagan's Caribbean Basin Initiative in this regard. He emphasizes that dictatorships, social inequities, and violations of human rights must be met with strong disapproval. At the same time, however, the prime objective of the United States should be to increase the productivity of the Latin American countries through economic incentives and support for the Organization of American States as a forum for political cooperation and stability. Such a hemispheric policy could "lead the way for collaboration of the industrialized countries with the Third World and for the progress of the poorer majority of mankind. It might help to lay to rest the idea that there is any acceptable alternative to freedom and democracy."

Senior Fellow and East Asian Curator Ramon H. Myers analyzes the principal economic and political problems that threaten to destabilize the Pacific Basin's current prosperity. Although this region has greatly benefited from U.S. aid and military protection since World War II, developments of the 1970s and 1980s, such as the Soviet military buildup in the region, pressure from China for the United States to weaken its relationships with Taiwan, and new pressures for protectionist trade policies, now require a different U.S. posture toward the countries of Asia. By remaining committed to free trade, assisting the Basin states on a bilateral basis, and recognizing that Japan—not Communist China—must be the linchpin for Pacific Basin peace and prosperity, the United States should be able to foster and strengthen the economic development and the security of the region throughout the 1980s and beyond.

The problems and prospects of war and peace in the Middle East are as numerous as they are complex. Senior Research Fellow George Lenczowski presents a fascinating picture of one of the most volatile areas of the world. Dr. Lenczowski points to the spread of Soviet and communist activity, to the availability of energy resources, and to the politics in the Palestinian region as the pivotal factors in U.S. foreign policy in the Middle East. In the 1970s, the forces hostile to the United States' influence in the Middle East greatly challenged its ability to promote stability, as crises of major proportion developed in Iran, Afghanistan, and Lebanon. Arab concessions to U.S. companies, which began a half-century ago, ensured access to oil in a buyer's market until the 1973 OPEC price increases disrupted energy-dependent markets around the globe. Thus, economic interests in Middle Eastern stability were added to U.S. political concerns in the region. In the author's view, political and strategic issues continue to occupy a dual focus of U.S. policy regarding Arab-Israeli interests. The national interest of the United States will best be served, the author concludes, if U.S. policymakers formulate strategies for territorial stability in the Middle East based on a sustained awareness of potential Soviet encroachment.

Senior Fellow and Coordinator of the Hoover Institution's International Studies Program Peter J. Duignan also serves as the Curator for the Institution's African and Middle East Collection. The need for increased U.S. political and economic influence in Africa is the subject of Dr. Duignan's essay, which explores the many tensions within the continent that make it increasingly vulnerable to Soviet domination. The author analyzes the inconsistencies of past U.S. policy in Africa, which has not prevented the steady growth of Soviet influence through communist front organizations. U.S. support of three critical African regions—the northwest, the Horn, and the south—is vital, the author argues, to contain Soviet aggression and foster self-reliant economic development. He sees the growth of private enterprise as a stabilizing factor that will counter the spread of socialism, which is heavily dependent on foreign aid. Dr. Duignan warns that Afro-Asian countries "can afford the luxury of neutralism" only if the West remains strong. A combination of diplomatic effort, economic support, and military assistance, in his view, should be the major components of the United States' African policy. Through the promotion of peace and economic development, the United States can unequivocally demonstrate that it has common interests with Africa as a continent and with African states as independent governments.

Senior Research Fellow Robert Conquest, Curator of the Institution's East European Collection, examines the psychological and historical background of the Soviet leadership, establishing its basic motivations in the field of foreign affairs. He discusses Soviet conduct in recent years and suggests its further development, both in the field of armaments and in various areas of the world. He concludes with a long-term evaluation of the Soviet future, suggesting that if the West properly understands its opponent, there are reasonable prospects for a more peaceful world.

The significance of Soviet military power is analyzed by former National Fellow H. Joachim Maître in an essay focusing on its growth and particularly on its effects on arms control negotiations and on the credibility of NATO. The author describes the alternative confronting the West as either rebuilding its military forces or risking eventual defeat at the hands of the Soviet Union. NATO no longer faces a Soviet state that is a European power, but a global power that has expanded into Africa, Asia, the Middle East, Central America, and into the five oceans. At the same time, the United States has assumed increased responsibilities throughout the world, while the Western Europeans have not significantly upgraded their military obligations to the alliance. Dr. Maître stresses that the "Should the U.S. pull out of NATO?" debate can "no longer be seen by Europeans as merely a revival of discredited isolationism." On the contrary, it should be recognized as an indication that the Soviet Union is moving closer to realizing its objective of removing the U.S. military presence from Western Europe and establishing Soviet hegemony over the entire continent. His conclusion argues that the resources to prevent such a development are there and that "only will is required."

The essay on Eastern Europe is a penetrating analysis of an extremely complex set of concerns. The dilemma facing the countries of Eastern Europe is that they lie between *Freiheit und Diktatur*. These states are both an asset and a liability to the Soviet Union. On the one hand, writes Senior Fellow Milorad M. Drachkovitch, the role played by some countries of Eastern Europe, particularly East Germany, serves to promote Marxist-Leninist revolutionary goals in different parts of the Third World. On the other hand, the author quotes a leading expert on Eastern Europe who emphasizes that "when basic incongruity exists between the political culture and the system, as in Czechoslovakia, Poland, or Hungary, especially if reinforced by modernizing pressures, such a conflict breeds demands for democratization and generates instability leading to revolutionary situations." Of equal significance, Dr. Drachkovitch writes, is that "East Europeans overwhelmingly identify with Western ideas and realities of representative governments, genuinely free elections, and authentic pluralism of political and social life." The author concludes that Soviet leaders are "fully aware of the flammable potential burning under the surface in Eastern Europe" and, as a consequence, may in the future conclude "that it is not in their interest to suppress militarily the ultimately irrepressible democratic aspirations of the East Europeans."

In Senior Research Fellow William R. Van Cleave's assessment, U.S. strategic and arms control policy has failed to keep pace with continually expanding Soviet military power, in particular Soviet nuclear forces. This military imbalance poses serious problems that require solutions, for the "essence of U.S. strategic policy over the years has been deterrence of attacks on the United States and its allies through retaliatory forces that are both capable and credible." Dr. Van Cleave's emphasis on U.S. vulnerability to the Soviet Union includes criticism of Reagan administration opponents who reject increased defense spending for deterrence and nuclear weapons and who do not acknowledge that U.S. spending has previously been inadequate. The principal cause of the imbalance is the large gap in strategic capabilities. This gap may be reduced by the current administration's commitment, but Dr. Van Cleave believes that there is inadequate attention to force survivability and an inadequate sense of urgency in the administration's program. If the United States is to endure as a major power, it must possess credible military capabilities supported by a citizenry that has the will to defend itself. Thus, while the United States should pursue arms control negotiations, it should not forget "that arms control was never more than a modest supplementary means of national security, the success of which required that the United States first assure that security through its own means."

Of critical importance to the maintenance of peace and security is the existence of an intelligence establishment that provides accurate information. Arnold Beichman, a Visiting Scholar in residence at the

Hoover Institution during 1982 and 1983, has written an essay addressing this point. He gives particular emphasis to the necessity to understand, for example, the intentions of the Soviet Union so that U.S. policymakers can develop effective political and military policies. This conclusion applies to all aspects of foreign relations of the United States. Dr. Beichman stresses the need for rebuilding the United States' intelligence system precisely because it can preclude confrontation and in turn promote peace.

The essays contained in this volume do not deal with all of the foreign policy issues that confront the United States. Each, however, has an important bearing on the kind of world in which we will live. For this reason, I hope the views expressed in these essays will stimulate the imaginations of their readers and provoke discussion. The open exchange of ideas is the essence of a free society. We must make full use of this great strength if the foreign policy of the United States is to promote peace in freedom.

Dennis L. Bark
Senior Fellow

Stanford
December 1983

1
Development Without Aid: Aid Without Development

Melvyn Krauss

T here are only two ways to improve living standards in the world's poorer countries. The first is to increase the rate of growth of the world economy—not only that of the less developed countries (LDCs) themselves but of the developed ones as well. The second is to improve efficiency in the international allocation of the world's resources. A third approach—transferring wealth and income from the have to the have-less countries—has been championed by left-leaning economists and social-democratic politicians. But this approach to improving Third World living standards is a fruitless one. The "international transfer of prosperity" via rapid growth and liberal foreign-trade policies is preferable to the "international transfer of income"—at least if one's objective is to help the Third World's poor.

Harmony or Conflict?

The first point to be made is that there exists an essential harmony between the economic interests of the poorer countries and of the richer countries. Economic growth in the developed world both stimulates and is stimulated by economic growth in the Third World.

According to Nobel Prize winner Sir Arthur Lewis, "For the past hundred years, the rate of growth of output in the developing world has depended on the rate of growth of output in the developed world. When the developed grow fast, the developing grow fast, and when the developed slow down, the developing slow down."[1] The developed countries, in other words, have been the engine for prosperity for both themselves and the poorer nations.

The principal linkage between the developed and developing world has been international trade. Lewis discovered that the growth rate of the developing countries' exports of primary products to the developed world was 0.87 times the growth rate of industrial production in the industrialized countries during the past hundred years. That is, a 1.0 percent increase of industrial production in the North, on average, was associated with a 0.87 percent increase of the South's exports of primary products. Thus, to improve living standards in the Third World, it is important not only to have rapid economic growth in the developed world but also to keep the avenue that links North and South—international trade—as free from obstacles as possible.

International trade is a two-way street, of course. Just as free trade ensures that the benefits of economic growth in the North spread to the South, free trade also ensures that rapid growth in the South spreads to the North. This is extremely important for the United States, in particular, since, quantitatively, the Third World accounts for an important share of the United States' exports. According to World Bank statistics, developing countries have accounted for a stable 35 percent of U.S. merchandise exports from 1960 to the present.

Increasing world economic growth is one way to improve living standards in the poorer nations. Greater efficiency in the international allocation of the world's resources is another. And, a harmony of interests between the have and have-less nations of the world exists as much in the latter case as it does in the former.

A long-standing and venerable principle of economic theory is that when countries voluntarily enter into economic exchange with one another, there is mutual benefit; otherwise, why would they trade in the first place? Marxists, on the other hand, do not acknowledge the mutual gains from trade. They see international trade as a "zero sum" game—one country can gain from trade only at the expense of another. But as well-known international economist Robert Mundell once pointed out, "zero-sum exchange" is virtually a contradiction in terms. International income and wealth transfers are "zero sum exchanges"—not international trade.

tries is borne by competitive industries in the Third World. Furthermore, workers in the less developed countries are being hurt not because the steelworkers in the welfare state face certain unemployment, but because the steelworkers refuse either to accept pay cuts in their present jobs or to accept jobs in other industries or geographical locales. The welfare-state worker makes exacting demands on the government. And it is the Third World worker who often must pay.

Note, the northern European social democrats and American liberals see themselves as the champions of Third World interests. But no amount of conscience money—that is, foreign aid—is going to change the fact that what the social democrats give in aid, they more than take away by restricting trade.

Because the internationalism of the Left is based on fashion rather than sound economic doctrine, its scope has been rather limited—restricted, in fact, to explicit international trade-restricting devices. The internationalism of the Left does not extend to international capital and labor flows. American liberals and European social democrats support both restrictions on capital outflows to protect against the alleged "export of jobs" to foreigners and restrictions on labor inflows to protect the bloated real wages the welfare state has bestowed on workers in the industrialized countries. Cheap wages in the South attract capital, while dear wages in the North attract labor. As noted above, international labor and capital flows are two of the three ways prosperity gets transferred from the North to the South.

Only when the welfare state in the northern industrial powers is dismantled will protectionism cease to be a problem for the Third World.

A further way the welfare state damages the Third World—in addition to promoting protectionism—is to downplay the importance of economic growth. Economic growth is said to ruin the environment. And in societies where leisure has become a way of life, the hard work that economic growth implies has become anathema. This is tragic for the poorer nations of the world economy, whose very survival depends on rapid growth in the industrialized countries.

Of course, fashionable "Club of Rome" biases against economic growth have something of the "let's make a virtue out of a vice" about them. When the northern European welfare states were growing well in the 1950s and 1960s, economic growth was not considered such a bad thing. But the "sick seventies" demonstrated that economic growth is incompatible with both the high taxes and many of the social welfare programs that are endemic to the modern welfare state. Rather than face up to the long-run consequences of this incompatibility, welfare-state advocates find it much more comfortable to put their heads in the sand and make believe growth no longer counts.

Foreign Aid Hurts, Not Helps!

The modern welfare state is committed to foreign aid as the primary means of helping the poorer nations of the world. This commitment is based on two pessimistic and fundamentally incorrect assumptions about the nature of and remedy for Third World poverty: (1) Third World peoples possess an inherent cultural and environmental inability to achieve rapid economic development, and (2) a distortion in the international system of capitalistic competition and free enterprise prevents the transfer of prosperity from the North to the South.

Sir Arthur Lewis wrote in his Nobel Prize lecture that in the late 1940s and early 1950s, "people were skeptical of the capacity of the LDCs to grow because of inappropriate attitudes, institutions, or climates. The sun was thought to be too hot for hard work, or the people too spendthrift, the government too corrupt, the fertility too high, the religion too other-wordly, and so on."[3]

These patronizing and quite frankly racist views provide one of the principal underlying assumptions behind the often-heard position that Third World poverty must be alleviated by massive transfer of income from the developed to the "backward" nations, as they then were commonly referred to. Post–World War II history and the outstanding economic performance of many Third World countries—indeed, the LDCs as an aggregate group—have shown these views, not the LDCs, to be backward. Consider what the Nobel Prize–winning economist Simon Kuznets has to say about Third World economic performance:

> For the LDCs as a group, the United Nations has estimated annual growth rates of total and per capita GDP (gross domestic product at constant factor prices) from 1950 to 1972. The growth rates of per capita product . . . for the twenty-two years was 2.61 percent per year . . . *such growth rates are quite high in the long-term historical perspective of both the LDCs and the current DCs* [italics added].[4]

The second assumption underlying conventional analysis of the economic development problem is an alleged bias in the system of capitalistic competition that deprives the LDCs of the benefits of international exchange. The crux of the argument is that, according to development economists Raul Prebisch and Hans Singer, there has been a long-term decline in the terms of trade for primary products, in terms of industrial goods, that has been adverse to the Third World. The Prebisch-Singer argument was first advanced in a U.N. document and, according to Oxford economist I. M. D. Little, "became enshrined in UNCTAD [United Nations Conference on Trade and Development] and in constant repetition by development economists . . . The fact that all scholarly work, to my knowledge, denies any long-term trend has probably still not fully exorcised the myth created by the U.N."[5]

Little is not alone in challenging the bogus Prebisch-Singer terms-of-trade argument. Harvard's Gottfried Haberler, the dean of development-trade economists, writes:

> What, then, are the facts about the alleged tendency for the terms of trade to change against the LDCs or for prices of primary products to fall in relation to manufactured goods? Fortunately, a definite answer can be given, for this is one of the most thoroughly analyzed and researched areas in international economics. There have been and there still are cyclical fluctuations, in the past at times violent and destructive.
>
> . . . But no long trend in the terms of trade for broad groups of countries, DCs or LDCs, or of primary against manufactured products has been established.[6]

The case for foreign aid as compensation to the poorer nations has been shown to be incorrect. But the case against foreign aid, and international income transfer in general, is stronger than this. Foreign aid *hurts,* not helps, the LDCs. Thus, even if aid-as-compensation arguments for LDCs were acceptable—which they are not—foreign aid would be a counterproductive way of effecting compensation. The most telling argument against foreign aid is that it encourages and finances destructive economic policies in recipient countries.

The "Gang of Four"—Hong Kong, Singapore, Taiwan, and South Korea—is frequently cited as an important success story for free-market economics.[7] But the identification of the free market with rapid rates of economic growth in Taiwan and South Korea has been challenged on the grounds that both performed their economic miracles with substantial U.S. aid. Foreign aid, it is argued, was the springboard for their rapid growth.

This argument is not only incorrect, but the reverse of what actually happened. In both Taiwan and South Korea, U.S. economic aid financed and sustained wealth-destroying protectionist and antiprivate capital-import policies. It was not until the United States threatened to cut off foreign aid in the late 1950s that both countries were constrained to adopt the free-market, pro-foreign capital-import policies that proved responsible for their success. Rather than preparing the Taiwanese and South Korean economies for takeoff, as alleged, foreign aid threatened to ground them permanently.

There were several motives for U.S. aid to Taiwan from 1950 to 1965. The least controversial was sustaining a strong Nationalist military posture vis-à-vis Communist China. The resources provided by U.S. aid—particularly clothing and food—let the Nationalists make necessary military expenditures without creating hyperinflation. Aid for this purpose is generally considered to have been quite successful.

By 1956, however, U.S. aid objectives gradually shifted from military strength to economic growth. Reflecting the conventional wisdom of the time, Taiwan's development strategy was to use government aid funds to build infrastructure (power, transport, communications), foster agriculture, and develop human resources. Industrial development was to be left in the hands of private enterprise. In other words, U.S. aid was intended to help create a booming private sector by making available increased power, transportation, efficient labor, and low-priced raw materials.

From 1951 to 1965, two-thirds of all U.S. aid went to projects run by public enterprises and agencies. Some 37 percent of the aid in this period went for infrastructure, 26 percent for human resources, 25 percent for agriculture, and 15 percent for industry.

Though designed to benefit private enterprise, the effect of U.S.-financed investment in "social-overhead capital" was to damage private enterprise by diverting scarce resources away from it. This "crowding out" of the private sector by public projects increased the cost of resources to the private sector as much as an explicit tax on their use would have. Reflecting this, private-sector gross investment in fixed capital formation in Taiwan fell from 56 percent in 1954 to 41 percent in 1958. From 1951 to 1963, the public sector accounted for 48 percent of total Taiwanese net domestic investment. U.S. capital assistance accounted for 80 percent of that figure.

Rather than creating a model for capitalistic development, as intended, it became obvious by the late 1950s that government-to-government aid was creating a strong socialist state in Taiwan that was suffocating the private sector. This was one of the main reasons Washington wisely chose to discontinue its aid to Taiwan.

The conventional wisdom that inspired the practice of letting the public sector crowd out the private sector in Taiwan is what one might call "cart-before-the-horse" economics. Social-overhead capital simply is not the horse to pull private business along with it. Indeed, the opposite is true. The lack of infrastructure may well be a bottleneck in economies already experiencing strong private-sector growth, in which case the rate of return from investing in infrastructure will probably be high. But in poor countries, as Taiwan and Korea were at the time, the absence of infrastructure is more a reflection of economic stagnation than a reason for it. The private sector must lead the public one—not the reverse.

An equally important purpose of U.S. aid to Taiwan and Korea during the 1950s was general economic assistance. Grants and concessional loans to finance perpetual balance-of-payments deficits and support the currency in foreign-exchange markets became an important factor in sustaining the protectionist policies of the Nationalists in Taiwan during the 1950s. These policies hurt Taiwanese industry in at least two ways.

First, they artificially restricted Taiwan's exports by drawing resources out of export industries into import-substitute industries. During the protectionist decade of the 1950s, the average annual growth rate of Taiwanese exports was 15.5 percent; during the free-market 1960s it was 31.5 percent. Second, protectionism helped create stagnation in Taiwanese manufacturing during the 1950s. The annual rates of output growth in the non-food-manufacturing sectors of the Taiwanese economy were (in percentages) 22, 23, 19, 11, 10, and 10 respectively for the six years from 1953 through 1958. The drop in output growth was particularly severe in textiles, wood products, and basic metals, all of which suffered from severe excess capacity.

In addition to economic stagnation, there were fears in Taiwan that U.S. aid had made the country too dependent on the United States. Independence from foreigners had been a central motif of Nationalist Chinese international economic policy since Sun Yat-sen. The result was that Taiwan, like many Third World countries, opted for protectionist policies in the early post–World War II period. The Nationalists rejected an export-oriented, free capital-import program precisely because they saw it as surrendering Taiwan's future development to private firms and foreign interests who, they thought, would be preoccupied with profit and unresponsive to the political and historical imperatives that President Chiang Kaishek had defined for his island-country.

Autarkic economic policies, however, did not bring independence.

They brought the opposite. By running the economy into the ground, protectionism forced Taiwan to depend increasingly on the United States for general economic assistance. The Nationalist fear of dependence on private foreign firms thus led to the reality of "aid dependency" on the United States. In the final analysis, the Nationalist government realized that only the prosperous are truly independent, and that Chiang's earlier fear of foreign capital had been misplaced, if not counterproductive.

Like aid to Taiwan, U.S. aid to South Korea in the early postwar period was linked to containing communism in the Pacific Basin. A food shortage resulted in South Korea from the massive migration south when the peninsula was split; the United States countered with free food and a half million tons of fertilizer. The fertilizer, in particular, is considered to have been instrumental in restoring agricultural production to its pre–World War II level by the time of the outbreak of the Korean War. Later, however, it was argued that surplus food imports were a prime factor causing stagnation in Korean agriculture because they kept food prices down.

After the Korean War, U.S. economic aid to South Korea was both more substantial and less successful. From 1953 to 1963, U.S. economic aid accounted for 13.4 percent of Korean GNP, 95.9 percent of Korean gross domestic investment, and 75.6 percent of government expenditure. It is no exaggeration to say that it misguidedly financed socialism in South Korea during this period.

Foreign aid on a large scale leads to corruption on a large scale. In the case of the Syngman Rhee regime in South Korea, aid-financed agriculture and industrial projects were used to prop up Rhee's political fortunes rather than the Korean economy. As a result, one-fifth of all such projects financed by U.S. aid from 1953 to 1963 proved unsound for reasons of bankruptcy and lack of managerial skills. Korean per capita GNP grew at an annual average rate of 1.9 percent during this period, compared with figures three times that magnitude after both aid and government size in Korea were scaled down in the 1970s.

It is sometimes argued that U.S. aid was vital in stabilizing such societies because it signaled American willingness to stand firm against communist aggression. This supposedly gave the Taiwanese and South Korean economies their attractiveness to private investment. In fact, however, foreign and domestic private investment did not take off until the governments changed their policy orientation from government-led growth and reliance on foreign aid to more emphasis on private-sector growth.

In short, so long as generous U.S. aid was forthcoming, Taiwan and South Korea could forgo private-capital import and export promotion for foreign-exchange purposes. But when the United States discontinued its aid, the generation of foreign exchange by the private sector became critical. It was no mere coincidence that both countries radically altered their domestic economic policies from import substitution to export-led growth in the face of the U.S. aid cutoff. It was a case of cause and effect.

Taiwan and South Korea are interesting for many reasons. Not the least is that they demonstrate the harm foreign aid can do in promoting wealth-destroying economic policies.

The Brandt Report

The pessimistic assumptions underlying the "transfer-of-income" approach to increasing living standards in the poorer nations are nowhere more apparent than in the recently released report of the Brandt Commission, published under the self-effacing title *A Programme for Survival*.[8]

The motivating premise of the Brandt Report is that the world is about to collapse. This cheerless outlook may reflect the misgivings and grievances of the commission's members, all former heads of state who had seen their own political careers collapse. These included, among others, ex-chancellor Willy Brandt of West Germany, ex-president Eduardo Frei Montalvo of Chile, ex–prime minister Edward Heath of the United Kingdom, and ex-premier Pierre Mendes-France of France.

The Brandt Commission's recommendation that substantial amounts of real resources be transferred to less developed countries reflects a strategic judgment that the Third World constitutes a future hot spot in the East-West conflict and that rather than rearming to discourage the Soviets from their special sort of troublemaking there, the West would be better off defusing possible exploitable local conflicts by ameliorating poverty in the Third World. European social democrats also fear a military buildup because financing this would undoubtedly mean a reduction of social expenditure—the lifeblood of their welfare states—and, finally, because they do not want to provoke the Russians. Put somewhat differently, the Brandt Commission feels—quite mistakenly, I believe—that it is cheaper to prevent East-West conflict through foreign-aid transfers to the Third World than by a Western military buildup.

Unlike the New International Economic Order with its heavily

Marxist overtones—that Third World poverty is caused by the industrial countries—the Brandt Report is the work of social democrats and clearly states their thinking on the causes of and solutions for the economic development problem.

The social democrats, for example, have an unshakable faith in the curative powers of income transfer. The Brandt Report therefore concentrates its recommendations on means of transferring income internationally rather than on means of creating it. But the left-liberals face a critical obstacle when trying to impose their transfer-of-income approach to economic development in the world economy—namely, government coercion is needed to effect income transfer and no world government exists. National sovereignty makes income transfer between nations purely voluntary.

The Brandt Report attempts to surmount this obstacle by introducing mechanisms that create the effect of world government without creating world government itself. To do this, the report adopts Jan Tinbergen's idea of "the introduction of *automatic* revenue transfer through *international* levies . . . on international trade, arms production or exports, international travel and the global commons, especially sea-bed minerals."[9] The report also advocates an *international* income tax based on ability to pay. Willy Brandt himself writes, "Why should it be unrealistic to entertain the idea of imposing a suitable form of taxation on a sliding scale according to countries' ability to pay?" Brandt continues, "It is our conviction that we will have to face more seriously the need for a transfer of funds . . . with a degree of *automaticity* and *predictability* disconnected from the uncertainties of national budgets and their underlying constraints."[10]

International taxation constitutes but one dimension of the Brandt Report's overall strategy for transferring political power (1) from the nation-states to international organizations and (2) from richer to poorer states.

The Brandt Report seeks to "reform" old international institutions, such as the International Monetary Fund (IMF) and the World Bank, and create new ones to give borrowing countries a greater role in management and decision making. The report recommends "the creation of a new international financial institution—a World Development Fund—with universal membership, and in which decision making is more evenly shared between lenders and borrowers."[11] This is part of the Brandt Report's plan to create "a more equal partnership" between the industrialized countries and the Third World.

Of course, what a "more equal partnership" means, in plain English, is that the industrialized countries, particularly the United States,

would make substantially more funds available to the Third World on
heavily subsidized terms with no strings attached—that is, regardless of
how foolish the economic policies of the borrowing country are, no
matter how antithetical to the lender's interest the foreign and economic policies of the borrowing country are, and no matter how bad a
credit risk the borrower is. One can believe in Christian charity, but
must the Christians throw themselves to the lions?

The supranationalism that masks the Brandt Report's intended
wholesale transfer of resources from the industrialized to Third World
countries is not an isolated incident but part of a left-liberal grand design. In 1982, the Reagan administration made headlines when it pre-
cipitously pulled out of the negotiations for the proposed Law of the
Sea Treaty. According to the proposed treaty, which has received almost universal approbation by leftists, all the treasures of the ocean
floor, manganese, cobalt, copper, would be controlled by a powerful
new international cartel, operated under the United Nations. William
Safire wrote that by signing the treaty,

> We would be party to the creation of a world economic govern-
> ment—an "authority"—with its own taxing powers, no longer
> dependent on its members' contributions for support. The min-
> eral riches of the next century would be consigned to a super-
> OPEC with the power to develop—or create artificial shortages
> of—the ingredients of tomorrow's technology.[12]

In addition to income transfer, the social democrats also believe as
a matter of faith that *economic incentives* should not be the basis for
economic behavior. Their credo appears to be "one should do it for
love, not for money." This belief has led the social democrats to discount heavily the "incentive effects" of their proposals—that is, the
effects their proposals have on the economic behavior of the concerned
economic actors. The Brandt Report contains several recommendations whose incentive effects would be negative not only for the world
economy, but for the poorer nations themselves.

Here are some examples

1. The report urges that loans be made on the most lenient
terms to countries that need them most. This seems commendable.
But what the report fails to consider is that usually there is a reason
a country needs the loan most, and that reason often is irresponsible economic management. By rewarding economic irresponsibility, the Brandt Report would encourage it.

2. The report is rightly impressed with the contribution that guest workers in the industrialized countries make to the economic development of the Third World countries from which they migrate. But, if implemented, the report's insistence that migrants be given their rights would increase the cost of migrant workers to prospective employers and thus decrease their employment opportunities.

3. The report recommends "legislation to regulate transnational corporation activities in matters such as ethical behavior, disclosure of information, restrictive business practices and labor standards." But by increasing the cost of doing business for the multinationals, such legislation would, in fact, ensure that they did less business. This would hurt the LDCs as well as the multinationals.

The Brandt Report has not been well received—and with good reason. Even left-liberal sympathizers sense that, like the Club of Rome and New International Economic Order preceding it, the Brandt Report arrived on the scene well after the party had ended. It is repetitive of the others, impractical, and, most important, irrelevant to the needs of the Third World in the 1980s.

Simply put, what the Third World needs most "for survival" in the 1980s is economic growth, not international income transfers that stunt growth. The Brandt Report realizes that economic growth in the industrialized countries is good for the LDCs, but fails to recognize that it is precisely the welfare-state, high-tax, egalitarian policies favored by the left-liberals that constrained economic growth in the advanced countries to unacceptably low levels during the 1970s. If the social democrats who wrote the Brandt Report took time off from lecturing others on how to manage world affairs to put their own house in order, the Third World, among others, would benefit immensely.

The World Bank

The tasks facing the Western economies after World War II were truly enormous. The war had ravaged the West European economies, and their reconstruction became an objective of the highest priority, both to the United States and to the European countries themselves. Moreover, there was a growing realization that a prosperous and stable world order could not proceed without the full participation of the poorer or less developed countries of the world. To many, the supply of private savings and capital appeared inadequate to accomplish these twin postwar tasks of reconstruction and development. The International Bank for Reconstruction and Development, or World Bank, was created after the war to supplement the supply of private capital with public capital. The original, and fundamental, purpose of the World Bank was to *create* wealth, not transfer it. It was to achieve this noble purpose by assisting the private sector.

The faith placed in the private sector by the international community in those early postwar years proved not to have been misplaced. Western Europe is not only back on its feet but a major economic force again (threatened only by its own welfare state), while the poor nations of the world have made remarkable economic progress. The World Bank, however, captured by people who have little understanding of, and faith in, the private sector, has veered dramatically from its original purpose. Instead of creating wealth, the World Bank today is more interested in transferring wealth. Instead of promoting Third World development by supplementing private capital, the World Bank today frustrates development by crowding out private capital.

Under Robert McNamara's leadership, the World Bank has become increasingly involved in direct income and wealth redistribution to help the poor in the Third World. Here are a few examples of specific World Bank loans for this purpose during recent years.

1. A $32 million loan to the Philippines: "About 180,000 residents of Tondo, one of Manila's worst slums, will benefit from an urban development project in which health, nutrition, and other social services improvements will be integrated with improvements in water supply, sewerage and drainage projects."

2. A $6.7 million loan to El Salvador: "A second urban development project consists of the construction of about 8,000 serviced lots, complete with social and economic infrastructure; squatter upgrading; credit and technical assistance to small businesses."

3. A $24 million loan to India: "Some 240,000 slum dwellers and other poor in Madras will directly benefit from residential sites and services; improvement of slum areas . . . "

What the Third World poor need more than anything else is relief from domestic government policies that impoverish their economies. By trying to help the poor directly, the World Bank bails out offending governments by negating the costs of their ill-conceived policies. In so doing, it encourages the continuation of such policies and thus the continuation of the poverty of those it pretends to assist. If the World Bank were to discontinue its poverty program from afar, the main beneficiaries would be the Third World poor themselves.

Occasionally, the World Bank's wrongheaded approach to helping the poor has involved it in projects that seriously jeopardize the human rights of the poor people concerned. An example is the Indonesian transmigration project. Despite the fact that McNamara was strongly criticized for his support, the World Bank has persisted in aiding the Indonesian government in forcibly uprooting 500,000 families from Java for *shipment* to several small, barren islands off the coast of Indonesia. In its annual reports, the World Bank justifies this Hitleresque moving about of poor peoples as if they were oranges or apples on the grounds of "upgrading crop production," "generating employment opportunities," and "improving livelihoods." So far, taxpayers throughout the industrialized world, through the World Bank, have subsidized the Indonesian government in this attack on the human rights of its own citizens to the tune of $785 million. This is precisely the type of thing that has occurred as the World Bank has moved into poverty areas, and it is not an isolated incident. There also have been newspaper reports that poor farmers in Tanzania have been herded, under World Bank auspices, onto cooperative farms "to increase agricultural productivity."

When the World Bank moved away from its original wealth-creating purpose to pursue social objectives, a Pandora's box of dubious projects opened up. Diversifying industry away from congested areas does not appear to be a policy geared to increasing economic growth. Yet the World Bank has made at least two loans for this purpose: one in Brazil, the other in Thailand. The justification of a recent loan to Brazil was that "industries will be diversified away from Sao Paulo and Rio de Janeiro areas"; that of the loan to Thailand was "to establish export processing zones away from congested Bangkok."

Perhaps the most serious charge against the World Bank is that it is financing socialism in the Third World by crowding out private capital in areas in which private capital has a comparative advantage. Consider the following loans that enable Third World governments to "capture" industries that properly belong to the sphere of the private sector.

> *Algeria:* World Bank—$46 million. This loan to a state-owned construction-materials enterprise will assist in financing the construction of a cement plant capable of producing a half million

tons a year. The distribution system of the enterprise, Société Nationale de Matériaux de Construction, will be expanded through the acquisition of 260 silo-railway cars and 1,980 trucks and reorganized through the execution of a program of studies. Technical assistance will be provided to the state auditing and accounting enterprise. Total cost: $214 million.

What is the government of Algeria doing in the cement business?

Brazil: World Bank—$60 million. This fifth loan for steel expansion in the country helped the Companhia Siderurgica Paulista (COSIPA) finance its Stage III expansion of steel-making capacity. The project was to expand COSIPA's raw steel production capacity from 2.3 million tons at the completion of Stage II to 3.5 million tons yearly. About 6,500 workers were to be added to the mill's labor force of 7,600 when Stage III attained full production in 1982. Other external lenders were the Inter-American Development Bank ($40 million) and bilateral sources. Total cost: $1,446.4 million.

What is the government of Brazil doing in the steel business?

India: International Development Agency—$105 million. The project was intended to help increase fertilizer production in the country's existing plants from about 60 percent of capacity to about 90 percent by 1979. It will assist in removing production bottlenecks, improving pollution control, and increasing the production of industrial chemicals. An additional 253,000 tons a year of nutrients is expected. Total cost: $239 million.

What right does the Indian government have to be in the fertilizer business? (This one speaks for itself.)

The following two loans are particularly important since they exemplify recent World Bank activity in the energy area:

India: World Bank—$400 million. The development of the southern and central areas of the Bombay High offshore oil field will be continued by drilling 64 wells and constructing fifteen production platforms, a processing platform, and a platform for living quarters. The production potential was expected to reach 12 million tons of crude oil a year by mid-1982. Co-financing ($30 million) is being provided by the OPEC Fund for International Development. Total cost: $858.2 million.

India: World Bank—$150 million. Facilities required to produce up to 140,000 barrels of oil a day and 2.2 million cubic meters of natural gas a day from the Bombay High and North Bassein oil and gas fields will be constructed, as well as facilities for processing, transport, storage, and delivery.

The Bombay High project is a good example of how the World Bank finances socialism in the Third World by allowing governments there to crowd out private investment. A U.S. Treasury study says that the two Bombay High loans are expected to have an economic rate-of-return of 70 percent and 100 percent, respectively. "From a purely nationalistic standpoint, it is understandable that India did not wish to share this project with a foreign company, or to pay market interest rates for loans. But given the high rate of return, commercial financing would most likely have been available."[13]

The World Bank loan to the Bombay High project has had, at least, two deleterious consequences. First, it has imposed an unnecessary cost on taxpayers in the industrialized world by offering a subsidy that was not needed to initiate the project. Second, it has enabled the public sector to crowd out the private sector from jobs that the private sector can do more efficiently. Beryl W. Sprinkel, under secretary of the U.S. Treasury, argues that it is folly for the World Bank to "throw massive money into those kinds of projects, when there is an industry that is the most highly financed of all, that is very competitive, that can do a marvelous job of bottom-line explorations."

The International Monetary Fund and Third World Debt

The history of the International Monetary Fund (IMF) has clearly paralleled that of the World Bank. Both institutions emerged as a result of World War II. Both were intended to supplement—and reinforce—the capitalistic free-market system. Both have veered dramatically from their original purpose to the point where they currently are encouraging and financing big government and socialism in the global economy. And, finally, both have enjoyed an increase in power and influence under the Reagan administration.

The latter is surprising not only because of Reagan's free-market rhetoric, but also because the IMF presumably was made redundant by the move to flexible exchange rates after the breakdown of the Bretton Woods international monetary system during the Nixon years. The central function of the IMF under Bretton Woods was to help member-countries finance "temporary" balance-of-payment deficits so that fixed rates of currency exchange could be maintained. When fixed rates went by the boards, the IMF was widely expected to share a similar fate. But rather than wasting away, the IMF has staged a remarkable comeback. Indeed because of the problem of Third World debt—or, more precisely, because of the Reagan administration's approach to this problem—the influence of the IMF has increased to the point where it once again has become a major player in the international money game.

The reason is that the Reagan administration—led by Treasury Secretary Donald Regan—has chosen the IMF as its "bailout mechanism" to save both the banks that have lent enormous sums of money to Third World countries and the Third World governments who borrowed those sums. In the face of the unpleasant reality that the Third World debtors did not have—and could not develop—the economic and financial wherewithal to repay either the principal or the interest on their debt, the Reagan administration had three options. It could have done nothing and let the banks and LDCs work the problem out for themselves. It could have opted for a bilateral bailout, in which case the IMF would have been bypassed. Or it could have done what it in fact did—opted for a multilateral bailout via the IMF.

The reasons why the multilateral route was favored are easy to explain but difficult to defend. At the time the critical decision was made—early spring, 1983—the Reagan administration was excessively influenced by the gurus of Wall Street, whose primary concern was to lower interest rates—the alleged *sine qua non* of the hoped-for economic recovery. Many considered the financial fabric of both the U.S. and the world economy to be so thin that the slightest hint of default and/or bank failure could spark a financial panic that would not only damage the economy but damage Ronald Reagan's chances of being re-elected if he chose to run for a second term.

The risk of letting the free market or, more precisely, the debtors and creditors unaided by government work out the debt problem for themselves was thought too great. The Reagan administration had confidence in the free market, it is true, but not that much confidence. Accordingly, it sought a bailout mechanism, preferring the multilateral route because it was—to put it bluntly—cheaper. Never mind that instead of the private-sector-loving free-marketeers of the Reagan administration imposing conditions on the recipient LDC "bail-outees," the faceless bureaucrats at the IMF would have the honor. The important thing was that the bailout should be achieved at a minimal cost to the

U.S. taxpayer (a strange neglect of the argument that no bailout would have been cheaper yet). And, for this, the IMF was judged to be the perfect conduit.

Not only was the bailout of the international banks shameful for an administration that preaches the disciplinary role of the marketplace, but, more important, it was counterproductive to the legitimate aspiration of ensuring that the present situation never happens again. The bankers have not been disciplined. Instead they have learned that high-interest loans to risky clients are profitable indeed, for when push comes to shove, Uncle Sam will bail them out. And the offending LDC governments also have been able to avoid the fundamental reform of their economic policies that the no-bail-out solution would have compelled.

Of course, the bailout does not compel recurrence—it only encourages it. But if it has happened once, there is no reason to believe that it will not happen again, particularly since the bankers and LDCs have learned that they can avoid the costs of their economically irresponsible policies by threatening the West with a financial panic. The incentive effect of the IMF bailout, in other words, is the wrong one if a repeat performance is to be avoided.

The arguments against the IMF bailout are the same as those against foreign aid. Just as foreign aid discourages reform of destructive domestic economic policies in recipient countries, the IMF bailout does likewise. Just as foreign aid finances exports from the transferor to the transferee, the IMF bailout finances the interest payments on Third World debt to the international banks. And just as foreign aid encourages "big government" in the developing world, so do IMF loans.

The magic of the marketplace that Ronald Reagan often invokes to justify domestic policies extends past the United States' national boundaries. The free-market approach to global economic development is incompatible both with foreign aid and IMF bailouts. And the free-market approach is the only one that works.

Notes

1. W. Arthur Lewis, "The Slowing Down of the Engine of Growth," *American Economic Review* 70 (1980): 555.

2. Melvyn B. Krauss, *The New Protectionism* (New York: New York University Press, 1978).

3. Lewis, "The Slowing Down of the Engine of Growth," p. 555.

4. Quoted by Gottfried Haberler, "The Liberal International Economic Order in Historical Perspective," in R. C. Amacher, G. Haberler, and T. D. Willet, eds., *Challenges to a Liberal International Economic Order* (Washington, D.C.: American Enterprise Institute, 1979), p. 51.

5. I. M. D. Little, "The Developing Countries and the International Order," in ibid., pp. 261–62.

6. Haberler, "Liberal International Economic Order," p. 55.

7. See Melvyn B. Krauss, *Development Without Aid* (New York: McGraw-Hill, 1983).

8. *North-South: A Programme for Survival* (London: Pan Books, 1980).

9. Ibid., pp. 244–45.

10. Ibid., p. 22.

11. Ibid.

12. William Safire, "The Great Ripoff," *New York Times*, March 19, 1981.

13. Quoted in Shirley Hobbs Scheibla, "McNamara's Bank," *Barrons*, August 17, 1981, p. 11.

2

The Churches, Peace, and Communism

Alain Besançon and L. H. Gann

The existence of quite another system of opinions and interests [opposed to Protestantism and Catholicism] is now plain to the grossest sense . . . It is the new fanatical religion . . . which rejects all establishments . . . and which will lay prostrate your Church . . . This religion, which laughs at all creeds and dogmas and confessions of faith, may be fomented equally among all descriptions and all sects—among nominal Catholics, and among nominal Churchmen, and among those Dissenters who know little and care less about Presbytery . . . Against this new, this growing, this exterminatory system, all these churches have a common concern to defend themselves . . . How the enthusiasts of this rising sect rejoice to see you of the old churches play their game . . . in order to keep up the execution of their plan for your common ruin.[1]

Edmund Burke, in his time, presented an eloquent case against those churchmen willing to compromise with Jacobinism. He would have been yet more outspoken against those ecclesiastics determined to pursue a pacifist policy with regard to the challenge from communism—a system far more sophisticated and antireligious in scope than Jacobinism with its naive faith in reason, virtue, and the Rights of Man.

There are many different forms of Marxism-Leninism. Marxist-Leninist parties may quarrel among themselves; many follow different lines. But when in power, they share certain features. They profess a doctrine of "democratic centralism" that requires—at least in theory—total adherence to the party's decisions in every sphere of life. The parties represent the interests of a new class of functionaries and ideologues whose privileges derive their legitimation from the party's exalted role. The party is more than a mere political authority. It sees itself as the demiurge of a new world to be shaped through the instrumentality of "scientific socialism" and "dialectical materialism"; its basic assumptions run counter to those of all traditional religions. The party's claims to omnicompetence are startling—and they are not made lightly. One-third of the globe has now fallen under the sway of Marxist-Leninist parties. Among them, the Communist Party of the Soviet Union is the most powerful; it controls the greatest concentration of military might that has ever existed on this globe. According to Soviet theoreticians, socialism—as represented by the USSR—and capitalism—as embodied by the United States and its allies—are locked in a fateful struggle. This must be waged on many planes, economic, military, political, diplomatic, and ideological. Final victory must go to Marxism-Leninism, a philosophy destined ultimately to create a New Man.

Such claims should make a churchman tremble. Yet it is indeed astonishing how the churches have widely placed themselves at the head of pacifist movements as far afield as Germany, Holland, Belgium, and Great Britain, though not in France or Italy. The Communists profit from the movement and in many cases direct it, but they did not create pacifism; nor can they supply it with its requisite moral energy. This force derives from the churches themselves. But why? For many centuries the churches, while preaching peace, have accommodated themselves to war; churchmen have been pacific, but never pacifists. The present situation, of course, does not derive from a classical conflict between states, as in 1914, but results from a global conflict between the communist world and the noncommunist world. Once again the churches' attitude seems surprising: according to its basic principles, communism is anti-Christian; communists in power have always persecuted believers. One might therefore expect a very strong ecclesiastical reaction.

Nevertheless, it is precisely because communism is the potential enemy that the churches of Western Europe are paralyzed and capable of being manipulated by Communists. This phenomenon has its roots in religious, intellectual, and political history. The concepts that underlie modern pacifism first appeared at the beginning of the nineteenth century; the political situation making churches vulnerable to pacifism took shape during the period immediately before, during, and after World War II. In its present form, pacifism derives from an even more recent concatenation of circumstances. Pacifism, as presently preached, is but a symptom of a profound crisis, one intelligible only in historical terms.[2]

The Romantic Heritage

Pacifism today stands mainly to the Left; its intellectual origins, however, derive from the Right—from the conservative romanticism that flourished at the beginning of the nineteenth century. The churches at that time had barely escaped disaster as a result of the Enlightenment, including the Jacobinism against which Burke had inveighed. The churches therefore formed an alliance with romanticism, a force that was widely supplanting anti-Christian rationalism and criticism. Having been traumatized by the revolutionary experience and having committed themselves to fighting against the remnants of the Enlightenment and its antireligious convictions, the churches permitted themselves to be infused with romantic notions foreign to their traditions, even though those concepts frequently took fervently religious forms. Modern pacifism owes a profound debt to several of these concepts.

The Organic Ideal.   Throughout its existence, the church—especially the Catholic church—had learned to accommodate itself to struggles of princes and nations. The churches had formulated a *jus pacis et belli* (law of peace and war) justifying "just wars" as well as imposing sanctions against "unjust wars." The new liberal regimes involved the churches in a new order characterized by the rule of secular states and by conflicts between classes, social groups, and lobbies. The churches widely turned to the ideal of an organic society where, by definition, conflicts would cease to exist. This ideal took the form of a retrospective utopia with regard to Christendom, found equally in Chateaubriand and Novalis, and among the Russian Slavophiles. These notions easily fused with a futurist utopia in which a *nouvelle chrétienté* (a new Christendom) would create an organic community of classes and nations free from oppression and strife.

Antijudicialism. For untold centuries sages have pondered the legitimacy or illegitimacy of property and the question of man's right to defend his property and motherland by force of arms. The churches have always proclaimed man's right to sacrifice his life for supernatural ends—for the soul's salvation or the worship of the true God. In addition, the churches have permitted man to take up the sword for "natural" ends—allowing men to fight *pro aris et focis* (for altars and hearths), to battle to the death in defense of liberty, honor, and property. This right, according to the churches, springs from Natural Law—one that does not depend on revelation but derives, more properly, from the human condition. Natural Law aims at a just apportionment of material goods among free people (*suum cuique*—to each his own). These concepts, inherited from Aristotle, the Stoics, Roman jurists, and medieval canon-law theorists, were wrecked by romantic historicism. Humanity, according to the romantics, is being carried forward by the tide of evolution: law is not absolute but relative in character, dependent always on society, its time and place in history.

In addition, the concept of Natural Law was undermined by pietism and evangelicalism. These two trends, powerful among both Protestants and Catholics, devalued law in favor of grace—the Old Testament as against the New Testament. Pietists dreamed of a society in which law would be rendered superfluous through the triumph of Love, while private property would become nugatory at the onset—here and now—of a messianic era. Duty, private property, and obligations assumed an unworthy quality and were subjected accordingly to moral censure.

Antichrematistic Values. At the beginning of the nineteenth century, romantic conservatives elaborated an anticapitalistic philosophy that rejected the legitimacy of complex financial transactions, industrialization, the profit motive, and finally the free market. As Macaulay put it trenchantly in a polemic against poet and historian Robert Southey:

> There is nothing which he [Southey] hates so bitterly [as the industrial system]. It is, according to him, more tyrannical than that of the feudal ages, a system of actual servitude, a system which destroys the bodies and degrades the minds of those who are engaged in it. He expresses a hope that the competition of other nations may drive us out of the field; that our foreign trade may decline, and that we may thus enjoy a restoration of our national sanity and strength.[3]

The romantics detested and vilified money, a measure of economic realities, in and of itself. Christian antichrematicism thus listened sympathetically to the imprecations against the bourgeoisie that were heard all over Europe. Moreover, Christian antichrematicism introduced a geographic dichotomy between those countries where commercial values ruled supreme and those lands where the remnants of a partriarchal order still held sway. Antichrematicism favored the economically more underdeveloped sections of Eastern, as against Western, Europe. The romantics on the continent also developed their own peculiar prejudices against the Anglo-Saxon world and its supposed penchant for materialism, selfishness, and mediocrity.

Spirituality. Its enemy is the world as it exists. Spirituality rejects the oblique, patient, and imperfect ways of politics. It instinctively seeks the *Aufhebung* (the magic disappearance of all social and political "contradictions"). It searches for a mystical short circuit that will lead to a general reconciliation. Spirituality rejects wealth, even simple comfort, in which it sees man's surrender to matter. Spirituality aspires to unselfishness and praises gifts and feasts provided gratuitously; it therefore undervalues the more modest precepts of the Ten Commandments. In their place, spirituality looks to the morality of the Beatitudes, even though the latter were intended not to replace, but to extend and fulfill the Ten Commandments. The commandments of the Old Testament become optional; the counsel of the New Testament becomes obligatory. It is excusable to steal but not to own property. Influenced by romanticism, Christian spirituality evinced a tendency to oppose the God of Moses to the God of Jesus, returning spontaneously to Gnosticism and to the heresy of Marcion.[4] Spirituality regarded with suspicion the Creation itself; in its place, it placed its hope in a New Creation—the destruction of the existing world and formation of a new order that would free humanity from the debasing constraints of the body, of the economy, of society, and history at large.

Such are the characteristics of the philosophical-religious syndrome developed by those Christian thinkers who rejected the modern world, industrial society, and liberal democracy. During the Revolution of 1848, this congeries of ideas became the property of the Left. In France the key figure was Félicité Robert de Lamennais, who began his spiritual career as a follower of ultra-Catholicism and, having been converted to the religion of humanity, thereafter looked to the future and to socialism to realize his utopia. In Russia, it was Alexander Herzen, who grafted on populism the Slavophile themes of an organic community. In Germany, the Hegelian Left adopted the same ideas. In most cases, these movements explicitly rejected Christianity and the churches. Yet Christians who verbally attacked the revolutionary Left for its atheism often came to share its contempt for the modern bourgeoisie. Such, in particular, was the position of Dostoevsky and of the French Catholic polemicists Léon Bloy, Charles Péguy, and Georges Bernanos in France. Christian conservatism therefore can at any moment mutate into revolutionism; the moment is apt to be decided by political circumstance.

The Politics of Utopia

In the many denominations (with their varying hierarchical systems) that constitute Protestantism, it is difficult to determine specific political trends within the ecclesiastical realm. The Catholic church rests on a hierarchical organization headed by the pope, and its political blunders are therefore more visible. Widespread pacifism within that church appears at first sight to derive from an inadequate analysis of the current political situation. However, the church has also become entangled in errors that spring from different sources and lead back to mistaken assumptions of previous generations regarding liberal society, nazism, and communism.

Liberal Society. During the nineteenth century, French and German thinkers (especially Jean Baptiste Lacordaire, Marc Sangnier, Karl von Vogelsang, and Wilhelm von Ketteler) had created what has become known as Catholic "social doctrine," which later found expression in the celebrated encyclicals *Rerum novarum* (Of new things; 1891), *Quadragesimo anno* (In the fortieth year; 1931), and *Mater et magistra* (Mother and teacher; 1961). This doctrine rests on a positive theory of what the "good Christian society" ought to resemble. The doctrine assumes that this society can be created only by making a simultaneous break with liberal society, socialism, and the centralizing state. The doctrine extols a social, corporate-type organicism with roots in the romantic movement, one that had a considerable impact in the Catholic states of Europe—in Mussolini's Italy, Salazar's Portugal, and Dollfuss's Austria. This doctrine in some respects also departs from traditional notions of Natural Law. Until then, the church had demanded that justice must be based on existing regimes, but it did not call for a commitment to work for an ideal regime. Thereafter the church began to veer toward utopia.

Catholic conservatives committed another serious error in widely stigmatizing liberalism and socialism as parallel evils. By doing so, conservatives imputed to these movements similarities that did not exist. By attempting to create an organic society in which conflict either did not exist or would be settled automatically, conservatives ran the risk of diminishing the autonomy and freedom of the various social actors. In addition, organicists erred in adjudging moral worth by considering organizations or "social structures" rather than individuals. In fact, social structures in and of themselves are neither good nor bad; it is only individuals who commit or abstain from committing evil.

Relations with National Socialism

The compromises of the Catholic church, especially the Catholic church in the Third Reich, to the Nazis can be explained in part by the Nazis' apparent commitment to an "organic" ideal and also by the church's perfectly legitimate fear of communism. The church on the whole failed to perceive the totalitarian, indeed the Gnostic, nature of nazism. (Alfred Rosenberg, one of the chief nazi theoreticians, indeed identified in his book *Der Mythus des 20. Jahrhunderts* the heretical and Gnostic "Albigensians, Waldensians, and Catharites" with the spirit of Germanic heroism.) Nazi philosophers envisaged history in terms of an eternal struggle between the forces of light embodied by the Aryan race and the forces of darkness represented by the Jews. The nazi faithful put their trust in Adolf Hitler, a messianic leader who would lead Germany from servitude to salvation, to the splendor of the *Tausendjährige Reich* (Thousand-year Reign). The new millennial empire would vindicate the sacrifices of the nazi martyrs done to death by *Rotfront und Reaktion,* the Reds and reactionaries denounced in the nazi party anthem. But apparently oblivious to the history of heresy, the church was apt to confuse nazism with authoritarian fascist regimes—straightforward tyrannies with which the church had managed to conclude legitimate compromises.

Even more fateful was "the silence of Pope Pius XII," the *de facto* abandonment of the Jewish people. This essay does not propose to examine the extenuating circumstances that the churches could plead in their defense—above all, the difficulty of understanding an atrocity as alien to humanity as the Final Solution. The church's failure, however, was fraught with fateful consequences. The church was burdened with a bitter sense of guilt, although responsibility did not lie with the churches alone. Roosevelt and Churchill also knew what was happening at Auschwitz, and neither acted in a more positive fashion than Pius XII. But Pius was the pope, and the victims were Jews. The churches thereafter would have done better to examine their own consciences than to make excuses. In equating their duty toward the Jews with their duty toward the persecuted of every kind, the churches moreover forgot their natural solidarity with the synagogue. The churches failed to see that in attacking the Jewish people, the nazis in fact also attacked the church—a fact that had been obvious to many ordinary German Catholics during the *Kristallnacht* (a pogrom launched in 1938, resulting in the destruction of all German synagogues). While formally rejecting anti-Judaism, the churches allowed themselves to be pushed into a *de facto* Marcionism. Marcionism in turn entailed a secular drift into antinomianism, antijudicialism, spiritualism, and a sense of distrust toward the created world and society at large. The churches therefore rendered themselves more vulnerable than earlier to the challenge of communism.

Relations with Communism

During the interwar period (1918–1939), few temporal and spiritual authorities condemned communism as vigorously as did the papacy. Unfortunately there was a wide gap between condemnation and comprehension. Separated from the liberal world by a great barrier, the papacy considered communism a continuation of liberalism and democratic socialism, a catastrophic aggravation of evils already in existence. Having failed to understand the rift between the Mediterranean fascist movements and nazism, the church equally failed to grasp clearly the novel aspects of communism—an all-embracing, supposedly scientific, ideology. The church was inclined to consider communism a society, a civilization, a culture—admittedly evil, but nevertheless a society. In fact, there is no such thing as a communist society; there is only the domination of an ideocratic party over the ruined remnants of society.

During the aftermath of war, the European churches found themselves in a very vulnerable position vis-à-vis both communism and the USSR. Communism had actively striven against nazi anti-Semitism; it claimed to put an end to social injustice and to create an organic society in which the poor would come first. Moreover, communism vowed to put an end to wars between nations by crushing imperialism—the ultimate cause of war according to communist doctrine. Communists proclaimed their commitment to peace. Their apparent commitment heightened the churches' sense of guilt (by reason of their previous attitude toward fascism and the Jews and their former political and social conservatism). The sense of guilt became all the more bitter as the churches widely equated part of the communist program with their own.

Present-Day Problems

Pope Pius XII unfailingly denounced communism until his dying days. The 322 bishops assembled at the Vatican Council in 1964 demanded that communism should be condemned as such in a conciliar document. For obscure reasons, however, this petition was not discussed; thereafter the word "communism" disappeared from official documents issued by the magisterial authority of the Catholic church. At about the same time, the World Council of Churches began to embark on a rapprochement with the communist world. The new policy entailed some major misconceptions.

The Symmetrical Vision. Many churchmen have become accustomed to condemn in equal and symmetrical fashion the real or supposed evils both of "capitalism" and "socialism." The churches do not comprehend that in doing so, they unwittingly commit themselves to an ideological mode of thought. The Communists' theological dualism in fact divides the world into two opposing camps—two antagonistic "realities"—one of which is destined to prevail over the other. A nonideological thinker, however, cannot simply subsume modern society under the concept of "capitalism"; such an assumption makes sense only within the framework of Marxist-Leninist doctrine. Neither is there any such thing as a "socialist" society. Utopia remains beyond the reach of utopians in power. Communism's crushing machinery of domination attempts to persuade men that socialism already exists— even though nowhere has it come into being.

It is a serious matter for the churches to have unwittingly accepted this dualism, this ontological equation between the so-called capitalist world on the one hand and the socialist world on the other. If socialism is to be considered an existing system, the churches should subject it to the criteria of divine law and seek to convert the Communists. But having accepted communism as a project already half put into practice, one designed to install "social justice" on the earth, the churches can only criticize communism on the grounds that it has not fully met its promises. The churches would then have to call for a new declaration of the Rights of Man; they would have to demand that the Communists be more faithful to their own declared program of social justice as well as recognize the reality of the human soul and man's religious aspirations.

Many clerics believe that a communist society that also believes in God would be more naturally Christian than our own. In doing so, however, they go astray. The trouble with communism is not that it lacks a program, or that it is unjust, tyrannical, or even atheist. Communism, by its very nature, is false; it does not exist; it is of itself one universal lie. By taking seriously, even for the purpose of censure, communism's instrumentalist ethic, its philosophical pretension, and its "achievements," a critic already concedes to communism an ontological consistency that it does not possess. The churchmen engaged in a "dialogue" with communism unwittingly fall into what Alexander Solzhenitsyn describes as the moral sin of personal participation in the Big Lie.

On the other hand, if the Western world is envisaged as "capitalist," the innumerable injustices occurring every day are interpreted only in one sense and deriving from one side cause: capitalism. Hence the churches make more radical claims with regard to capitalism than to socialism; to them, if capitalism exists, it is unjust by its very nature. Churchmen then call for changing a capitalist structure that is supposedly both iniquitous and unacceptable. The churches thereby drift even further into ideology: socialism should be improved; capitalism must be changed. The Communists say the same thing.

Clerical Para-Marxism. The search for a synthesis between Marxism and Christianity has a long history. The Marxist camp has furnished "god-builders" such as Lunacharsky and philosophers such as Ernst Bloch and Roger Garaudy. Christian synthesizers include Karl Barth, the greatest of Protestant theologians, who was a socialist all his life and participated in the first "peace movement" by signing its Stockholm manifesto. The popularity of Teilhard de Chardin, a Catholic priest, derives from his evolutionary globalist cosmology that wishes to accommodate the communist phenomenon.

What were once the beliefs of individuals have become the beliefs of mass movements. Guilt-ridden because of past errors, churches accuse themselves of imaginary errors. Hence they succumb to Marxist pressure and allow themselves to support almost any kind of social claim—often the most demagogic ones—for fear of failing in their duty toward the poor on the one hand and of compromising with the rich on the other—of doing the very things of which they stand accused by their opponents.

Regarding recently decolonized countries and the Third World at large, for example, the churches accept as self-evident current theories that Third World poverty derives from imperialist domination, neo-colonialist manipulation, capitalist exploitation, and the transfer of wealth from the Third World to Europe or the United States. In order to find forgiveness for past indifference toward the Jews, the churches back the Palestinians. These emotion-laden creeds have hardened into a new doctrine that finds expression in theological thought. European seminaries have thus elaborated, for the benefit of Third World clergy, a new "theology of liberation" based on Marxism-Leninism. Para-Marxism of the ecclesiastical sort represents a new crisis of faith—one much more serious than the unbelief fashionable among so many enlightened churchmen during the eighteenth century and gently satirized by historian Edward Gibbon, who imputed contemporary skepticism to the pagan priests of Rome at the decline of the empire.

> Viewing with a smile of pity and indulgence the various errors of the vulgar, they diligently practiced the ceremonies of their fathers, devoutly frequented the temples of the Gods, and sometimes condescending to act a part on the theater of superstition, they concealed the sentiments of an Atheist under the sacerdotal robes.[5]

Para-Marxism represents not so much unbelief as a distortion of religious commitment. During the nazi era, a number of variegated clergymen, the *Deutsche Christen,* had attempted to build a theology that would sacralize the nazi dictatorship and keep Christianity abreast of history. Christian para-Marxists of a later generation imagined that a sacred empire was emerging in the shape of the people's democracies, represented by revolutionary leaders such as Fidel Castro. The so-called liberation theology spread among the demi-intelligentsia rather than among the rank and file of believers. The views propagated by the World Council of Churches with regard to the alleged evils of capitalism or the malevolence of Israel are popular with leftist clergy rather than with the individual in the pew. Practicing Christians, whose numbers are constantly diminishing in Europe, derive mainly from the middle classes and vote for conservative parties. Ideologically minded clergy count themselves as members of a progressive vanguard called on to "enlighten" and manipulate the masses, while paralyzing the authority of their own clerical superiors. The latter, fearing dissensions and schisms, are apt to remain silent and make concessions rather than resist.

The Nuclear Menace.   Mankind today faces a terrible threat: the accumulation of nuclear weapons so powerful that their employment might end life on this planet. No church can remain indifferent to this peril. According to the theory of the "just war," the cause for which a conflict is waged must be just; there must also be a proper relation between the means employed and the ends pursued. Nuclear weapons, however, have introduced an element of disproportion between means and ends. Means as horrific as the atomic and the hydrogen bombs cannot easily be reconciled to an end that would justify their employment. Since their use could entail absolute destruction, no combatant is morally entitled to wield them except for the purpose of resisting an absolute evil. It is almost certainly a historical tragedy that the bomb was not dropped against Hitlerism, which could justly be identified with total iniquity, rather than against the Japanese, who pursued a classic war of conquest that was no better and no worse than preceding wars of imperial conquest in human history. During the aftermath of war, men of good will widely became convinced that life under a totalitarian regime, either nazism in Germany or Soviet communism in Russia and Eastern Europe, was so debased that even atomic death was preferable. This commitment found expression in the slogan "Better dead than Red," a sentiment not evoked by historical wars of conquest. No Alsatian, for example, would ever have said "Better dead than German" or "Better dead than French."

The churches in the past had sometimes condemned wars of conquests, but they had rarely called for revolts against the conquerors, not even in pagan or Moslem countries. There were some exceptions to this rule: the papacy during the sixteenth century had demanded of English Catholics that they should rise against Queen Elizabeth I, a heretic, and support Philip of Spain. Submission to *de facto* kings, however, had been the norm. In medieval Russia, for example, the church had officially prayed for a Moslem ruler, the Tatar khan. The churches had rarely envisaged civil disobedience or resistance to the death such as that practiced by Judas Maccabeus. Resistance seemed justified only when the conqueror seemed clearly resolved to annihilate a society or absolutely to go counter to the precepts of Natural Law and morality. It was on these grounds that Pius XII had condemned communism. Hence the churches did not initially object to the creation of the U.S. nuclear arsenal; the United States clearly did not intend to launch an attack. The defensive use of nuclear weapons seemed legitimate not for the purpose of resisting Russian expansionism, but to defend the West against communism—considered a mortal evil threatening human society.

The churches today have largely lost the conviction that communism stands for absolute evil. Instead, they are more inclined to regard communism as a relative evil confronting the Western world, a world that is likewise and symmetrically wicked. These views are particularly popular among young seminarians desperately anxious to halt the exodus from the churches by finding a social gospel that will appeal to the broadest number of people. Assumptions concerning the assumed symmetry of evil between the United States and the Soviet Union have also become widespread among the literary intelligentsia. As Günter Grass, a moderate and a friend of former West German chancellor Helmut Schmidt, as well as a courageous critic of the New Left in Germany, put it:

> I am convinced that in the United States, in the so-called silent majority, strong fascist tendencies have become apparent in recent years and that a land, such a rich land that to this day practices racism—with disastrous consequences, as we know—that such a rich land in which I don't know how many millions live below the poverty level, such a rich land relies—now under Reagan—on early capitalistic methods of exploitation and develops them anew, that this land has no right, or has lost its right, to point critically at others.[6]

Günter Grass did not ask the Boat People (the Vietnamese refugees given shelter in the United States) their opinion. But his books found a wide readership; his views regarding the United States hardened into a new orthodoxy on both sides of the Atlantic.

In addition to intellectual reasons, the churches were influenced by new political circumstances. Statesmen such as de Gaulle and Henry Kissinger, both proponents of détente, were convinced that the USSR could be admitted to a concert of powers by taking due regard of Moscow's legitimate interests as a great power. In doing so, they unfortunately forgot the essentially ideological nature of communism, and the asymmetry that existed between the Western countries and the communist movement headed by the USSR. The churches embarked on an *Ostpolitik* of their own. They desired to protect their coreligionists, to contribute to détente, and perhaps to embark on a dialogue that many vaguely regarded as a means of converting Communists. The churches came to think in terms of two rival empires, the Soviet and the American, which supposedly had divided the globe between them. A considerable body of clerical literature began to compare the situation in Poland with conditions in Chile, and in Latin America with Eastern Europe.

When the communist movement and its allies launched the first peace movement (the Stockholm manifesto) in 1950, the churches stood aside. Subsequently, the churches found many reasons for joining the second movement in the 1970s. For many churchmen, the new campaign seemed a kind of revival. There were, of course, many exceptions. Many believers remained committed to militant anticommunist creeds, including evangelical Christians (fundamentalists) and adherents of new churches such as the Unification church ("Moonies"). The Moonies' anticommunism offended the Establishment churches more than their absurd metaphysical doctrines and bizarre theology. The Church of Scientology's implied libertarianism, its dislike of both psychiatry and the welfare state, and its conviction that communism is a "suppressive" creed troubled liberal critics more than the Scientologists' tenets on humanity's immortality or assumed ability to lead successive lives. While calling for a dialogue with the Communists, the Establishment churches failed to embark on a dialogue with either evangelical Christians or so-called cultists. Unable to provide good reasons for preferring an evidently guilty West to a probably guilty East, the churches were inclined to adopt "peace"—namely, the preservation of human life at any price—as their supreme value.

Having accepted these premises, churchmen turned the disarmament question into the main political issue. Some pastors in fact called for unilateral disarmament, including Bishop John Baker of Salisbury, who insisted that the British government should relinquish all its nuclear weapons—even at the risk of "blackmail and defeat" by an enemy: "Better Red than dead" (with a curious lack of logic, no advocate of unconditional disarmament argues "Better Yankee than dead"). For the time being, however, the Establishment churches, including the Anglican and the Catholic, contented themselves with bilateral disarmament.

We do not rejoice at the churches' attitude. Indeed, we must confess to a certain measure of sympathy with Queen Elizabeth I, who, in 1579, ordered preachers

> that in their sermons and preachings they do not intermeddle
> with any such matters of state, being in very deed not incident or

> appertaining to their profession . . . but rather teach the people to
> be thankful towards Almighty God for the great benefits both of
> liberty of conscience, peace, and wealth which they have hitherto
> enjoyed by her Majesty's good means.[7]

Pacifist pastors have good reason to ponder Queen Elizabeth's past pronouncements while pondering the Soviet Union's present position. The Soviet Union clearly has not the slightest intention of disarming; Soviet leaders stand committed to the intensification of the international class struggle. Soviet military theoreticians reject a defensive doctrine and preach, instead, the merits of a sustained offensive. The Soviet armed forces do not exist merely to defend the motherland and the other socialist countries. The Soviet armed forces also support "national liberation movements" and stand ready to resist "imperialism" in the most distant corners of the globe.[8] Given such Soviet assumptions, the West—in our opinion—remains fully justified in continuing its efforts to maintain a balance of terror. But if we commit ourselves to a doctrine of symmetry between East and West, we help to legitimize the communist system. By doing so, we may in the long run weaken our commitment to legitimate defense.

The present political drift has already continued for two decades (the Second Vatican Council formed a milestone). In the religious sphere, the trends developed over a period of two centuries. This evolution is perhaps so profound and far-reaching that the chances of a reaction seem slight. In the political field, the West must surely arrive at a clear understanding of communism's true nature and of the danger that it poses to human society. Elected officials who practice politics as their trade rarely arrive at such a grasp. Why, then, should the clergy be expected to think in a more lucid fashion? Nevertheless, communism is not merely a political phenomenon. It is also a metaphysical system— it posits an all-embracing vision of the physical world and history and performs a religious mission in seeking secular salvation.

It has often been from a metaphysical standpoint that communism has been criticized most profoundly. We can only hope that the churches will come to understand the threat that communism poses through its perverse imitation of the Judeo-Christian tradition and that they will begin one day to rid themselves of trends and attitudes that favor this perversion and thereby involve churches in moral complicity. By doing so, the churches would return to a just appreciation of Natural Law, the legitimacy of society's natural ends, its autonomy, and the dignity possessed by the created world. Such a return would be a true "reformation," that is to say, a reversion to the established norm.

Notes

1. Edmund Burke's undated letter, probably about January 1797; Edmund Burke, *Selected Writings and Speeches*, ed. Peter J. Shalis (Gloucester, Mass.: Peter Smith, pp. 270–71.

2. See Alain Besançon, *La Confusion des langues* (Paris: Calmann-Lévy, 1978).

3. Lord Macaulay, "Southey's Colloquies on Society," *Critical and Historical Essays* (New York: Armstrong & Son, n.d.), p. 104.

4. Marcion belonged to the Roman clergy, from which he was expelled in A.D. 144. His heretical system contains the following elements: (1) rejection of the Old Testament, rewriting of the New Testament; (b) distinction between the God of Abraham and Moses and the God of Jesus. The former, creator of this imperfect world, represents Fear, Justice, Punishment; the latter, who sent Jesus to liberate humanity from the bondage of matter, justice, sexuality, and property, represents Love and Spirituality. Although condemned, Marcionism revived many times in the history of Christianity.

5. Edward Gibbon, *The Decline and Fall of the Roman Empire: An Abridgement*, ed. D. M. Low (New York: Harcourt, Brace & Co., 1960), p. 13.

6. "Gunter Grass: An Interview," *New York Review of Books*, February 23, 1983, section BF, p. 2.

7. Paul Johnson, *Elizabeth I: A Biography* (New York: Holt, Rinehart & Winston, 1974), p. 354.

8. Marshal A. A. Grechko, "The Leading Role of the CPSU in Building the Army of a Developed Socialist Society," *Voprosy istorii KPSS* 1974, no. 5 (May), in *USA/FN Soviet Press Translations*, July 31, 1974, pp. 74–77.

3

Leadership in Times of Crisis

James Bond Stockdale_____

S everal years ago I found myself cooling my heels in the offices of NBC Television in New York, waiting for a stage to be set up for the filming of a public service talk show in which I had been invited to participate. I had arrived several minutes early, and an accommodating receptionist suggested that I might enjoy visiting with one of the NBC executives while I waited. Agreeing, I was escorted into a magnificent suite and on into the large inner office, where a dozen TV screens were embedded in the wall, all videos on, all sound off. The suite's sophisticated master was standing behind his large desk, arms folded, keeping an eye on the television world so to speak, ready to turn up any audio should something catch his eye. He was not of my generation; he was a younger man with a modish haircut and a turtleneck sweater under an expensive sport coat. I sighed to myself, "Here's fifteen minutes shot."

Not so. The man stuck out a friendly hand and said, "I'm Lester Crystall, president of NBC News." (Our acquaintance continues; in March 1983 Crystall stepped down from the NBC post to become executive producer of the MacNeil-Lehrer Report.) My Navy uniform gave him a lead-in for the opening of an impromptu conversation neither of us had anticipated: "Do you think the Navy is being well served by the national news media?" Startled, I muttered something agreeable, then immediately regretted that I had missed a golden opportunity to get on a soapbox.

"Well let me tell you," Crystall was already saying, "I think that in an important way, the television news industry is doing the whole country a continuing disservice. We constantly reinforce a bad idea that we helped invent—the idea that the key to being a good citizen, a discerning voter, is to know where all the candidates stand on all the *issues*. The issues are given the center of the stage, and the politician is cast as their suitor. We have made the expression 'So much for philosophy, let's get down to issues' a maxim of conventional wisdom. And at newstime every evening, all networks project scenes of harassed men and women being nailed down by stubborn interviewers who insist on quick answers on where their victims stand on gun control, abortion, and so on and so on. It's as though the merits of a political leader are known only if he is first carved up into twenty or thirty sections, each representing his ten-second position on every news item of the day, and then his being reassembled and analyzed as a composite whole, as a 'Mr. Blockhead' build-it-yourself educational toy. Because this fractionation and reassembly of a candidate lends itself to simplified, marketable news-theater, we have taught a nation to analyze people in this very shallow way."

Crystall continued. "What's important is not a person's current views on transient issues, but his *character*. Thinking back, I have seldom been surprised at a position held or action taken by a political figure. Once his true character is grasped, his policies and actions are almost always predictable fallouts. To test this idea, I went back and studied the Lincoln-Douglas debates in detail. And let me tell you, Douglas was all issues. He pandered to the mob on every little issue of 1858—and had our current style of television coverage prevailed in those pre–Civil War years, we would have made him the darling of America. We could have got him elected and the country ruined in one simple operation. Abraham Lincoln on the other hand was weak on some issues and indifferent about quite a few others. But you can't read the speeches he wrote and not get the message that he was all character. It comes through, even amidst his somewhat off-color jokes."

About that time I was summoned to go down to a stage to be filmed discussing Shakespeare's famous soliloquy in *As You Like It*, "All the world's a stage . . . ," with Lynn Redgrave, General Andrew Goodpaster, and a couple of his West Point cadets. (What did we think of Shakespeare's characterization of a soldier: "full of strange oaths . . . jealous in honor, sudden and quick in quarrel . . . "?[1])

But I never forgot those words with Crystall—though it's hard to reconstruct his list of examples of hot issues of that day years ago, issues that made or broke candidates in the 1976 elections. Today the list is completely different—nuclear freeze, Central America, draft registration . . . In a year from now the list will again be different. And yet it will be a big deal when put to candidates who will serve in office in 1985–1989 terms—terms in which the main issues to be faced will not even have surfaced by the time of their election.

Isn't Crystall right that *character* is what counts in leadership? Character is probably more important than knowledge. It was so in the case of Lincoln. Of course, all things being equal, knowledge is to be honored. People who at the drop of a hat can give the last word on "The U.S. and the Third World," "The U.S. and the World Economy," "The U.S. and the Soviet Union" are valuable and sometimes good candidates for leadership roles. But what I'm saying is that whenever I've been in trouble spots—in crises (and I've been in a lot of trouble and in a lot of crises)—the *sine qua non* of a leader has lain not in his chess-like grasp of issues and the options they portend, not in his style of management, not in his skill at processing information, but in his having the character, the heart, to deal spontaneously, honorably, and candidly with people, perplexities, and principles.

But discussions of ideas like "character" and "heart" have to be well ordered lest they slide into flabby generalities like "strong character," "weak character," "good hearts," "soft hearts," and all the rest. To avoid that quagmire of rhetorical fuzziness, I'm going to delineate the personality traits of several common types of American public figures, then bang such traits against a worst-case crisis predicament, and finally have a look at how they fare under the gun. The method, like that of the old alchemists, is to base judgment only on the outcome of tests conducted over a hot fire, to draw conclusions only after you have brought out with heat and pressure the *essence* of what's being tested. To isolate essences, I will evaluate typical sets of character traits while exposed to obligations of leadership under the greatest heats and pressures I know—those demanding the generation and maintenance of that moral ascendancy indispensable to nurturing others to prevail with pride under the guns of an extortionist political prison.

I am affiliated with Harvard psychoanalyst Michael Maccoby in an organization called the American Leadership Forum. A few years ago he wrote a popular book entitled *The Gamesman* based on considerable data he had acquired in a study of how new technology was affecting society. Much of this data came from in-depth interviews with 250 top-level business executives, commencing in 1969 in a project called "Technology, Work, and Character." With a lot of historical background, Maccoby set down four sets of character traits, each set being commonly found in one of four types of leaders who at least until 1976 had historically run America. We all know many examples of each of the four types in our midst right now—they've always been around. But by a kind of economic determinism, each of these archetypes had his day in leadership limelight roles in particular historical periods. Maccoby named these: the Craftsman, the Jungle Fighter, the Company Man, and the Gamesman. I'm going to use these models up to the point where I develop a "fifth man," whose time has now come.

Ben Franklin is Maccoby's prototype of the craftsman, and craftsmen prevailed as the leaders of American society from the Revolution until the national banking and credit system emerged soon after the Civil War. This character type is self-contained, inventive, thrifty, resolute, sincere. But Maccoby doesn't play with plaster saints. Craftsmen, like all men, typically have certain negative traits: they are generally obstinate and suspicious and, expecting no favors or handouts from anybody, are often given to hoarding and stinginess. Their motto is "God helps those who help themselves." You know them today as people like Hyman Rickover and Jimmy Carter.

But Benjamin Franklin's type gave up center stage as the industrial revolution enveloped America after the Civil War. It was Andrew Carnegie and his jungle fighters who then became the prime movers of our country. But whereas the craftsman is *not* a game player, not a man who devotes his energies to one-on-one competition but rather to mountain climbing, to pitting himself against the world as he strives for self-improvement, jungle fighters *do* play games. They play zero-sum games—the winnings and losses at the table always adding up to zero. The jungle fighter sees his universe as having a finite amount of business out there, and he strives to get his share—sometimes more. He is tough but, like the craftsman, is also a man of conscience and heart—not the soft heart, certainly not the bleeding heart, but the Old Testament heart (about which more later). He works for himself, for his company, and frequently for his community and country. He can sit at a board table and figuratively decapitate incompetents with ease. But he looks them in the eye as he does it. And he can grieve for them as he sends them on their way. He is bold; he is paternalistic (like old Henry Ford, like old Tom Watson); he is authoritarian; he is intensely competitive.

After World War I, when public relations images and agencies became a fact of life, the jungle fighters' industries, railroads, and banks became more like government bureaucracies than the freewheeling entrepreneurial enterprises they had formerly been. And those tough old competitors themselves were gradually displaced by the less abrasive "company men." Like the jungle fighters, the company men were paternalistic and authoritarian. But unlike those pioneers of industry and finance who were motivated primarily by competitive zeal, these company men, our psychoanalyst believes, were more typically motivated by a fear of failure. Maybe the country sensed that; popular authors pictured them as just warmed-over jungle fighters lacking even the prime virtue of their predecessors—guts. (During the 1950s *The Man in the Gray Flannel Suit* and *The Organization Man* sold very well.) But their most recent progeny (Eisenhower, Jerry Ford) were characteristically honest and cautious men of conscience. They looked men in the eye when they fired them. They were "men of the heart," possessing qualities with an emotional content: a sense of commitment, a sense of loyalty, a sense of humor, spontaneity, and intellectual honesty at the gut level.

In the early 1960s, a fourth leadership style emerged. John F. Kennedy and his whiz kids took center stage explaining that we had made this whole business of running a country too hard. Maccoby identifies practitioners of this style as "the gamesmen." The gamesmen, impatient under the yoke of their paternalistic and authoritarian fathers, and educated more often than not in the game-theory-oriented elite business schools in the country, turned over a new page in leadership practices. The gamesmen believe that if one properly analyzes the "game" of life, the "game" of management, the "game" of leadership, one sees that it is not necessary to frame the problem as a zero-sum game. Rather, in their minds, American life can be analyzed as just one big "game" in which any number can play and win. "Join the meritocracy!" "On to the moon!" "On to Vietnam!"

Now, these gamesmen were relaxed, objective, open-minded, detached, and cerebral. Such emotional baggage as commitment or conscience they deemed unnecessary, inefficient, and overweight. "Play your cards rationally to win, drop the emotional baggage, and go to bed and sleep like a baby without remorse." Some bothered with love and families; many gave them a tentative try and quit when they found them too burdensome, too hard to deal with close up. Maccoby said that there was a theatrical production that typified the leaders of each of these four American eras and that the drama of the time of the gamesmen was portrayed in the movie *The Sting*. You might remember that screenplay; in it, fair, competitive, cooperative swingers, with the aid of teamwork and technology, destroyed the emotional, hung-up, authoritarian Godfather.

The gamesmen, concluded psychoanalyst Maccoby, were basically "men of the head": cool intellectual types, walking calculating machines. Men of the head do many things well, but they usually have trouble coping with unpleasantness. Having confrontations is such a close-up thing, and it's so uncomfortable, so personal, so creepy to have to actually look at emotional faces while you talk to people. These cool, flexible, accommodating guys don't like to discipline people, and they don't like to look people in the eye when they fire them. (It's so much cleaner and easier just to reorganize and eliminate their jobs— "Sorry about that.") Moreover, the typical gamesman craves to be admired, can't stand not to be loved, and that is a great leadership weakness. True leaders must be willing to stake out territory and identify and declare enemies. They must be fair and they may be compassionate, but they cannot be addicted to being loved by everybody. The man who needs to be loved is an extortionist's dream. That man will do anything to avoid face-to-face unpleasantness; he will sell his soul down the river for praise. He can be had.

And the gamesman can have *you,* too, if you are at his bidding and get caught out on the point when he confronts the unexpected, is threatened with facing unpleasantness, and gets cold feet. Although these gamesmen sail under the banner of compassion and benevolence, by being unable to face up to unpleasantness they pull the rug out from under law and tradition and affront the sense of fairness that good men intuitively possess. I digress with a few true stories about how modern political leaders, seeking public adulation, pulled the rug out from under some good men left out on the point.

I used to keep a list of all the American government's own violations of that Code of Conduct which that government's presiding gamesmen sent us military aviators off to war, bound to uphold. The gamesmen inherited that Code. It was old and it was good; it set forth rules befitting honorable conduct of men in battle and in prisoner of war camps. During the early 1960s, as these gamesmen were positioning the country to enter the fighting in Vietnam, we were continually admonished to take that Code seriously and prepare ourselves to uphold its demands. (Just before the Tonkin Gulf events of August 1964, I remember reading a particularly strong admonition signed by Cyrus Vance demanding: "a positive and unswerving acceptance of, belief in, and devotion to the spirit and letter of the Code of Conduct, and the recognition that the Code is a binding military obligation."[2])

You can imagine the dismay of those of us who were shot down in enemy territory and then spent seven or eight years and no small amount of blood, sweat, and tears upholding that Code in Hanoi prisons, out of touch with America, hanging in no matter how tough the going got, to come home and find that stringent codes had long been ignored back in America itself. Rather than obey its own laws, our government had avoided unpleasant confrontations by opportunistically putting all that honor and discipline stuff on the back burner.

For instance, the Code specifically prohibits the making of false confessions. Some in Hanoi prisons gave their lives to avoid it. But our gamesmen dropped that obligation like a hot potato when the North Koreans demanded that our government make a false confession, a public false confession in the name of our president no less, as a *quid pro quo* for the release of USS *Pueblo* prisoners who had been held for less than a year. Our morale would have hit rock bottom if we had been permitted to read the front page of the *New York Times*, December 23, 1968: "The United States Government has deliberately signed what it termed a false confession of espionage inside North Korean territorial waters . . . Secretary of State Dean Rusk said tonight that lengthy negotiation had turned up no other way . . . 'I know of no precedent in my 19 years of public service,' Mr. Rusk said." According to the text of the statement issued by President Johnson, our negotiator "preserved the integrity of the United States." The *Pueblo* had *not* been inside North Korean territorial waters before it was captured.[3]

The Code prohibits the acceptance of parole—the trading of a concession for freedom. (The concession demanded in North Vietnam was the making of treasonous statements.) We senior officers in Hanoi prisons forbade American prisoners to accept this sort of freedom. They stayed in jail, willingly and pridefully stayed in jail in accordance with our orders, our laws, which we derived from the Code. Yet when the few who violated our orders and bought their way home with those treasonous statements showed up in America, the gamesmen greeted them with open arms, made no charges, and even neglected to extend the statute of limitations so that we whose sense of decency they had offended by their conduct might present our case in court against them when we returned.

As a matter of fact, the responsibility for the discipline of all prison informers and collaborators was abdicated by our government and dumped in the laps of us who wrote and enforced the American laws of those prisons. Our government leaders, avoiding unpleasantness, would bring no charges even though their own lawyers (judge advocates) certified that our evidence was complete and sufficient. The cases were few, but those that were on the docket were serious and by being ignored left dangerous precedents. This is a matter of continuing interest and concern to those of us who were involved; there is a good deal more about these matters that belongs in the public domain.

Of course we were all encouraged to look on all these matters as our national leadership's commonsense response to unprecedented circumstances. But "unprecedented circumstances" has become a code word for the cop-out of authority, a code word for a politician's license to steal. By invoking that empty phrase, gutless leaders make exceptions to law, custom, and morality in their own favor on the grounds that the world is becoming new and different. Who's kidding whom? Such an "all previous bets are off" attitude undermines institutions. One man's exception is another man's betrayal.

And so it was in these cases so familiar to me that what was touted as benevolent forgivenesss of the "suffering prisoners of war" was a thinly veiled case of a government's lack of moral courage under pressure. This was met by the vast majority of returning prisoners of war—certainly by all those who served most bravely in Hanoi—with an enraged demand that the score, the score of misery and pride under whose banner they had fought versus the score of self-serving pusillanimity that they held in contempt, be publicly settled. If the government had no belly for unpleasantness, hundreds of these returned prisoners of war demanded that private charges be brought to set the record straight for future wars. It was my constituency who demanded this justice, and thus my duty to serve the charges. For the first six months after I limped out of prison, I spent ten hours a day trying to satisfy that demand, performing that duty. The faceless government bureaucracy was willing to supply massive investigative and legal support, even prepare the legal charges, but of course they insisted that I sign them as a private citizen. Meanwhile they remained on the sidelines, shoulders in the hunched position, palms up, smiling quizzically, while the press treated the affair not as the ex-prisoners' ground-swell attempt to set correct precedents for the next war, but as a simple grudge fight between individuals.

Leadership of that sort—"nice guy," detached, open, evasive, emotionally neutral, a legacy of those "men of the head"—is still *de rigueur* in too many high places. Never mind that it leaves it to the cop on the beat to take the gas and then to read the hate mail. Such leadership comes from people who are not able to experience reality, to deal with fear, guilt, and truth. And that kind of leader will never do if our institutions are to survive. When the going *really* gets tough, the people will read him for what he is, a threat to those institutions, and just calmly disregard him and walk away.

*   *   *

What, then, of "men of the heart," men having Old Testament qualities of heart, the qualities of heart Islam's philosopher Ibn Khaldun attributed to it, the qualities of heart the ancient Greek philosophers attributed to it? That heart was the center of wisdom, the shock absorber of guilt, the source of courage. (Courage comes from the Latin *cor,* the French *coeur;* under "courage" Webster's says, "the heart as the seat of intelligence or of feeling.") The pre-Socratic Heraclitus said the development of the heart has to do with the capacity to face and experience reality. The capacity for that experience is also the capacity for courage. The heart wills, it is the seat of conscience, it introduces *purpose.* The heart is not a neutral processor of data.

In that same age-old sense, the head *is* neutral about knowledge. Ibn Khaldun wrote that no amount of knowledge of the head by itself can give a sense of what is good, what is true, or what is beautiful.

Solomon said to the Lord in a dream: "Give therefore thy servant an understanding heart to judge thy people, that I may discern between good and bad . . . " And the Lord replied: " . . . lo, I have given thee a wise and an understanding heart; so that there was none like thee before thee, neither after thee shall any arise like unto thee."[4] It is not enough that a crisis leader be rational, flexible, open-minded, and cool under stress; without those hearty qualities with an emotional content—spontaneity, compassion, sense of humor, loyalty—he rings hollow.

No one can develop a strong heart, a hard heart, if he is not capable of experiencing the pain of guilt, of admitting to himself that he has acted in a way that has been harmful to others, of being able to repent, and of being able to stand the full experience of reality. The Prophets have told us that it is only the hard heart which can properly repent. If we have leaders who have not developed hard hearts, leaders who cannot face up to guilt and use it as a cleansing fire, we are under the sway of people who cannot act on hard truth and real experience, and believe me, they are a hazard to navigation.

Simple "nice guys"—soft and friendly and always assuring everybody that they feel it "way down here" for the little folks—were hazards to navigation where my data came from. And of course those data came from that very confined, pressurized, intensely heated laboratory-like cauldron of personality distillation—the extortionist prison where, as in the hermetically sealed retorts of the alchemists, essence and change are highlighted, accentuated, and observed on a faster-than-life time base.

There is no way our government, let alone a university, could afford a leadership laboratory like that. You would need a score of human subjects—all of high intelligence, nearly identical in cultural backgrounds, all being well-educated (in our case, 30- to 45-year-old males, all aviators with college degrees and most with advanced degrees from good universities)—all facing a common danger of the most destabilizing sort, that is, the destruction of their personal reputations. Such threat of destruction would be backed up by a force of skilled tourniquet-wielding maulers with unlimited rights of torture—all subjects first undergoing about a two-year solitary confinement "softening up" period before the experiment proper started, then each subject being locked in a concrete box ten feet by four feet, in leg irons, able to communicate only by clandestine wall tap.

At that point the subjects' group project would be assigned: to establish and maintain a prison society that breeds unity, pride, mutual trust and confidence, and high-mindedness. The idea of the experiment would be to collect data over a two- or three-year period, data that would provide insight into the nature of leadership in times of crisis and allow the pinpointing of leadership character traits that succeed or fail in crisis circumstances.

Clearly soft hearts will not do. A crisis leader must be able to handle fear. A crisis leader must be able to handle guilt. A person is thrown into a political prison either to have his mind changed or to be used, or both. People with experience know that the tools of the trade in an extortion operation are only secondarily the infliction of pain and the condemning of people to months of isolation; those are just catalysts for the one-two punch that lies within all effective systems of compulsion—the one-two punches of fear and guilt. That fact has been part of the wisdom of the ages. In the second century, the Stoic Epictetus was lecturing in the area of Epirus on the eastern shore of the southern Adriatic: "For it were better to die of hunger, exempt from fear and guilt, than to live in affluence and with perturbation."[5] Eighteen hundred years later, Carl Jung, Swiss protégé of Sigmund Freud, was describing the process as destabilizing victims with fear and then polarizing them with guilt. He who would prevail when these forces are set upon him must handle that fear and guilt, or die, or worse—collaborate.[6]

In Hanoi, the inducement of fear was not subtle. Physical abuse to the point of unconsciousness was commonplace. But what haunted the prisoner was not pain, but the threat of disgrace. One learned that the maintenance of *moral* authority was crucial to minimizing an interrogator's gains in the eyeball-to-eyeball, hour-after-hour, one-on-one sessions. You learned that to keep from being had you had to develop a private reservoir of willpower, spirit, and moral ascendancy from which you secretly drew solace when the going got tough. That reservoir had to be yours alone, with no access ever given to foe or friend. It was a trinity: you, where you lived, your power source. From it you had to generate a personality that kept all outward signs of fear or guilt obliterated, contained within you where you could deal with them properly, alone. (I used to perform a ritualistic chant under my breath as I was marched to the interrogation room with a bayonnet pricking the middle of my back: "Show no fear, show no fear; don't let your eyes show fear.") To handle fear, you had to become a sort of Knight of Selfhood, as playwright Robert Bolt described Sir Thomas More in his play *A Man for All Seasons*: "Thomas More, as I wrote about him, became for me a man with an adamantine sense of his own self. He knew where he began and where he left off, what area of himself he could yield to the encroachments of his enemies, and what area to the encroachments of those he loved."[7]

The handling of guilt was generally a more formidable problem. Of course I'm *not* talking about guilt vis-à-vis our military duties in the war; that problem did not exist. Of course the North Vietnamese took a crack at trying to make such feelings exist. From the very first we were tortured to follow their script of our being remorseful for having bombed their "schools, churches, and pagodas." But that sort of statement was so patently unreal and so ludicrous that it left no psychic scars on the way through us. True debilitating guilt has to be based on reality, and the big reality in Hanoi on the guilt score was that many of the American prisoners there had been needlessly shot down while following Washington-issued, lock-step operation orders dictated by politicos who had grown more concerned about creating a national image of compassion than saving American airplanes and lives. We had no feelings of owing any Vietnamese remorse. My friend and prison mate Jim Kasler was a Korean War fighter ace against the MiGs at the Yalu and veteran of scores of bombing missions in North Vietnam. He described the maneuvering restrictions put on him as leader of the war's first raid against Hanoi's oil storage tanks in an article in the *Air University Review*:

> The operations order had also directed that all attacks would be executed on a south-to-north heading to preclude tossing a hung

bomb into the city of Hanoi. Approaching from the north, we
[Kasler was leading a flight of sixteen supersonic Thunderchief
fighter-bombers] had to make a 180-degree pop-up maneuver to
strike the target as ordered. What the attack order meant was that
every aircraft would be rolling into the bomb run at the same
spot, heading in the same direction. Not too smart from the pi-
lot's viewpoint, but in the interest of protecting civilian populations such orders were commonplace in Vietnam. (Ideally, attacks
should be on divergent headings to confuse the gunners and thus
prevent them from zeroing in on one spot.)[8]

Our feelings of guilt were not about what we did to the Vietnamese, but about what they were forcing us prisoners to do to each other
through torture—their shutting off the blood circulation in our arms
and beating us while our heads were stuffed into suffocating claustro-
phobia-inducing positions until we "submitted" and gave the names of
co-communicators, the duties of specific camp mates in the clandestine
underground American prisoner organization, and so on. Like as not,
as soon as this material was extracted, we involuntary informers were
whisked out immediately and isolated in a separate location where we
would eat our hearts out in solitude in the months that followed—
cursing our inabilities to stand more pain, feeling remorse for the harm
we were sure was being visited on those most precious beings in our
lives, our friends back in the cell block from whence we had come.

This feeling of rottenness was made all the worse by the degrading
dictatorship-of-the-proletariat rules of procedure in those dungeons.
An American had to bow at the waist 90 degrees whenever meeting any
Vietnamese guard or officer. He could never look at the sky but always
had to keep his eyes cast toward the ground. When brought to interrogation, he was to take the inferior position—on the floor if the interrogator was in a chair, and so on. All in all it was designed as a
guilt-inducing and debilitating environment, against which one had to
work at the very point in time when one was trying desperately to mus-
ter courage and keep his spirits up.

In that "make or break" situation, one learns that there are two
self-destructive routes to degradation: to become consumed by guilt on
the one hand or to practice self-delusion and deny its existence on the
other. To become consumed is to lose all willpower; when you feel
yourself sinking into that funk, you have to force yourself to pull out of
the slump by emphasizing the reality of the situation: "After all, I *was*
tortured." But that reality can be exaggerated into fantasy and followed
over another cliff: when you start denying *any* personal responsibility,
you are on another mud slide to self-destruction. In that case, you

know in your heart of hearts that you could have done better, and you know that there is no one magic point in time when you are suddenly transformed from a person of free will to a blameless victim of outside compulsion. Would that life were so simple; we all spend our most important hours in that ambiguous zone, part volition, part compulsion. (It was none other than Aristotle who told us that compulsion and free will can coexist.) Honest men in prison know that there is no such thing as "brainwashing" or "breaking." These expressions of self-delusion never find use behind bars. They are just unfortunate metaphors that allow people outside prisons to be less uncomfortable in discussing human limitations.

To either hide from guilt or let it consume you are gamesman-like escape routes from the truth—and he who cannot bite the bullet and use that guilt for its intended purpose, as a searing fire to cauterize the wound, as a goad to better resistance next time, is doomed. He who cannot cope with reality himself is certainly lacking the heart to lead others through crises.

In times of crisis the wise and courageous handling of the twin fires of fear and guilt has historically been one of mankind's greatest challenges. All too many who can't face up to dealing with them forthrightly have discovered the cheapest escape route of modern times: jump on the bandwagon of a social determinism that holds that all men are victims of their environment, that moral decay is the natural product of hardship. In that world everybody escapes responsibility for his actions, and guilt not only ceases to be a problem, it becomes an ornament of chic affectation. (Many of these social determinists delude themselves into ascribing nobility to feeling guilty about having power or wealth.) The notion that human beings are always victims of their circumstances is an affront to those bold spirits who throughout history have spent their lives prevailing over adversity.[9]

In my data bank, the facts show that the more the degradation, the more the pain, the more the humiliation, the more the human spirit was challenged, the better it performed. A sense of selfless unity, a nobility of that spirit that seemed to run counter to conventional views on survival instincts grew up among us. It became commonplace for one man to risk greatly to save another. I don't believe it *always* happens that way. There are stories of those in crisis who savagely turn against each other—all against all. Whether the best or worst in men emerges as they face crises together swings on the quality of leadership available to them.

I say leadership "available to them" because people in true crisis usually beg for leadership—seldom is it a case of some authoritarian master imposing it on them. Although conventional wisdom has it that the human condition is optimized when each individual has a maximum of autonomy, when true crisis prevails, when life really gets chaotic, when the dividing line between good and evil ceases to be clear-cut, when no consensus exists as to what is the right and what is the wrong thing to do, people demand to be led, regimented, and guided. The neophyte senior spending his first month in a cell block, grasping after a fashion the great dilemmas of human choice on every hand, typically launched his career of giving prison orders by whispering under his door something like, "In this situation where we're being forced to do things against our will, all I can ask is that you do what you think best." About two days later, said senior would be accosted by his juniors with outrage: "You have no right to dump these decisions in our individual laps; we deserve to live in a sensible society in which we have some idea about what is considered unavoidable and what is considered totally repugnant. Tell us just exactly what specific enemy demands you want us to refuse and take torture for. It is not fair for you to proclaim that all should try to do good; you owe it to us to set down rules of behavior and tell us just exactly what the good is."

Anyone who has lived in a severe extortion environment realizes that the foremost weapon of the adversary is his manipulation of his victim's shame. If when the people call for a leader in extremes, a guilt-ridden whimp (one who manufactures guilt for which there is no way to atone) takes the seat of authority, they are doomed. Only if a man with a hard heart answers is there hope.

This "fifth man," this hardhearted leader who can deal with fear, guilt, truth, and reality is one who would come across in the prison society as a moralist. I do not mean a mere poseur, one who sententiously exhorts his followers to be good. I mean one who has the wisdom, the courage, indeed the audacity, to elucidate just what, under the circumstances, the good *is*. This requires a clear perception of right and wrong and the integrity to stand behind one's assessment, to persevere when the going gets tough.

*   *   *

In 1940, as the British were being crowded toward Dunkirk, the seaport in the far north of France, a message was received in London from a certain element of those British forces about to be involved in the long-shot mass evacuation attempt. The message was made up of just three words: *"But If Not."* A sharp-eyed biblical scholar saw it immediately as a quotation of the three key words in a scripture story of ultimate commitment. The words were lifted from the Book of Daniel, chapter 3, where the conceited and domineering King Nebuchadnezzar was laying down the law to Shadrach, Meshach, and Abednego: either serve Nebuchadnezzar's god and worship the golden image he had set up, or get thrust into the fiery furnace.

The king gave the three a chance to think it over, and they answered as follows:

> O Nebuchadnezzar, we have no need to answer you in this matter. If it be so, our God whom we serve is able to deliver us from the burning fiery furnace; and he will deliver us out of your hand, O king. *But if not,* be it known to you, O king, that we will not serve your gods or worship the golden image which you have set up.[10]

What is needed in times of crisis are leaders with the character to stand up like Shadrach, Meshach, and Abednego when challenged. The test of our future leaders' merit may well lie not in "hanging in there" when the light at the end of the tunnel is expected, but rather in their persistence and willingness to commit us to honorable action when there is a distinct possibility that the light will never appear at all. These are people with Old Testament hard hearts who can deliver the ultimate stultification and turn the Nebuchadnezzars of the world around:

> Mr. Nebuchadnezzar, we've thought your proposition over, like you said. We've decided on the furnace.

Notes

1. William Shakespeare, *As You Like It*, act 2, sc. 7, lines 150–51.
2. Quoted from Paragraph B. (2) of *Department of Defense Directive*, 1300.7, July 8, 1964.
3. F. Carl Schumacher, Jr., and George C. Wilson, *Bridge of No Return: The Ordeal of the USS Pueblo* (New York: Harcourt Brace Jovanovich, 1971), p. 86.
4. I Kings 3:9, 12 (King James version).
5. Epictetus, *The Enchiridion*, trans. Thomas W. Higginson (Indianapolis, Ind.: Bobbs-Merrill Educational Publishing, 1955), p. 21.
6. C. G. Jung, *Psychology and Alchemy*, vol. 12, 2d. ed. (Princeton, N.J.: Princeton University Press, 1968).
7. Robert Bolt, *A Man for All Seasons* (London: Heinemann, 1961), preface, p. xii.

8. *Air University Review* (Montgomery, Ala.), November–December 1974.

9. In April 1983, the FBI reported that in 1982, the worst year of the recession, national crime declined by 4 percent—the steepest decline in five years (see R. Emmett Tyrrell, Jr., "The Continuing Crisis," *American Spectator*, June 1983, p. 4).

10. Daniel 3:16–18 (Revised Standard version).

4

Why U.S. Monetary Policy Should Be Internationalized

Ronald I. McKinnon

No one doubts that the world economy is in serious trouble, but the monetary origins of the disorder are not well
understood. Main-line Keynesian and monetarist theories suggest that
by floating its exchange rate, each nation can—and should—freely exercise national monetary autonomy. These theories induce policymakers to ignore valuable information provided by the foreign exchange
markets and by monetary events in other countries.

Fortunately, practical central bankers in today's increasingly open
economies do not always stick with these insular doctrines. For example, in the 1970s both the Bank of England and the U.S. Federal Reserve System (the Fed) abandoned their (Keynesian) targets for
domestic interest rates because of unexpected domestic inflationary
pressure and because of even more pronounced depreciation of their
national moneys on the foreign exchanges.

In 1979, both central banks realized that disinflation was imperative, and each then adopted the monetarist principle of prespecified
(and declining) rates of *domestic* money growth as their new operating
target. Subsequently both countries were hit with unexpectedly sharp
exchange appreciations—sterling in 1979–1980 and the dollar in

1980–1982—that converted disinflation into depression. Again chastened, each central bank wisely abandoned rigid adherence to domestic monetarism—the Federal Reserve being somewhat more explicit in suspending its MI (currency in circulation plus checking account deposits) target in October 1982. But the result is an apparent analytical vacuum regarding the future conduct of monetary policy.

There is a way out. By shifting the focus of monetary policy from a national to a carefully specified international level, each central bank can avoid severe and disruptive exchange-rate disalignments. But more is required of the Fed because it is at the center of the world dollar standard. To stabilize world prices successfully and avoid the boom and bust cycles characteristic of the recent past, the Fed must act as the balance wheel of the international system—explicitly compensating for shortfalls or excesses of monetary growth in other hard-currency countries such as Germany and Japan.

Dollar Appreciation and the Slump of 1981–82

Before examining the reconstruction of the international system, let us try to understand why the slump of 1981–82 was worldwide. Embracing accepted monetarist doctrine in October 1979, the Fed slowed money growth in the United States without reference to the foreign exchanges or monetary conditions in other industrial countries. Annual growth in M1 fell moderately from about 8 percent in 1977–1979 to about 5 to 6 percent from 1980 to October 1982. But such a moderate decline in U.S. money growth does not explain the severe slump in the industrial economies, accompanied by a global banking crisis arising from economic deterioration in less developed debtor nations. What went wrong?

In late summer 1980, the dollar unexpectedly began to rise against other hard currencies (see Figure 4.1). The origins of this sharp appreciation now seem partly political and partly economic. The anticipated election of a conservative U.S. president strengthened political support for Fed Chairman Paul Volcker's policy of disinflation. Dollar assets suddenly looked more attractive to multinational firms, Arab sheikhs, foreign central banks, and others—particularly those that had reduced their dollar holdings (in favor of European currencies or yen) during the great dollar depreciation of 1977–1978.

In Europe, the Polish crisis threatened German banks and Euro-

Figure 4.1

The Power of the Dollar*

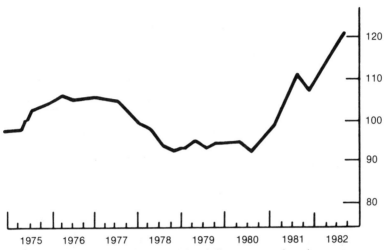

*Average trade-weighted value of the dollar measured against seventeen currencies of major industrial trading partners, 100 equals the average in 1975.

SOURCE: International Monetary Fund, *International Financial Statistics*, 1983.

pean military security. In early 1981, France elected a socialist government—with an inflationist bent—that promised to tax and expropriate private wealth. In several smaller European economies, unsustainable welfare burdens precipitated political and financial crises. Thus over 1980–1982, political and economic accidents prompted investors to move from European currencies into dollars.

With U.S. encouragement, the Tokyo capital market was first opened to foreign borrowers in 1980. Because interest rates abroad seemed excessively high to the Japanese government, however, it prevented yields on yen loans and deposits from rising to international levels. The resulting capital outflow exceeded the Japanese trade surplus, causing the yen to depreciate against the dollar. Despite the competitiveness of Japanese exports in U.S. markets, this unfortunate financial imbalance caused the yen to stay weak until November 1982, when dollar interest rates finally decreased and the Japanese political crisis was resolved with the selection of Yasuhiro Nakasone as prime minister.

The Fed's Blind Spot

These seemingly nonmonetary and largely unforeseeable events aggravated the great dollar appreciation of 1980–1982; they also had grave monetary consequences. The upsurge in foreign demand for U.S. Treasury securities, industrial bonds, equities, bank deposits, real estate, and so on, indirectly increased the demand for money in the United States. But the Federal Reserve had committed itself to a fixed rate of domestic monetary growth. With increased demand and unchanging supply, the result was unexpectedly tight money.

In the United States, the resulting deflationary pressure worked, in part, through the overvalued dollar. Between 1980 and the fall of 1982, the dollar rose about 20 percent against the yen and 25 percent against the mark. But Germany and Japan had much lower rates of domestic price inflation over the same period. The result was a loss of international competitiveness by those U.S. industries most exposed to foreign trade—manufacturing, mining, farming. They became severely depressed, leading to an unfortunate outbreak of protectionist sentiment.

Because the dollar had far overshot its norm in the foreign exchange market, people began to anticipate—incorrectly, for all of 1981 and most of 1982—that the dollar would depreciate to its purchasing-power parity. But this expectation contributed to keeping short-term interest rates on dollar assets much higher than on yen or mark assets, a further source of deflationary pressure in interest-sensitive industries in the United States. Instead of falling in response to the upsurge in foreign demand for U.S. financial assets, U.S. interest rates initially moved in the wrong direction because the dollar had been allowed to appreciate too much.[1]

If the Fed followed an internationalist monetary policy, a stable exchange rate would be an important monetary target. Then upward pressure on the dollar in the foreign exchanges (against other hard currencies) would clearly signal that U.S. monetary policy was too tight. In the United States, money supply would automatically expand, allowing interest rates to fall and rebalance the international bond market without having the dollar overshoot its appropriate value in the foreign exchanges.

The Impotence of Foreign Central Banks

But why should foreign economies become depressed just because the U.S. Fed fails to respond correctly? At first glance, one might expect offsetting inflationary pressure in those industrial economies whose currencies had become undervalued. Unfortunately, the overvalued dollar triggered two sources of deflationary pressure abroad in addition to the depression emanating from the United States.

First, after watching their moneys depreciate, some foreign governments worried about a possible run on their currency and about provoking increased U.S. protectionism. Many resisted depreciation by intervening in foreign exchange markets to repurchase their own currency (with dollar reserves), thus contracting their domestic money growth. In Germany and Japan during 1980–1981, growth in M1 fell sharply and magnified the worldwide deflationary effect of the Fed's more modest slowdown (see Figure 4.2).

Second, the *private* sectors in foreign countries usually have dollar debts exceeding dollar assets, reflecting the facts that the United States is an international creditor and that the dollar is the dominant international reserve currency. An unexpected appreciation of the dollar tends

Figure 4.2

Swings in Money Supply
(Annual percentage changes in M1)

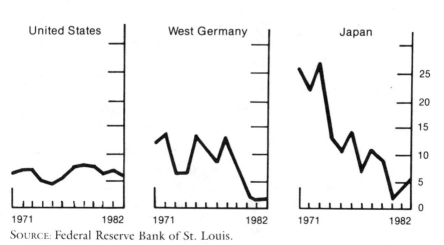

SOURCE: Federal Reserve Bank of St. Louis.

to increase foreigners' debt burdens measured in their own currency and so curtails private spending. Indeed, massive private bankruptcies could result from a depreciation of the domestic currency. For heavily indebted less developed countries, this reduction in net wealth is further aggravated when world depression reduces the dollar prices of their primary products.

In summary, with heavy speculative pressure in favor of the dollar and no compensating action by the Federal Reserve System, foreign monetary authorities are hard-pressed to avoid an ensuing depression. If a central bank intervenes successfully to prevent exchange depreciation, its domestic money supply contracts. Simply letting its domestic currency depreciate may provoke harmful protectionism in the United States and make the financial position of its dollar-indebted private sector precarious.

Obversely, foreign central banks are no better able to avoid worldwide inflation on their own. The two great inflationary explosions of the 1970s can be traced to speculation *against* the dollar, leading to dollar devaluation and uncontrolled monetary growth in other industrial countries. Of course, the open U.S. economy felt the full impact of each inflationary episode.[2]

The Need to Coordinate Central Bank Policies

Sustained recovery—where future cycles of inflation and deflation are avoided—is only possible if the principal central banks jointly agree:

1. to avoid major disalignments in exchange rates and sudden changes in the international competitiveness of different countries; and

2. to adopt a new international standard for controlling world money growth in order to stabilize the prices of internationally traded goods and thus allay inflationary (or deflationary) expectations for the future.

Fortunately, among the world's 150-plus countries, only a small group (from Western Europe, Japan, and North America) provides effectively convertible (hard) moneys usable for international trade and capital flows. And only among these countries is agreement necessary or indeed even possible. Because the deutsche mark is the central hard currency of the European Monetary System (EMS), "Germany" will be a shorthand designation for "Europe" in the following discussion. Countries such as the United Kingdom and Switzerland, currently not members of the EMS, would be welcome members of a broader agreement.

To simplify discussion, however, let us concentrate on how monetary relationships among the larger economies of the United States, Germany, and Japan should be harmonized.

A New Operating Principle for the Fed

Because Germany and Japan intervene continually to mitigate disalignments in their dollar exchange rates, their monetary policies are already significantly internationalized. Still, since 1970 Germany and Japan have suffered unduly large fluctuations in their currency's exchange rate and in their national money supply that magnified world business cycles. The crux of the problem is the failure of the Federal Reserve System to support these well-intentioned foreign interventions.

If the Fed contracted the U.S. money supply when foreign central banks were induced to buy dollars because their own currencies had appreciated unduly or expanded U.S. money when foreign central banks had to sell dollars, the system would be more stable. Exchange rates would move within a much narrower range. Most important, growth in the *sum* of the money supplies of hard-currency countries would be smoother: the Fed would naturally increase U.S. money when foreign money growth decreased, and vice versa. The international cycle of boom and bust, which we have experienced since 1970, would be greatly dampened.

In general and nontechnical terms, how could the Fed best announce its new operating principle—without panicking the always panicky gnomes of the financial community? British journalist Samuel Brittan has kindly volunteered what the Fed's spokesman should say:

> "In fixing its short-term monetary growth objectives, the Fed now intends to take into account the overseas as well as the domestic demand for dollars . . . When the dollar was particularly strong against other currencies, the money supply target would be increased; when it was weak the target would be reduced." [*Financial Times*, July 12, 1982.]

This much the Federal Reserve System could do without any formal pact with foreign central banks and without any new legislation from the U.S. Congress.

A Tripartite Monetary Agreement?

A formal agreement for harmonizing monetary policies among the three countries might make this new procedure securer. The Bundesbank, Bank of Japan, and U.S. Federal Reserve could jointly agree to fix a trend rate of growth in the monetary base for the system as a whole, while encouraging (offsetting) variances in national money growth rates according to the international ebb and flow of demand for each of their currencies as indicated by pressure on their exchange rate. Targeting base money growth would be designed to stabilize a broad price index of internationally traded commodities, an index that could be common to all three countries once exchange rate fluctuations diminished.

Although not to be underestimated, the technical difficulties of implementing such a pact are no greater than trying to run each national monetary policy separately without the cooperation of foreign central banks. Changing international asset preferences has made the demand for each national money too unstable for independent national monetary policies to be successful. And a formal tripartite agreement, signed with due pomp and circumstance, would dramatically signal international investors that their future would be secure whether they be in yen, deutsche marks, or dollars.

Milton Friedman objects that the political difficulties of securing such agreement are overwhelming:

> The economic objections to the proposal are dwarfed by the political objections. A verbal agreement is possible, but a credible and enforceable one, next to impossible. But even if it were, the proposal involves giving great and essentially discretionary powers to an international body independent of any political control by citizens of each member-country short of withdrawal from the agreement.[3]

Yet to successfully circumscribe the autonomy of central banks as Friedman wants requires that the monetary authorities be given the correct guidelines: rules that, if followed systematically, would indeed succeed in stabilizing the domestic economy. To this end, stabilizing the exchange rate against other hard currencies is a necessary condition (even for the U.S. economy of the 1980s). Moreover, it is relatively easy to monitor whether central bankers do stabilize exchange rates.

Somewhat more difficult to agree on, and to monitor, is the appropriate rate of growth in "world" money: the weighted sum of monetary aggregates. But this problem is very similar to that already faced by each national authority operating independently. Should one target M1 or M2 or M3? How can the short-run rate of growth of any broad monetary aggregate be stabilized when money multipliers vary unpredictably? For international coordination, I have shown that emphasizing control over the joint monetary base is a way of potentially finessing these ambiguities.[4]

Apart from these rather arcane technical questions of monetary control, however, the U.S. government would be more politic with its allies if ongoing monetary cooperation succeeded in preventing sharp fluctuations of the dollar against other hard currencies and prevented the accompanying cycles of worldwide inflation and deflation of the past dozen years with which we are all too familiar.

Recovery in 1983

Unduly sharp deflation and dollar overevaluation precipitated the worldwide slump of 1982. Starting from this disequilibrium, how should the monetary policies of Germany, Japan, and the United States be ideally coordinated to overcome depression on the one hand and correct the overvalued dollar on the other? (Readers may judge for themselves how much the policies actually followed differed from this ideal.)

Getting out requires some carefully formulated, once-and-for-all monetary expansion (in 1983) above the normal trend of monetary growth in this triumvirate. Because near-term inflationary expectations were sharply reduced in the United States, one expects an upward shift in the demand for base money in dollars that the Fed should accommodate.

To allay legitimate fears of future inflation, however, any monetary expansion in 1983 is best coupled with the Fed's adopting a more internationalist operating procedure: one that convincingly limits future monetary growth in the world system in general and in the United States in particular. Subsequent monetary growth in the three countries (the Fed could hypothetically explain) would slow to a normal rate designed to secure zero price inflation in a broad basket of internationally traded manufactured goods and primary commodities. More-over, the Fed would make clear that extraordinary monetary expansion in the United States would only continue as long as the dollar re-mained overvalued against the yen and the mark and the threat of dol-lar price inflation was minimal. This strategy is fully credible only if the Bundesbank and the Bank of Japan agree *not* to expand until the dollar is properly aligned.

In summary, monetary expansion for the system as a whole should always be concentrated in that country whose currency is unusually strong in the foreign exchanges.

What if international investors become disturbed, dump dollars in favor of yen and marks, and thus precipitate a further sharp devaluation of the dollar? When the dollar exchange rate becomes approximately correct in terms of marks and yen, the three central banks would sim-ply switch roles: monetary growth would be curtailed in the United States and be increased in Germany or Japan, depending on whose cur-rency was the strongest.

This plan requires that the three central banks agree on an "equilib-rium" set of dollar-yen and dollar-mark exchange rates for approxi-mately aligning national price levels, as they have evolved into early 1983. It does *not* involve any mercantilist juggling of exchange rates for the purpose of fully eliminating bilateral trade surpluses or deficits between any pair of countries. To a considerable extent, surpluses and deficits in current balance of payments accounts are a natural and desir-able consequence of allowing capital to flow freely from one country to another. They are heavily influenced by fiscal deficits or surpluses in each trading partner.

For all the ills of the international economy in 1983, the unexpect-edly sharp deflation in the United States has brought its basic inflation rate much closer to those prevailing in Germany and Japan. Conse-quently, once dollar-yen and dollar-mark exchange rates are appropri-ately realigned in the course of our once-and-for-all monetary expansion, future significant exchange adjustments would likely be un-necessary and unwise.

Fiscal Deficits and International Competitiveness

But monetary policy, however well managed among the three countries, cannot do the whole job. The sorry state of the public finances in the United States will continue to disrupt the interna-tional economy. By appropriating almost all personal savings, the federal budget deficit of over $200 billion severely damages domestic industry through high U.S. interest rates that crowd out productive investment. And the Japanese government is inhibited from relaxing interest-rate ceilings in Tokyo, with the unfortunate consequences discussed above.

Massive dissaving by the federal government literally forces the U.S. economy to rely on the savings of other nations. High rates of interest attract financial capital from Japan, Europe, and the Third World, thus forcing greater real appreciation of the dollar in foreign exchanges. The resulting decline in the U.S. net exports merely reflects the trade deficit necessary to absorb capital from abroad. The trade deficit is thus caused and dominated by the much larger U.S. fiscal deficit.

Without the benefit of a Japanese trade surplus and savings transfer to the United States, real rates of interest in the United States would be even higher—making economic recovery more difficult. But the burden of absorbing this foreign capital falls disproportionately on U.S. tradable goods industries, which are understandably upset.

In short, correcting the trade deficit and preventing a severe outbreak of protectionism require that the United States put its fiscal house in order. This would free surplus Japanese saving to provide yen-dominated finance for the Third World—a more appropriate role for Japan as a natural international creditor.

Conclusion

Among financially open economies, the exchange rate indicates when national monetary policies are relatively too tight or too easy. Since 1980, the overvalued dollar has been sending a clear signal to U.S. monetary authorities that they should ease up relative to their German and Japanese counterparts. Criticism of the Fed for unduly rapid monetary expansion in 1982 and in 1983 was unwarranted. There is scope for harmonizing the monetary policies of Germany, Japan, and the United States with great mutual benefit—even if the United States' fiscal problem is not satisfactorily resolved.

Notes

1. For readers interested in a more technical description of the failure of interest rates to adjust correctly leading to an overshooting of the exchange rate, see

Ronald McKinnon, "Why Floating Exchange Rates Fail," Working Papers in Economics, Domestic Studies Program, Hoover Institution (June 1983).

2. For a fuller examination of foreign-exchange-based inflation in the 1970s under the world dollar standard, when there is speculation against the dollar, see Ronald McKinnon, "Currency Substitution and Instability in the World Dollar Standard," *American Economic Review*, June 1982, pp. 320–33.

3. Milton Friedman, "Monetary Policy for the 1980s," in John H. Moore, ed., *To Promote Prosperity: U.S. Domestic Policy in the Mid-1980s* (Stanford: Hoover Institution Press, 1984), chap. 2.

4. For the specific technical procedures by which monetary coordination among the U.S. Federal Reserve, the Bank of Japan, and the Bundesbank could be carried out in practice, see Ronald McKinnon, "A Program for International Monetary Stability," Richard Levich, ed., *The Future of the International Monetary System* (New York: New York University, 1984). The need for detailed monetary cooperation among the principal industrial countries was first broached many years ago in Ronald McKinnon, *A New Tripartite Agreement or a Limping Dollar Standard?* Essays in International Finance, no. 106 (Princeton, N.J.: Princeton University Press, October, 1974).

5
Energy and Peace

Edward Teller

The interrelationship of energy supply, economic well-being, and political power is obvious. The significance of these interrelationships has, since 1945, become much clearer, as oil dependence has rapidly increased in both the industrialized West and the Third World. Reliance on energy from nations that are not secure from Soviet takeover or that have political aims divergent from Western values is a threat to the stability of peace. These insecure sources of oil could be replaced by developing alternative energy supplies from domestic sources. The United States could even become an energy exporter by the end of the century—a position that would add considerable strength to the stability of peace.

The Energy Weapon

The connection between energy supply, diplomacy, and war is not a novelty of the second half of the twentieth century. At the start of the First World War, Italy dropped out of an alliance with Germany and the Austro-Hungarian monarchy and, nine months later, declared war on its former partners. One frequently mentioned (though clearly not exclusive) reason was Italy's dependence on Britain for coal, the prevalent energy source at that time.

Between 1950 and 1975, world coal production increased about 60 percent, while world petroleum production increased 400 percent. By 1975 the world economy received almost twice as much energy from oil as from coal. According to U.N. statistical reports, over the same period the per capita energy consumption of the developing nations increased threefold, while consumption in the United States and other industrialized countries increased 70 percent. Most of that increase was supplied by oil.

Oil is an unique energy source: it is easily produced and transported and can be used in machinery that is both relatively inexpensive and simple to operate. These qualities made it ideally suited to the needs of the developing nations. Without oil, these countries would not have developed, and without the enterprise and innovative research of the multinational corporations, the oil would not have become available.

Without oil, people in the Third World would not merely have failed in their initial development effort but would have perished in great numbers. During the 1950s, they lived on the edge of starvation. Since that time Third World populations have doubled as a consequence of improved medical care and decreased infant mortality. This accomplishment should, of course, not be deplored even though it has led to an ominous population explosion.

Food production has stayed a little ahead of this unprecedented population growth, and the credit for this goes to the Green Revolution, a nonprofit venture of capitalist countries. The Green Revolution began with the work of the International Rice Research Institute, established by the Rockefeller and the Ford Foundations at Los Banos in the Philippines. It was continued by the International Maize and Wheat Improvement Center in Mexico City under N. E. Borlaug. The Green Revolution doubled, sometimes quadrupled, agricultural yields per acre. I often wonder about the juxtaposition of this development and the widely used expression "neocolonialism."[1]

Unfortunately the new crops developed by the Green Revolution are better than the old only if irrigated and supplied with nitrogen-based fertilizers. Both requirements depend on energy. Thus without oil, not only will the developing countries fail in their further development, they will also be deprived of sufficient food to support life. The coal supply had political effects in 1915, but the oil weapon could have far more terrible repercussions were it to be used.

Western oil companies explored and developed the Persian Gulf's rich oil deposits, whose existence had been recognized since ancient times.[2] The expertise and technology of the Seven Sisters (Exxon, Shell, British Petroleum, Gulf, Texaco, Mobil, and Chevron), perhaps unfairly noted more for their wealth than the effects of their contributions to postwar reconstruction, enabled the Persian Gulf nations to produce oil at $0.10 per barrel and sell it for $2.00 per barrel. Even this pricing produced considerable profit, though not much of it was left in the Middle East. However, the owners of these oil wells could hardly be called poor, even in comparison with their flashy Texan colleagues.

In 1968, representatives of the oil-producing nations that considered themselves underprivileged formed the Organization of Petroleum Exporting Countries (OPEC) to increase their share of the profits. At the time, economists paid scant attention because one of the well-established facts of economics was that producers of raw materials cannot form a successful cartel.

When, in autumn 1973, the Arabs attacked Israel and successfully concealed their plans from the Israeli intelligence service, OPEC suddenly changed from a modest defensive position to a strongly offensive one. The oil weapon produced an effective shock that isolated Israel from practically all external help but that of the United States. The attack on Israel failed. But the oil weapon, wielded not only by the oil-producing nations of the Persian Gulf and Africa but by Venezuela and Indonesia as well. was established. Today, the effective price of oil—discounting inflation—is ten times as high as it was prior to 1973. The effects of all this are felt both in economic conditions and in international politics.

Prior to 1973, economists were steering a careful course between the Scylla of unemployment and the Charybdis of inflation. While Odysseus managed to avoid both, since 1973 we seem to have experienced them both simultaneously. In economics it is probably a mistake to give only one reason for one result. But both timing and logic indicate that stagflation is at least in part caused by a shortage of inexpensive energy and the transfer of great amounts of capital from established industrial countries to less experienced hands. At the same time, many Third World nations without domestic oil have been granted—for extraordinarily strong political and humanitarian reasons—uninsured credits to purchase oil. These loans are apt to endanger many economies in the future. The oil weapon's assault on the free industrial world has indeed shaken its financial structure.

Obviously, the way to render the oil weapon harmless is to develop new sources of energy. Indeed, many potential substitutes for oil exist, but establishing them requires capital, time, and an innovative spirit. We appear to be short of all three.

National Energy Resources

Nuclear Energy

The prime example is the use of nuclear power for generating large amounts of electricity. Nuclear power should, from a technical point of view, be preferred above all other forms of electrical generation: it is least expensive, cleaner than all forms except wind and hydropower (which are sharply limited in availability), and, contrary to popular opinion, the safest major energy source available.

In 1982, 294 reactors were operating throughout the world. An additional 215 were under construction, 156 were in the design stage, and 7 new reactors (4 in France, 3 in Japan) were ordered. That same year, plans for 18 reactors were canceled. Two of the reactors were to have been built in Italy. The remaining 16 cancellations were in the United States.

The International Atomic Energy Agency, founded in 1957, has made the safety measures that originated in the United States available to all interested nations. They include, during the construction phase, an intensive inspection of all crucial parts. Once operation begins, safeguards include continuing ultrasonic and visual inspections and humidity and airborne dust detectors for early warning of even tiny leaks. The automatic water-cooling system is safeguarded by several alternative systems, including one driven by a diesel engine to ensure against power failure.[3] The containment chamber, the last line of protection, consists of three feet of specially designed concrete, heavily reinforced, coated inside with thick, welded steel plates; it is built to withstand tornadoes, plane crashes, or even large explosives detonated against it. Perhaps these extremely comprehensive and redundant safeguards have in themselves contributed to the creation of unwarranted anxiety. Misinformed people may translate great caution into great danger.

The redundancy makes it easier to understand how more than 200 large industrial reactors have operated for an average of ten years without a single health-damaging accident due to their nuclear nature. Technical improvements instituted since the industry began—new steel alloys for reactor vessels and for piping and modified welding techniques—have offered extended plant durability. In the history of energy generation, no other industry—even many decades after its establishment—has a safety record comparable to the one reactors have had from their initial commercial development. Yet this incredibly successful proof of design safety seems to be largely unrecognized.

Malfunctions in early small experimental reactors caused several fatalities, but the antinuclear forces have not been critical of these accidents. Without entering into the conscious (and more important, unconscious) motivations of nuclear critics, it should be observed that they have attacked industrial reactors only if they are operated in a noncommunist country. One remarkable case is that of the Tullnerfeld reactor located in Zwentendorf, 30 kilometers from Vienna. Permission to open the completed Austrian reactor was denied by popular vote in 1978. The opponents of this reactor managed to avoid mentioning that a reactor of Soviet construction (whose safety measures have not been analyzed outside the Soviet Union) was operating in Czechoslovakia at approximately the same distance from Vienna.

Nuclear energy is not without hazards. Radioactive gases in uranium mines can cause damage. Uranium mining began in 1911, greatly increased during the late 1940s and 1950s, but only in 1968 were ventilation problems in uranium mines adequately addressed. The health histories of a group of 4,146 U.S. uranium miners who were employed prior to 1964 have been followed since 1950. At last report, during the period ending in 1974, 156 of these early miners had suffered respiratory cancers, almost five times the number that would be predicted among the general population.[4] To clarify comparative risks, however, in 1975, government figures listed 93,000 production workers in coal mines, 139,000 widows of coal miners who had died with black lung disease, and 165,000 miners disabled by the disease.[5] Per unit of energy produced, uranium mining has been tens of times less risky than coal mining. With modern methods, this ratio will grow larger.

France, Sweden, and Taiwan have demonstrated that when all of the safety precautions are observed, nuclear reactors can be built in six years. Because of repetitious protests and hearings, the time needed in the United States is approximately twelve years. Since 75 percent of the cost of nuclear-generated electricity results from the initial capital investment of construction, this pointless delay greatly increases the cost to the consumer. Indeed, at the present high interest rates, the length of the construction period in the United States has brought the economic feasibility of new nuclear reactors into serious doubt.

These difficulties are due not to technical problems but rather to bureaucratic actions based on misinformed public opinion. Within a year, U.S. oil imports could be reduced by one million barrels per day (and a corresponding outflow of capital by $12 billion per year avoided) simply by licensing completed but idle reactors and removing the unjustifiable limitations on the operating power of existing reactors.

The most widespread objection to nuclear power is that no safe and reasonable method exists for disposing of the by-products. As early as 1973, Dixy Lee Ray, the last and best head of the Atomic Energy Commission, called this objection the greatest contemporary nonproblem in existence. France and Sweden have accepted the substance of the waste disposal method that was reviewed and unanimously approved by the American Physical Society.[6] Military waste disposal in the United States has been handled in a much less careful manner than is now planned for reactor wastes. Although the quantity of military wastes exceeds all industrial wastes, they have harmed no one in any way.

In 1982, nuclear energy accounted for a little more than 11 percent of electrical generation and 4 percent of total energy consumption in the United States. What is worse is that no new reactors have been started in the United States since 1978. The nuclear energy industry remains comatose in spite of encouraging statements by the Reagan administration. It is most important that it be revived.

Coal

Next to nuclear energy, the most obvious resource is coal. In the eighteenth century in England, coal replaced firewood as the principal fuel.[7] Coal, which burns at a higher temperature, made iron available at lesser cost and in greater quantity. It may even make sense to place the beginnings of the iron age in the eighteenth century. Iron and coal have remained the twin foundations of technology well into the twentieth century.[8] During the past decade, however, U.S. coal production has increased by less than 3 percent per year.

One reason that coal has lost its predominance is that coal mining is dangerous. Safety measures as well as increasing wages have made coal more expensive. Coal production has shifted to areas where labor costs are cheap. That Poland should be a case in point is a noteworthy comment on the relationship of communism to a workers' paradise. However, even a communist government has difficulties in maintaining work in the coal mines.

A second reason is that burning coal produces pollution. During five days in December 1962, a fog in London was said to be the cause of 137 deaths and the hospitalization of some one thousand persons. Now, strict regulations limiting the use of coal in London's private fireplaces have made such fogs a thing of the past; but since the beginning of the Industrial Revolution, at least a million lives have been cut short by coal burning. Pollution control devices to clean coal smoke are now available, but they add considerably to the expense of coal-generated electricity.

The last but possibly not least objection to coal is the difficulty and expense of its transportation and storage. Any breakdown, regardless of its cause, endangers the supply, as the winter of 1978–79 (when stored coal in several areas of the northeastern United States could not be delivered as the snow covering it had frozen solid) demonstrated. Offsetting these difficulties is the abundance of coal. Supplies will remain plentiful under any usage conditions for at least another century.

Coal is a fossil fuel, like oil. The origin of neither is completely clarified, but it seems that organic material is much more commonly converted to coal than to oil, and accessible coal is at least ten times more abundant than accessible oil. These numbers will shift further in favor of coal as technically feasible mining methods for deep deposits are brought into practice.

The problems with safety, pollution, and transportation must be overcome if this comparatively abundant resource is to play an important role in the U.S. energy economy. In regard to coal-mining safety, either of two approaches could suffice. Surface mining radically reduces miner health hazards, and the United States has many coal deposits near the surface. In Montana and Wyoming, deposits in layers exceeding fifty feet in depth can be mined simply by removing the overlying material.

Preserving the environment in the broadest sense is obviously a good objective. Mining a coal seam that is fifty feet thick will yield revenue considerably in excess of $100,000 per acre. For a small percentage of this amount, replacement and reconstruction of the former environment (including sufficient irrigation) can be accomplished. At the same time, the health hazards of underground coal mining can be almost totally eliminated. This protection of health, unlike that required to prevent air pollution from coal burning, is very inexpensive.

Another method that solves both the safety problems and the difficulties of mining deep deposits of coal is the process of in-situ coal gasification. The coal seams mentioned in Montana and Wyoming dip as one proceeds south. Thick layers of coal several thousand feet underground occur in Colorado, Utah, and, to some extent, in New Mexico.

In-situ coal gasification begins by fracturing the coal formation with high explosives. Oxygen (to produce high temperatures and to avoid contaminating the resulting gas with nitrogen) is then pumped in, and the coal is burned underground. Water, often present in coal, must also be present to furnish hydrogen. The water added need not be fresh, and saline water can usually be found in more or less adjacent deep layers. This process produces useless carbon dioxide (water soluble and easily removed) and useful carbon monoxide and hydrogen—components of what is called "producer gas."

Such gas has been obtained by aboveground gasification for many years. Unfortunately, the energy content per unit value is only one-third of that found in natural gas. Consequently, transporting producer gas by pipeline over long distances is not practical, but burning it within a few hundred miles of the coal deposits is. Alternatively, producer gas can be converted into a more energy-rich gas or into methanol, which may be used as automobile fuel. One of the great advantages of coal gasification is that most polluting materials are left underground.

Other methods can ease the difficulties of transportation and also of pollution. Coal can be turned into a slurry by suspending it in some appropriate liquid such as water, oil, or methanol. In the case of a water slurry, most of the water must be removed before the coal is burned. In the case of an oil or methanol slurry, the whole liquid may be burned. If coal is ground so that the particle size does not exceed one one-hundredth of an inch, it can be readily suspended in methanol. Methanol, the simplest alcohol, easily penetrates the smallest cracks and firmly attaches to the coal surface, but not to inorganic dirt. As a general rule, one-half of the polluting sulfur is found in this inorganic dirt. Once raw coal is suspended in methanol, the denser inorganic substances can be eliminated by centrifuging—one of the methods of coal purification.

The material formed can be transported by pipeline or oil tanker. Although the methanol suspension cannot be burned in automobiles, it can be used in current stationary oil-burning electricity generators with a modification costing less than $100 per installed kilowatt.

The process, patented as Methacoal, is in the planning stage. Final cost per barrel of oil equivalent is estimated at $20–25, about one-fifth less than the current price of oil.

By the end of the 1980s, more emphasis may be put on the use of coal even if present techniques are continued. But innovations, as illustrated above, may greatly ease and accelerate a return to more intensive use of coal.

Natural Gas

Natural gas is more generally used in the United States than in any other part of the world. This by-product of oil production could have much more widespread use since it is often flared at oil well sites. Its utilization requires either a network of pipelines, conversion into easily transported substances like fertilizer or methanol, or liquification of the gas for transport in special tankers.

Unfortunately, liquid natural gas (LNG) is a most dangerous substance. If it spills, the high density of the cool gas will cause it to stay near the ground. In the absence of strong winds, it would spread overground, mixing with air and producing a highly dangerous combustible mixture. For this reason and because of the expense of liquefying and transporting LNG, the importance of LNG seems to be declining.

The deregulation of domestic gas prices has stimulated gas production from deeper layers. So, even with increased drilling expense, such gas remains competitive with oil costs and is apt to play an important role for some time to come. Coal and particularly nuclear energy, however, will remain useful for longer periods. In the case of nuclear energy, this period could easily be extended into millennia.

Synthetic Fuels

The conversion of more abundant coal into more easily used oil is currently being considered. The process essentially involves adding more hydrogen to coal under the proper chemical conditions. Practical execution was developed during World War II in Germany but at a cost justified only by wartime necessity. In the 1950s, South Africa, with plenty of coal and practically no oil, decided to guarantee its oil supply. Using their plentiful coal, the cheap capital of that period, cheap labor, and an improved modification of the German process, they developed not only synthetic oil but many other chemicals ordinarily derived from oil. It is doubtful that similar methods can currently be made to work in a profitable manner in any other nation.

Solar Energy

The potential shortage of oil and other raw materials has led people to wish for "renewable" energy sources. The argument for renewable resources is in fact less than convincing. The availability of fuel or energy is useless until equipment exists to turn this energy into useful work or needed heat. The source of solar energy is, of course, free and renewable. This has made solar energy extremely popular. Unfortunately, people tend to forget that the equipment needed for its use is not renewable, nor is it free or everlasting. In spite of many intensive attempts to develop practical applications, solar energy is still not able to play an important role in the U.S. or the world economy.

The easiest way to use solar energy is to produce low-temperature heat of the range required in hot water heaters and residential space heating. Air conditioning, by a clever use of temperature differentials (but without the use of electricity), also seems possible. These projects are approaching the margin of economic feasibility.

Using solar energy to produce high-temperature heat or to generate electricity is much more difficult. The last objective has elicited considerable interest, but it has led—on the whole—to many disappointments. One straightforward method is to use a great number of plane mirrors whose orientation is changed by a clock-driven mechanism. Solar energy falling on one square mile of ground can be concentrated on a boiler on top of a tower, and ideally it would generate 1,000 megawatts of electricity (the equivalent of a nuclear reactor). The main expenditure would be the capital investment, which, unfortunately, is considerably higher than the cost of a nuclear plant. In the case of the solar plant, the particularly disturbing feature is that even under favorable conditions, energy is available only one-third of the time. Indeed, the estimate of power given above applies only to peak power.

Direct conversion of solar light into electricity requires exceedingly ingenious devices called solar cells, developed and used successfully as a power source in space exploration. Such solar cells employing crystalline semiconductors were a thousand times too expensive for general economic use. Diligent work has reduced the cost to merely ten to thirty times that of other sources. Further improvements are anticipated, and in this rapidly developing field, the economic exploitation of solar energy is possible, particularly if only small quantities of electricity are needed. A new type of solar cell proposed by Stanford Ovshinsky employs an amorphous semiconductor. The important factor is that such solar cells can be fabricated less expensively. There is a hope, rapidly approaching certainty, that such cells can actually be mass-produced by 1985.

Other Methods

The enumerated energy sources are the most popular and frequently discussed. Others, like wind and geothermal energy, will play some role, but in the context of the U.S. or world economy, these sources are not apt to be decisive, as they are available on a practical scale only in very specific areas. For example, geothermal energy in New Zealand and wind energy in the Hawaiian Islands could have considerable local success. Other possibilities such as tidal energy are farther from realization. Methods to exploit temperature differences in the ocean (OTEC) may never reach an economic stage.

The Outlook

The continuing rise in the price of electricity has been reversed at least temporarily. The price of oil, which peaked at a value slightly above $40 per barrel in 1978, dropped to $29 per barrel in 1983. Several reasons are involved: further oil has been discovered;[9] other energy sources have become available; the use of oil has decreased because of its expense and through conservation measures. Worldwide demand at the 1978 peak was slightly under 70 million barrels per day. Usage in 1982 amounted to less than 60 million barrels per day.

More important, the proportion of oil supplied by the Persian Gulf region has been reduced. In 1973 it constituted one-third of the world's oil supply; in 1982, one-fifth. Saudi Arabian sources have played the role of the flywheel in OPEC's economic functioning. In order to keep the price up, the Saudis had voluntarily reduced their peak output of nearly 11 million barrels per day to about 4 million barrels per day by 1982. This mechanism may have reached the limit of its usefulness.

The economic theory that raw material suppliers cannot form a cartel may have some truth to it after all. The oil companies made the mistake of concentrating development on too few regions—only the most promising. OPEC's years of success can be understood because new oil wells and most other new energy sources cannot be developed easily in less than ten years. Even with extreme effort only a few exceptional energy sources can be made available in less than five years. A decade was required for the rest of the world to develop competing energy sources. Then OPEC experienced difficulties. OPEC's role in the future is a question of great interest both from theoretical and practical points of view.

Energy and Peace

An obvious connection exists between a continuing energy shortage and the danger of war. The desperation created by the Great

Depression in Germany brought about Hitler's rise and a war of un-paralleled destructiveness. Our energy shortage could have consequences that no one can foretell. The final effects of the recent use of the oil weapon are unknown, but related events clearly endanger peace.

The Soviet Union has surrounded the Persian Gulf. South Yemen is a Soviet satellite with an immense number of Soviet tanks in place. The invasion of Afghanistan gave the Soviets control of the roads and communication centers of that country. Iran has been destabilized. Internal fighting has hurt all political parties, but, in spite of setbacks, the communist Tudeh party continues to be a menace. Israeli armed forces defeated Syria and the PLO—both armed with Soviet weapons, but the Soviets have sent many advisers to repair this weak link in the chain that encircles the Persian Gulf.

The Soviets seem to be seriously considering the possibility of taking over the Persian Gulf. Whether they will attempt this by slow penetration or by military attack cannot be foreseen. Restraints on military attack might be U.S. aid, Israeli resistance, and dissatisfaction among the sizable Soviet population of Moslem descent. Of these, the last could have the greatest weight. A strong Israel may be of some help, but direct armed resistance by the United States would have almost no chance of success.

The enormous advantage that the Soviet Union would gain with control of the Persian Gulf should not be underestimated. Even though a Soviet takeover would be less dangerous now than it would have been a few years ago, Soviet oil (itself the world's single biggest source) combined with Persian Gulf oil could amount to 30 million barrels of oil per day—approximately one-half of the world's needs. If this oil were for sale—not for dollars or rubles but for political obedience—it is by no means fanciful to say that the Soviet Union could deliver the coup de grace to NATO.

A serious consideration of appropriate countermeasures is long overdue. The increased development of various energy resources is a step in the right direction, but it should be accelerated. Development of energy conservation methods is also important. For neutralizing the oil weapon, however, the potential of energy conservation is more important than its current exercise. In case of an emergency that potential (as well as stored oil) would soften the blow that the oil weapon could deliver. Conservation can be implemented rapidly, but development of new resources takes years. To that extent, conservation is a more powerful defensive weapon.

In all this the United States needs to consider not only its own requirements but also those of its allies and the Third World. Today the United States is the leading food-exporting nation. It could aim beyond energy self-sufficiency toward the ability to export energy to the rest of the world. If it succeeded, it could peacefully negate the effects of any energy weapon the Soviets might establish.

The best and most lasting antidote to war is a commonality of interest that would obviously be endangered by war. To the extent that the United States can establish common interests and shared perceptions throughout the world, including those regarding energy production, and to the extent that its contribution to such cooperation would become both essential and obvious, it will have enhanced its security and its ability to enhance the well-being of the entire world.

Notes

1. While these new and better crops based on Mendelian theory were being initiated, the Soviet Union's food imports were sharply rising. By the late 1940s, the Soviet geneticist T. D. Lysenko had discarded Mendel's theory for one of his own and convinced Stalin to purge all Soviet geneticists who disagreed. The Soviets have never admitted the damage thus done to the agricultural productivity of the Soviet Union, nor to date have they effectively repaired it.

2. Greek fire, a substance used to repel the first Moslem invasion of Constantinople in the eighth century, was composed of unslaked lime, sulfur, and naphtha, a dense form of oil from Mesopotamia.

3. These automatic systems can be turned off manually by the operators, as was the case, unfortunately, at Three Mile Island.

4. Victor E. Archer et al., "Respiratory Disease Mortality Among Uranium Miners," *Annals of the New York Academy of Sciences* 271 (1976): 377–83. The high radiation doses received in the early uranium mines should be clearly differentiated from the dangers of low-level radiation. These latter effects have not been observed because a sample of 10,000,000 people would be required to demonstrate statistically whether so small an effect is present.

5. U.S. Department of Commerce, Bureau of the Census, *Statistical Abstract of the United States, 1980* (Washington, D.C.: Government Printing Office, 1980), pp. 413, 344.

6. Study Group on Nuclear Fuel Cycles and Waste Management, "Report to the American Physical Society," *Reviews of Modern Physics* 50, no. 1, part II (January 1978).

7. At its introduction, contemporary environmentalists strongly opposed the use of coal. In some cases they even succeeded in legislating the death penalty for those who burned it, although the penalty seems never to have been imposed.

8. Prior to the introduction of widespread coal usage, iron was so expensive that it was used almost exclusively in warfare. Indeed, the concepts of war and iron are closely linked in more than one language.

9. A huge discovery was made in Mexico, a smaller one near Santa Barbara, and the earlier North Sea discovery began producing oil.

6

Post-Collectivist Politics in Europe and Great Britain

Gerald A. Dorfman

U.S. foreign policymakers have long recognized the importance of union power in European politics and foreign policy. Industrial strife, recurring government crises, and the seemingly endless series of demonstrations protesting various policy issues illustrate how much the behavior of the labor movement in Europe affects contemporary economic and political life. Moreover, the labor movement operates from a crucial position at the center of national decision making. Unions in every major West European country have been active bargaining partners with their respective governments over almost every question of public policy from the national political agenda to the terms of specific legislation. U.S. leaders have worried about these relationships because they so often produce economic stagnation and political instability, which inevitably threaten the Western alliance.

U.S. policymakers need to recognize that this long-standing collectivist relationship between labor and government in Europe is changing in significant ways. Clearly, the most striking feature of this change is the decline of union power. High unemployment is sapping union strength in a number of ways. Most important, it is causing unions to lose members at a rapid pace. Union leaders, not surprisingly, are thus in a weaker position, more divided about their goals and strategy, and frequently confused about the course of contemporary affairs. At the same time, European political leaders in several countries are profiting from union weakness to reverse—fundamentally and permanently—the collectivist relationship. Although continuing to declare their fidelity to the goal of full employment, for example, they often implement policies that maintain high levels of unemployment. This serves as leverage both against renewed inflation and against the resurgence of union militancy. Concurrently, these political leaders are working to enforce legislated requirements on union behavior for strike ballots and to impose other restraints on rank-and-file members, as well as their leaders. Finally, political leaders are consciously reducing the frequency and quality of union-government interaction over the terms of public policy.

Although these changes have been developing for little more than a half-decade, they are already having a profound effect on the political process. U.S. leaders will need to understand a whole new set of relationships and anticipate new policy outcomes during the balance of this decade. The move into what can best be described as a post-collectivist era offers the possibility that European nations may avoid the stagnation and paralysis of public policy that have occasionally weakened the Western alliance in recent years. Yet, at the same time, U.S. policymakers also need to be aware that these changes may produce destabilizing conflict. Union leaders will not give up their place at the national bargaining table without serious resistance.

Origins of Union Influence

The contemporary power of labor is due much less to the skillful strategy of aggrandizing union leaders than to their relatively passive role as beneficiaries of an upsurge in government responsibilities.[1] Unions are so powerful because government has become so powerful and pervasive since the end of the Second World War.

Political decisions in the Western democracies in the mid-1940s to adopt Keynesian theory ensured that producing groups such as unions would play a new and very powerful role. Government became directly responsible for managing the economy and for developing and administering the welfare state. Both these responsibilities are among the central concerns of trade unionism and act to create a new and necessary relationship between government and labor. Government became the natural object of union attention and, in turn, needed the support, advice, and sometimes the acquiescence of the union movement to make its policies viable and politically successful. Unions were drawn from the fringes of power, where they had operated during nearly all of their history, into the corridors of power and influence. Inevitably, the two sides found themselves in a new relationship best described as collectivist or group politics.

In the early postwar months, when these relationships were being fashioned, there was considerable optimism throughout Europe that cooperative producing groups could do much to ensure that governments kept their commitment to stave off depression and create sustained prosperity. It was widely reasoned that government nationalization of leading portions of industry, its management of the economy in general, and a partnership with unions would create an ideal climate for progress.[2] After all, many reasoned, union members could take great satisfaction and encouragement that governments were now operating "our own industries" for "our own best interests."[3] Less noticed, unfortunately, was the risk of this relationship. What if unions did not believe that cooperation was in their interest? If government needed the cooperation of producing groups to carry out its commitments, including full employment, how would it be able to proceed if that cooperation were not forthcoming? We have learned painfully that these crucial questions need to be answered. The failure to answer them effectively during the past four decades has meant that governments have had no antidote to the stagnation, paralysis, or even outright conflict caused by disagreements between the two sides.

Unions and governments can easily agree on the need for full employment and growing prosperity. Arguments arise, however, because they can almost never agree on the policies for achieving these objectives. It would be difficult—perhaps impossible—for any two sides with such weighty and complex responsibilities to find common ground on a continuing basis. There is an inherent contradiction between the commitments of government to create and maintain prosperity and the purposes of unions to get "more and better for their men."[4] It was inevitable that if government were to maintain full employment, it would need the cooperation of unions in restraining the militancy full employment produces. Yet union leaders just as inevitably found themselves in trouble with their members if they refused to press for the highest wages possible. Although the record of cooperation between the German government and the German union movement may seem an exception, that record is affected by the unusually strong German fear of inflation, which stretches back to the horrors of superinflation during the early 1920s. For unions and governments in most other European countries, this problem has been central to their difficult, often paralyzing, relations.

The Example of Britain

The British case is the most notorious example of the problem of collectivist politics in Europe. Policymakers in Washington have worried at times during the past ten years when the United States' closest ally was shaken by destabilizing confrontations. The British example is important because the British union movement is the largest in Europe, both in number of members and percentage of the work force unionized. It is also important because it is led by a coherent national spokesgroup, the Trades Union Congress (TUC), which was founded with and continues to have close ties to the Labour party, one of Britain's two major political parties. Because unions enjoy such strength and coherent leadership, the British collectivist process offered the greatest potential from the beginning for the most effective collectivist government. Yet, for the same reasons, the potential for conflict with attendant paralysis of policy was equally great—and conflict certainly best describes the relationship during the past four decades.

Wage politics has been the great battleground in Britain, as in every country of Western Europe.[5] No issue is more crucial to union-government relations or to each side's fundamental interests. As a vital consequence of its economic management, government has needed union cooperation in exercising wage restraint. Unions, in turn, constantly need to address this issue, which more than any other impinges on their institutional reason to exist. Wage politics thus became in Britain and other countries the cornerstone for broad-gauged interaction. The TUC sought to gain the greatest possible access to and influence on policymaking, while the government sought to win the greatest possible cooperation from unions for what it wanted to do.

The TUC's performance has been uneven. It won initial access and influence because full employment after 1945 created pressure for higher wages, placing the TUC in a crucial bargaining position with government. Yet its influence was almost entirely negative. It could paralyze, even veto, government policies it did not like, but it could rarely influence government to adopt alternatives it suggested or endorsed. The problem for the TUC as chief spokesgroup for unionism was that government demands for wage restraint stirred resistance by individual unions. This, in turn, reinforced the natural inclination of these individual unions to guard their right to operate independently and to deny power to the TUC. Thus as government demanded more and more cooperation as the price for successful management of the economy, including full employment, the TUC became less rather than more able to deliver that cooperation.

The history of collectivist politics in Britain since 1945 painfully illustrates this process and its consequences. Both Labour and Conservative governments repeatedly bid for union cooperation. The TUC response varied depending on the party in office, economic circumstances, and the nature of internal union politics. But in general, the TUC, with only a few exceptions, would not or could not deliver its cooperation even though its intransigence damaged union interests as well.

The whole process exposed the TUC's fundamental weakness while paralyzing collectivist policymaking in Britain. During many of the negotiations, even the TUC's staff and leadership were in favor of agreeing to some form of union cooperation with government. They reasoned that wage restraint made good economic sense; moreover, sensible cooperation with governments of either party would improve the TUC's general bargaining ability in favor of other union interests. But matters have never been very much in their control, and instead of cooperation, the TUC regularly delivered policy vetoes and policy stalemate—or watched helplessly from the sidelines as they were delivered by rebellious members in local organizations.

The sorry record of the British economy over the past several decades and the difficult and often stormy history of industrial relations are tangible evidence of the failures of group politics in Britain. Britain's economic decline is not entirely due to these events, but its failure to become more competitive in the world economy is closely bound to the frequent paralyzing of its economic policies.

The Failure of Government Counterattack

Political leaders in Britain as well as on the continent were quick to recognize these defects in collectivist decision making.[6] It took only a few years for them to see that it was unlikely that the labor movement would be willing or able to deliver the kind of effective cooperation, including wage restraint, needed. The problem for European political leaders in launching a counterattack was twofold. First, they were highly vulnerable to the same negative union power they were attempting to curb. In short, unions and any other producing group could use their key veto powers at the bargaining table to defeat measures designed to alter the collectivist process. Second, and just as important, most political leaders wanting to change the system had championed its development and owed their incumbency in office to their advocacy of it. Many of them were even supported financially by the same unions that they now sought to curb. And even if monetary considerations did not play a role, personal ties of loyalty and shared viewpoints certainly did.

Given these facts, it is not surprising to discover that the attempts by several European governments before the mid-1970s to change the collectivist process were dismal failures. In each case, the labor movement or some other producing group such as farmers delivered powerful defeats using the very process government leaders were attempting to change. Some of the failed counterattacks actually enhanced the powers of these groups. The union-government confrontation in Britain in early 1974, for example, caused the electoral defeat of the Heath Conservative government. It was replaced by a Labour government committed to restoring peace with the union movement at any price, even if that meant giving the TUC a greater role in national policymaking.

Post-Collectivism

The height of producer group power throughout Europe was reached during this period. Labor militancy had been rising for more than a decade, and industrial disruptions painfully reminded political leaders everywhere that their strategy for counterattack was, in fact, creating even more of a problem. Social scientists confirmed these pessimistic assessments in conferences with such despairing titles as "Unions: Threats to Democracy?"[7]

It is ironic that at this moment of supreme union influence, the most potent economic recession since World War II delivered the first real challenge to that power. Recession almost perversely came to the rescue of battered political elites. Raging inflation, declining industrial production, and financial and monetary crises all worked to undermine union power. Their effectiveness was due to the challenge they posed to the Keynesian theories on which postwar economic, social, and political processes had been built. Full employment, the linchpin of the approach, began to slip away in 1975. Governments in Europe began to implement very different kinds of economic management in response to these new circumstances—most of them without understanding the blow they were delivering to collectivist politics.[8]

In retrospect, it is possible to see that this was a watershed. The underpinnings of producer group power were ebbing even at the moment that it seemed union power was out of control. Their awesome power to cause industrial disruption remained every bit as potent, but the will to use that power declined as growing unemployment defused a considerable amount of militancy. These changes did not occur suddenly. Politics is often a very subtle process, and in this case, it only gradually became clear that government had improved its leverage at the expense of its adversary. It was only by the end of the 1970s that it was possible to speculate that collectivist politics was changing and might even be transformed into some unrecognizable post-collectivist form.

The British example again serves quite well to illustrate these changes. The last years of the Callaghan Labour government, in 1977–79, provided the initial test of TUC behavior in the context of post-Keynesian economic management.[9] Full employment had long endowed the TUC with impenetrable power. But after 1975, the TUC watched almost helplessly as unemployment lines grew and "its" Labour government systematically abandoned the array of other economic policy commitments that had produced the era of collectivist politics.

The dilemma caused by this situation placed the TUC under greater rather than less pressure to be an effective producer spokesgroup. This demand came from two important, and in combination, destructively contradictory—directions. On one hand, the Labour government continued to want and even demand cooperation in meeting the serious challenge of economic recession. On the other hand, individual unions insisted that the TUC become more aggressive and effective in defending their interests against what they believed were harsh government policies—especially on employment. These same unions had become so suspicious of the government's intentions and the TUC's weakness that they were even more reluctant than usual to defer to the formerly protective TUC leadership. In 1979, in what was termed the "winter of discontent," this unresolved crisis of TUC power led directly to its failure to deal effectively with the ultimate confrontation between the Callaghan government and individual unions. The election of the Conservatives led by Margaret Thatcher in May 1979 was the most striking illustration of how the decline of collectivist politics had rendered the TUC weak and ineffective.

The return of the Conservatives to office plunged the TUC into despair.[10] It well knew that this was not an ordinary change of government. Thatcher had promised repeatedly over several years that she would bring an anti-collectivist purpose to office with her. The TUC knew that she would press vigorously to minimize their participation in national policymaking and otherwise act to limit union power. From the first moment, the course of the relationship between the TUC and the new Thatcher government showed these fears to be well founded.

The two main areas of interaction were economic policy and industrial relations. Both are at the heart of traditional union-government relations, but the economic tends to be consistently the more important. In this case, the government particularly stressed the economic because it was committed to a radical break with Britain's postwar Keynesian tradition. Even though the previous Labour government had already gone some distance in this direction, Thatcher's purpose was considerably more thorough and aggressive. She was determined to reverse the pattern of pervasive government intervention and "lavish" spending. She was also just as determined to change the rules of economic decision making so that government would no longer be so dependent on the willingness and ability of the trade union movement to deliver advice and cooperation.

The first weeks of the new government's incumbency proved to be decisive in setting the pattern for the following years, as well as providing clues to the shape of post-collectivist politics in Britain.[11] Each side worked during those early days to test the resources and resolve of the other. The Thatcher government, for its part, sought to seize the policy initiative while avoiding open confrontation with the unions. At the same time, the unions, through the TUC, tried both to overcome and to hide their own weakness and confusion, as well as their despair at the events that had led to Thatcher's election. The TUC sought during this period to convince the new government that it had the will and authority to inflict unacceptably damaging conflict if the government insisted on pressing ahead with its well-advertised plans.

The government had much the best of the struggle, as it succeeded in imposing its economic policy without consultation. The TUC vociferously opposed the government's monetarist approach, but it was abundantly clear that it lacked the access, influence, or ideas to obstruct or even delay the government's initiatives. Within a very few months, union leaders despondently retreated to self-serving assertions that although they could have no effect on the prime minister directly, they were confident that she would soon destroy her own government by her policies. The truth was that while they realized there would be "disastrous" unemployment and a fall in the standard of living of their members, they were at a loss to know what to do about it.[12] They promised to organize protests and campaigns against the government's policies even though they knew these would have little effect. They counted on time and the "mistaken" theories of Thatcher and her colleagues to prove them right and cause a policy reversal. This kind of passive criticism from a distance stood in striking contrast to the heady days when TUC leaders appeared weekly, and sometimes daily, at Number 10. Now they had to content themselves with rallies, pamphlets and occasional interviews with the press. Clearly, the era of collectivist politics was beginning to pass.

In sum, the beginning of the Thatcher government offered a disturbing preview for unions, both of their relations with the new Conservative government and of post-collectivist politics generally. The despair that TUC leaders had felt at the Conservative victory in May 1979 was well founded. The loss of full employment and the consequent rise of high unemployment had been the key factors undermining union power and the political process. British leaders were surprised not so much by the change itself as by its speed, intensity, and thoroughgoing effect.

British elites, including both political and union leaders, have long been especially sensitive to the issue of unemployment. The "guarantee" made by all political parties in 1944 that the government would achieve and maintain full employment illustrates this sensitivity. Scholars have, therefore, assumed that the union movement enjoys relative immunity from political counterattack because no government would dare allow unemployment to reach levels that would challenge union power. But during the past several years, there was surprisingly little protest against the rise of unemployment to previously unthinkable levels. There is no suggestion from any corner that these numbers could rise indefinitely, but it is evident that so far the electorate has tolerated much higher figures than anyone could have imagined.

Political leaders now know that they can live with a rate of unemployment high enough to do serious damage to their union adversaries, an important revelation for union-government relations.[13] Here, then, is the key to waging successful counterattack against union power and to changing the collectivist process permanently. British politicians are almost certain to continue to exercise this potent weapon—to keep unemployment permanently high by postwar standards—even while they continue to profess their determination to work for the restoration of full employment.

The Continental Labor Movement

The British example is striking because Britain has so large and powerful a labor movement. The example is also meant, however, to suggest a pattern of change encompassing political systems throughout Europe. Virtually every Western democracy made the same commitments to full employment, the managed economy, and the welfare state at the end of the Second World War, with similar consequences. Governments, as in Britain, needed union cooperation, advice, and sometimes acquiescence. They especially needed to restrain the bargaining leverage with which full employment endowed the unions. But, as in Britain, European leaders in nearly every country encountered the same contradiction between labor unions' desire to get more and better for their men and their own demands that labor act responsibly to restrain those demands in the national interest. In most cases, particularly in the 1970s, labor leaders paid more attention to their militant colleagues' demands for action than to government's call for patriotic restraint.

The effect of these conflicts in continental European countries was less striking than in Britain, though still significant in political and economic terms. The major differences related more to dissimilarities in union organization in each country than to differences in policy. Keynesian economic theory underpinned European economies everywhere in some degree, but each national union organization held quite a different position in national life. For example, unions in France have not been able to penetrate a similar percentage of the work force. Moreover, French unions have ties to one of three rather than to a single national spokesgroup. This means that French governments of all ideological persuasions face an inherently divided and weaker labor movement than does their British counterpart. The same divisions plague Italy as well.

Taking the European experience as a whole (including Britain), the profile that emerges is still one of a powerful union movement that has been very influential in determining the course of European economic affairs. The histories of each labor movement certainly differ, but the pattern of postwar influence reaching its height in the mid-1970s and then afflicted by the recession is held more or less in common. U.S. policymakers, therefore, have had to fret for several decades over the economic and political destabilization produced by collectivist politics. But they now must recognize and adjust to a new, post-collectivist era.

U.S. policymakers can best understand how post-collectivism has taken hold on the continent by examing some key events in the recent development of the European labor movement. The most significant of these has been the creation of the European Trade Union Confederation (ETUC) to press the interests of unionism within the European Economic Community (EEC), as well as with other European economic organizations. The ETUC is significant because its very development, in 1973, coincided with the onset of the decline of collectivist politics and its specific focus has been an attempt to halt or reverse this process. In short, the ETUC's existence and purpose confirm the presence of changes that threaten union power and participation in national decision making. So, too, does its history as an activist organization.

The ETUC is a fascinating barometer of union power in Europe in part because it is unique to the experience of the union movement on the continent. Until recently, the union organizations of individual countries had regarded the task of integrating trade unionism on a European scale as impossibly difficult.[14] Differences of experience, priorities, national environment, and organizational strength, as well as ideology, have all been complicating factors. And given the success of each union movement within its own country, the incentive for a collective European organization was very low.

All of that changed, of course, during the mid-1970s. The recession and consequent shift in economic policy away from Keynesian management and its stress on full employment produced new incentives. The historical impediments disappeared as European unions began to perceive advantages in collective organization. It was not so much that they came to value European-wide unionism for its own sake as that they began to believe that collectivism might enhance their individual strength, otherwise openly on the wane. In short, they hoped to build a European base from which they could argue with their own governments more effectively.

The continental and British dimensions of the problem dovetail here. The British TUC, itself long opposed to British membership in the EEC, ironically reached the opposite conclusion about European unionism at this time and took the lead in its development.[15] Simply, the British TUC moved into Europe in 1975–76 because it recognized that the domestic economic and political situation had eroded. It reasoned that such an initiative in Europe was worthwhile despite the threat collective unionism might pose to its own independence. It started with a whole shopping list of policy goals, headed of course, by the issue of employment. Like its continental brethren, the TUC was anxious to amass collective strength in order to convince its own government to adopt an aggressive reflationary policy based on classic Keynesian views.

What then, has been the result of this effort in Europe? After nearly a decade, the whole effort by the TUC and its compatriot unions in the ETUC has largely been a sorry disappointment. Their purpose had been to stop and then reverse the decline of collectivist politics, but instead that decline has continued apace. To be sure, the development of the ETUC has been an unprecedented achievement in organizational terms. European unions have overcome their traditional distance from each other to cooperate for the first time. The ETUC has attracted more than 30 organizations, from eighteen countries, with more than 40 million members.[16] By any measure this is an impressive figure. But to what purpose? The ETUC's representations to individual governments, as well as to the EEC and the Tripartite Economic and Social Conference, to name a few, have gone unrewarded. Governments have listened politely and even encouraged consultation, but they have remained undeflected from their policy intentions. The ETUC, in sum, has gained some attention and certainly real legitimacy as a European interest group, but it has not slowed down the development of post-collectivist politics.

Post-Collectivism and U.S. Interests

Finally, what does post-collectivism mean for U.S. interests and U.S. policymakers? It is still early in the process of change to be very confident about the outcome, but it is not too early to offer some speculations. Possibly the most important consequence is that U.S. planners can hope for more coherent and decisive economic policy making in Europe. Simply the absence of one key, contentious participant from the bargaining table makes the process easier to accomplish. And, of course, the substantive results of that bargaining are less likely to occur at the lowest common denominator level so frequent during the past decade and a half. This is not to suggest that unions have been entirely responsible for European economic stagnation or that European leaders inherently know what policy options are best at each point. The matter involves more than union participation. Rather, it means that these governments will be better able to proceed with clearer economic programs whose results can be judged both by a democratic electorate and by planners better able to refashion their strategies as policy outcomes dictate. Both of these changes should promote political stability because they will enhance more efficient and responsible government. U.S. leaders will certainly welcome these gains, which are likely to have a salutary effect on the Western alliance as well as on worldwide economic health.

The stagnation and paralysis of public policy in Britain and so many European countries in recent years have been a painful experience. Not only has economic life suffered, but conflicts have torn at social stability as well. It is, of course, extremely unfortunate that economic deprivation has been the motor for change. But now that it has worked a fundamental rearrangement in the political process, political elites in Europe are unlikely to allow a return to collectivism as soon as prosperity is re-established. Instead, they are likely to institutionalize buffering policies, including a relatively high level of unemployment, to prevent a reawakening of damaging union militancy. Therein lies the potential for trouble. Union leaders in every European country are anxious to re-establish their influence. Economic recovery will certainly stir their energies to counterattack. Thus, even while post-collectivism continues to emerge, it is quite possible that political leaders in Washington will have to contend with some measure of renewed industrial instability among the United States' closest allies.

Notes

1. This is drawn from the work of Professor Samuel Beer, who first offered his important view of collectivist politics in *Modern British Politics* (London: Faber & Faber, 1965).

2. Interview with George Woodcock, former TUC general secretary, August 1969.

3. Interviews with Lord Williamson and Lord Geddes, both retired British union leaders, June 1969.

4. Interview with Bill Callaghan, secretary, TUC Economic Department, July 1980.

5. This point is emphasized in a number of works, including Walker Kendall's *The Labour Movement in Europe* (London: Allen Lane, 1975).

6. Interview with Edward Heath, former British prime minister, April 1978.

7. This was the title of a conference at Oxford University in November 1974.

8. Interview with Robert Shephard, political adviser to James Prior, British minister for employment, July 1980.

9. For a discussion of the 1977–79 period, see Gerald A. Dorfman, *British Trade Unionism Against the Trades Union Congress* (Stanford: Hoover Institution Press, 1983), chap. 3.

10. I gained this view from numerous interviews I conducted at the Trades Union Congress during the summer of 1979.

11. Dorfman, *British Trade Unionism*, chap. 4.

12. Ibid.

13. Interviews with several TUC staff members and a Conservative politician, all of whom wish to remain anonymous, March 1983.

14. Interview with Peter Coldrick, secretary, ETUC, July 1977.

15. Interview with Michael Lloyd, director of labor affairs at the EEC office in London, July 1977.

16. TUC, *Annual Report 1981*, p. 206.

7

Reflections on the Western European Peace Movement

L. H. Gann

We do not share the view put forward even by progressive members of the peace movement that a just war is no longer possible in the nuclear age, or that a struggle waged with nuclear rockets no longer entails the continuation of politics by other means on the part of conflicting social classes, but only a nuclear inferno—the end of the world.

Heinz Hoffmann
East German defense minister, 1982

For they have healed the hurt of the daughter of my people slightingly, saying Peace, peace—where there is no peace.

Jeremiah 8:11

The autumn of 1981 witnessed some of the greatest demonstrations ever seen in Europe. Fifty thousand men and women marched through the streets of Paris, yet theirs was—by comparison—only a minor gathering. One hundred fifty thousand people tramped through Rome, London, and Helsinki. Public involvement was even greater in Bonn (with an estimated 200,000 to 300,000 participants), in Athens (300,000), and in Amsterdam (350,000). The

Spaniards beat all records with an estimated 500,000 marchers. The demonstrators' mood was one of commitment and celebration reiminiscent in some ways of both a huge holiday crowd and a revivalist meeting, with vows to end war and stay the specter of a nuclear holocaust. The leaders were not wholly one-sided in their assessment of the source of the danger. Some of them censured the military buildup of the Warsaw Pact as well as that of NATO. But the overwhelming majority condemned the West. In this respect, the organizers' success was stupendous. No demonstrations of a similar size had ever been launched against the Soviet invasion of Afghanistan, Soviet repression in Hungary and Czechoslovakia, or the horrors of the Gulag archipelago. For most of the demonstrators, the enemy was to be found at home and, even more so, in the United States—the world's supreme villain.

Had the Europeans become disenchanted with the Atlantic Alliance? Opinion polls seem to point at a different conclusion. In West Germany, the key to Western defense, the public appears to have become more rather than less favorable to NATO during the preceding two decades. (Between 1966 and 1980, the percentage of German respondents favoring continued membership in NATO on existing terms rose from 63 to 81. The percentage of those who desired their country to leave NATO fell from 3 to 1.) At the same time, the public seems to have become increasingly appreciative of the Bundeswehr; between 1974 and 1980, the percentage of those convinced that the Bundeswehr would strengthen peace increased from 69 to 90.[1]

Nevertheless, the critics of West Germany's military establishment had become a major force, all the more so since they drew support especially from the young and well educated. (In 1980, only 16 percent of the overall West German population disapproved of the Bundeswehr, but 20 percent of Germans aged 16 to 29 expressed disaffection with their country's military. On the average, those Germans most likely to be called to the colors disliked their prospective uniform more than the rest.)

The peace movement succeeded in exacerbating existing tensions between Europe and the United States, where, during the 1980 presidential election, defense had become a campaign issue and where students had widely deserted the cause of pacifism—sometimes to an astonishing degree.[2] The peace movement in Germany likewise won a psychological victory. Its proponents had persuaded millions of citizens that the danger of nuclear war derived from Washington, not from Moscow. Above all, the peace movement won by redefining the ideological debate; its members ended by appropriating the sacred word "peace" for their own political cause.

The peace movement was extraordinarily heterogeneous in composition; looseness and diversity constituted both its weakness and its strength. Its attraction depended heavily on local factors as well as on general considerations of policy. The crowds in Athens hated Turks more than Americans; the Greeks were concerned with Turkey's role in Cyprus and the assumed Turkish menace in the Aegean—as well as with the threat of a broader European conflict involving the use of atom bombs. The Spaniards remembered the attempt a few months earlier at a military coup; in addition, Spain was torn by a bitter internal debate over the question of joining NATO. (It did join.) Dutchmen may have hearkened back to their country's traditional neutrality.

But there were certain unifying trends. The participants in the peace movement mostly were at odds with what they regarded as the norms of an unjust society. The Book of Samuel describes the dissidents who secretly rallied to young David in the Cave of Adullam as "everyone that was in distress, and everyone that was in debt, and everyone that was discontented."[3] The peace movement was a Cave of Adullam gone public. It comprised a great aggregation of men and women who were psychologically alienated rather than men and women who were physically deprived. The marchers counted in their ranks socialists of every tune, from utopians to hard-line Marxist-Leninists. The free enterprise system, or modified varieties of it, may indeed have given prosperity to Western Europe, but it has never aroused much enthusiasm for its norms. Heine's satire of the fat, warmongering bourgeois, written a century and a half ago, has always evoked a popular response:

> He sits with his wallet under his arse
> While he drums with his fingers the *Dessauer Marsch*.

In addition to Marxists, quasi Marxists, and their allies, there were churchgoers who believed that nuclear war, or preparation for nuclear war, was incompatible with the Gospel. The churches, of course, were divided. (German Protestants, for example, contained within their ranks both proponents of unconditional Western disarmament as well as those who considered defense against aggression to be legitimate.) But by and large, younger churchmen were apt to lean to the Left. Many churchmen, moreover, had come to accept the new doctrine of moral symmetry between the USSR and the United States, that there was an equivalence between the real or assumed crimes committed by multinational corporations in the Third World on the one hand and the evils deriving from Gulag archipelagoes and universal thought control on the other. Many churchmen had begun to adjust their faith to what they considered the "realities" of the new world. (For an examination of this ecclesiastical revolution, see the essay by Alain Besançon and L. H. Gann in this volume.)

Within the secular peace movement, environmentalists played a particularly important part, especially in the predominantly Protestant areas of Europe—Britain, Scandinavia, and North Germany. In Catholic areas—Spain, Italy, France, and Bavaria—the ecological movement never attained the same status as a secular church with an earthly interpretation of salvation. There were nationalists and there were neutralists. The latter were of least significance in France and Switzerland, where the impact of the peace movement was less important than in the rest of Western Europe. Sweden, another neutral country, continued to maintain a substantial defense establishment and failed to be intimidated by incursions of Soviet submarines into its territorial waters. The French stood formally outside NATO's command; they prided themselves on their own nuclear deterrent—one that in fact might serve as a screen for an unacknowledged neutrality. Austria's neutralist position was embodied in its constitution. A first haven for refugees and persons expelled from the Eastern bloc, Austria was particularly apt to be pro-Western. Switzerland maintained a traditional neutrality based on a universal militia service almost uniformly acceptable to the citizenry. The demonstrators also contained men and women discontented with Europe's American connection and the assumed perils of "Coca-Cola-ization." And intermingled with them all were the numerous youngsters who enjoyed a rousing "demo" for its own sake.

"*Cui bono*—for whose gain?" Cicero once asked in a great oration. Who were the beneficiaries of these great demonstrations, the great campaign for peace through weakness? The Soviet answer depended on the demonstrators' target. Much to the surprise of its organizers, the British peace movement met with intemperate criticism from the Soviets on the grounds that END (the movement designed to end nuclear armament) sought to "split" the European peace campaign. The British might censure Washington more than Moscow, but END did not hesitate to condemn Soviet as well as Western civil rights violations and would not submit to the Soviet demand that END should "applaud without reserve all Soviet policies."[4]

The Soviets took a considerably more favorable attitude toward most of the peace movement on the continent of Europe, and with good reason: the Marxist-Leninist cause stood to gain from the endeavors of the peace campaigners. Wittingly or unwittingly, the peace movement would contribute to "peace" as understood by Marx and Lenin. The founding fathers of communism had been anything but pacifists; instead, they had condemned pacifism as an instrument of the bourgeoisie.[5] History, in their view, was a succession of class struggles; force was the midwife of history, an essential means on mankind's long progress from feudalism to capitalism, from capitalism to the dictatorship of the proletariat under socialism, and from socialism to communism—when all social contradictions and class struggles would be resolved and peace would stand finally assured. Mankind's destiny was already known to the initiates, the revolutionary vanguard of the toilers. This inherent knowledge required no empirical proof.

According to the theoreticians of the Communist Party of the Soviet Union (CPSU), mankind had fortunately made already great progress toward a destiny both blessed and inevitable. The world was now divided into two "camps," the camp of socialism and peace and the camp of capitalism and war. World capitalism was in decline, and it was the socialists' duty to hasten this inevitable process. Peaceful coexistence could be a temporary condition between capitalist and socialist states. But peaceful coexistence was itself an instrument for the intensification of the class struggle. Lenin's teaching on the subject was unequivocal. As Yuri Andropov explained in 1967, at a time when peaceful coexistence seemed unchallenged, although the USSR

> still maintains its economic and military power, the real danger remains for the people of our country, and for other socialist countries, for all progressive forces, and for world peace . . . Our party and the Soviet government firmly uphold the cause of peaceful coexistence between the States with different social systems. But the Soviet people remember:
> The more we provide for the security of our motherland, the more we close the borders of the Soviet Union against the agents of imperialism, the more energetic and the firmer will be our counterforce against the enemy, the better results this course [peaceful coexistence] will produce.[6]

Peace could be strengthened only by strengthening the armed might of the USSR and its allies, by weakening NATO militarily, diplomatically, and economically, by further shifting the international "correlation of forces" in Moscow's favor.

The USSR and its allies thus engaged in a series of so-called peace offensives, all of them linked to particular strategic objectives. In 1979, Brezhnev began a determined campaign against President Carter's previously delayed efforts to strengthen NATO's nuclear deterrent forces.[7] By 1980, the assault had gathered momentum as the Western European communist parties began to strengthen their position within the Western European peace movements. In this respect, the numerical power of these communist parties bore no relation to their impact. (In terms of the percentage of votes gained in parliamentary elections, the Communists were powerful only in Italy [29.9 percent in 1983] and, to a lesser extent, in France [16.2 percent in 1981]. In Great Britain, the German Federal Republic, Holland, Belgium, and Denmark, the Communists' share of the popular vote remained negligible [0.05 percent, 1983; 0.2 percent, 1983; 1.79 percent, 1982; 2.1 percent, 1981; and 1.1 percent, 1981, respectively].[8] But in terms of influence, organization, and publicity skills as well as financial support, the Communists had an impact that went far beyond their numerical strength; indeed, they prided themselves on their role in pursuit of this cause.

By 1980, the CPSU and its allies had fully mastered the primary lesson of the "neutron bomb campaign." The peace offensive, to party strategists, represented a popular front in novel format; wide-based participation in the CPSU's attempt to disarm the West by "bourgeois" pacifist, religious, and ecological groups not directly linked to the USSR could significantly help to influence public opinion in NATO countries on the nuclear weapons question. In order to achieve this aim, differences between Communists and the noncommunist Left must be downplayed on all nongermane issues, thereby allowing the Soviets to draw support from a broad-based alliance. Communists, moreover, would have to manipulate the European peace themes and popular dread of nuclear war carefully to gather to the movement alienated youngsters and alienated intellectuals who would otherwise be leaderless. The Soviet leaders took heart from the manner in which the struggle extended in 1981–1982 to include opposition to attempts to strengthen NATO's nuclear shield in Western Europe. As *Izvestiya* put it:

> A mass-based, truly popular movement is mounting in the Federal German Republic. Over 1 million people have already signed the Krefeld appeal calling on the federal government to reverse its agreement to the deployment of U.S. Pershing II missiles and cruise missiles in the Federal Republic. Ferment is growing in both ruling parties.[9]

How did this influence operate? The Soviets to some extent subsidized the movement. They employed journalists and academicians who traveled around Western Europe. In West Germany, the German Democratic Republic (DDR) played a peculiarly important part, profiting from the unique advantage of commanding the resources of an entire communist state linked to a major Western European power by ties of language and tradition. In West Germany, for instance, the communist-controlled Committee for Peace, Disarmament, and Cooperation staged an International Antiwar Day in 1980 supported by a variety of noncommunist groups such as the Association of German Students, Nature Friend Youths, local organizations of the Young Socialists, and the Catholic and Protestant churches. Even more successful was the German Peace Union, which, in the same year, took the initiative in the Krefeld Appeal, promulgated by representatives of the Green Party (Germany's left-leaning ecological party) and a host of religious groups, pacifists, and conscientious objectors, very few of whom had the slightest sympathy for the communist cause.

In addition, Communists used Moscow-sponsored front organizations such as the World Peace Council, the World Federation of Trade Unions, the Women's International Democratic Federation, the International Organization of Journalists, the Christian Peace Conference, the International Association of Democratic Lawyers, the International Union of Students, the World Federation of Democratic Youth, and the World Federation of Scientific Workers, all of whom loyally followed the Soviet line. The Soviets also received support from the Generals and Admirals for Peace (including French admiral Antoine Sanguinetti; Italian general Nino Pasti—an ex-NATO deputy commander; and German general Gert Bastian). In addition, the Socialist International began to take a pro-Soviet position on the so-called peace issue from 1976, after Willy Brandt had assumed the presidency. The World Conference of Religious Leaders, assembled in Moscow at the invitation of the official Russian Orthodox church, served as an even more straightforward "transmission belt."

Soviet participation in the peace movement did not go unchallenged. In 1981, for example, the Dutch government expelled a Tass "correspondent," who had openly boasted of Moscow's part in the peace movement; the Danish authorities asked a Soviet embassy secretary to leave the country; the Norwegians forced two Soviet embassy members to depart. Western intelligence services had their work cut out for them as copies of "top secret" U.S. nuclear plans were conveniently "discovered" and passed to sympathetic newspaper editors. But these were minor setbacks. Overall, the peace offensive turned out to be an enormous political and psychological success.

Communists, the point bears repeating, did not create the peace movement; neither were they the first to employ peace offensives as an instrument of foreign policy. Nazi propaganda had made a special appeal to an assumed international fraternity of former combat soldiers.[10] Nazi diplomacy, by a mixture of cajolery and threats, had benefited from antiwar sentiments in Western Europe and thereby contributed to Western appeasement. But even the appeasers of the 1930s had never succeeded in creating mass demonstrations of the kind that erupted in Western Europe during the late 1970s and early 1980s. The Communists for their part did not necessarily control these demonstrations; far from it. Their influence varied from country to country and region to region. In France, they were represented in the Mitterrand government, but did not dominate the peace movement. They played a minor part in Great Britain, a kingdom with a long-established pacifist movement of its own, traditionally stronger than its counterparts in Western Europe; moreover, Trotskyites formed an important part of the British movement. The British Peace Movement, END (founded in 1979 with support from men and women who had previously worked for CND [Campaign for Nuclear Disarmament] and ICDP [International Cooperation for Disarmament] and backed by a broad coalition of social democrats, liberals, trade unionists, and feminists), steered an overly independent course from Moscow's viewpoint.

Within many of the continental peace groups, the Communits had, however, secured a powerful position.[11] As for the non-Marxists among them, their divergencies did not matter too much to the Communists for the present. Whatever the demonstrators might think subjectively, objectively they were playing a "progressive" role at a particular moment in world history. Even when they were not anti-American, the demonstrators—like most European diplomats and government officials—had become consciously or unconsciously committed to the doctrine of symmetry—the unjustified assumption that there was an essential parallel between the two superpowers—between the USSR, with its totalitarian creed, and American democracy. Even the heroes of popular thrillers, characters such as the preposterous James Bond, adopted something of the new attitude when they ceased to chase KGB villains and, instead, went after unidentified private criminal organizations, identifiable all too easily with multinational corporations.

Neutralism was not a single doctrine; it came in many varieties. By reason of its geographic position, the Federal Republic of Germany

(FRG) had a greater stake in good relations with the USSR than did any of its NATO partners. *Ostpolitik* had facilitated relations between the FRG and the DDR and had resulted in increased trade with the East, apparently a more secure status for West Berlin, and permission for 300,000 ethnic Germans to emigrate from East Germany to the FRG. However, *Ostpolitik* conflicted to some extent with *Westpolitik*; hence neutralism was apt to become more respectable even within the Establishment than hitherto.

Neutralism also appealed to a number of soldiers; for instance, Major General Gert Bastian, a former commander of an armored division in the Bundeswehr, criticized Western rearmaments on more technical terms. To Bastian, NATO's projected new nuclear armaments would be useless, expensive, and dangerous to Western European security. NATO was already well supplied with nuclear weapons. Western Europeans would be insane to place on their soil land-based nuclear weapons capable of striking directly at the USSR. Soviet strikes on such emplacements would devastate Western Europe's densely populated industrial regions and occasion a general holocaust. Western Europe, more vulnerable than the United States strategically, could not afford to provoke Moscow by attempting to destabilize the existing nuclear balance in NATO's favor.[12]

Bastian ignored the offensive capacity of the Red Army, its unreservedly offensive doctrine, the Soviets' conviction that the military correlation of forces had shifted in their favor, the Western Europeans' unwillingness to create a joint defense force capable of defending Western Europe solely by conventional means, the fact that the initiative for placing land-based, intermediate-range ballistic missiles had come from the Europeans, and the unwillingness of so many of his supporters within the peace movement to consider *any* form of effective military defense. Nevertheless, Bastian's views found considerable support in the Dutch armed forces where men such as General von Mayenfeld and a number of lower-ranking officers shared similar views.

These peace generals evoked an equally powerful response among neo-nationalists, such as Helmut Diwald, who considered that peace could come to Europe only through German reunification. A united German state would break the cohesion of both NATO and the Warsaw Pact; Germany would cease to serve as a potential nuclear battlefield in the quarrels of foreigners; the danger of international confrontation would diminish if all Germans once more dwelt under a single flag, and if the Bundeswehr and the East German Nationale Volksarmee were no longer preparing for a fratricidal war. For Diwald, both East and West Germany were "occupied" territories—client states subject to the victors of World War II. Diwald—like other critics of NATO—assumed that there was a moral symmetry between East and West.[13] He overlooked that the Federal Republic—alone among the two German states—rested on a free constitution and was ruled by a freely elected government, whereas East Germany was a Soviet fief, subject to a self-appointed dictatorship of party functionaries and ultimately dependent on Red Army support. The advocates of reunification—like so many German nationalists in the past—moreover lacked all sense of what was politically attainable in given circumstances; reunification was out of the question as long as Moscow dominated Eastern Europe.

"Neutro-nationalism" made an equally strong appeal to the "Greens"—the ecologists and pacifists—who stood for what they called *Oeko-Pax* (Eco-Peace). By the early 1980s, the Greens had become a significant force in West German politics, having gained an increasing number of votes at the expense of the Free Democrats. Admittedly the Greens were badly divided. They ranged from moderate environmentalists to romantic anarchists who dreamed of a deindustrialized rural Germany, in effect promising to Germans as a reward what the ill-starred Morgenthau Plan of the 1940s, with its vindictive design for pastoralizing Germany, had intended as a punishment.

Nevertheless, the rising strength of the Greens was disquieting. In Germany (and also in Holland), the environmentalists gained no backing from those who made a living from nature—fishermen and farmers. Rather, they derived their support from those employed in such professions as teaching, journalism, television, the performing arts, academic research, publishing, and the welfare bureaucracies. They had become strong among the professional molders of public opinion. They were apt to assume, as the European gentry of old had, that a livelihood obtained from a monthly salary derived from public taxation was somehow more honorable (certainly more visible) than one sustained by the more uncertain profits made in business. The sympathies of the new diploma-bearing salariat, with its emotional and material stake in a state-regulated economy, therefore mainly supported the noncommunist Left, either of the Green or the moderate socialist variety.

These young men and women apparently had nothing to do with those of their forebears who had once constituted the Hitler Youth. The young of the 1970–1980s had no memory of the Wehrmacht; they did not enjoy marching to the tune of *Preussens Glorie* or the

Hohenfriedberger Marsch. They professed a commitment to peace; they were ready to declaim against the evils of neocolonialism and racism. They did not profess the Nazi version of inhumanity. But all of them drew on certain existing intellectual assumptions that predated Nazism. The Greens and the Nazis equally loathed parties and idealized *Bewegung* (the movement). They hated what they regarded as a despicable *System.* The Nazis had romanticized the peasantry in Germany; the Greens and the Socialist militants often, though not inevitably, idealized the peasantry in the Third World. The Nazis, though mainly city-bred, had censured the big city and its real and assumed ills; the Greens and Young Socialists were apt to dislike modern conurbations. They shared a similar *Kulturunbehagen* (malaise due to contemporary civilization), one that also found expression in the suddenly revived interest in emigration evinced by many young Germans in the early 1980s.

Kulturunbehagen in Western Europe has traditionally been associated with anti-Americanism, though not always for the same reasons. "Amerika, du hast es besser" (America, you are better off), Goethe had argued in a poem denouncing the ills of romanticism. Romantics such as Heine had not shared his standpoint. Neither had old-fashioned conservatives in love with a caste society or with the assumed merits of *Gemeinschaft* (an organic and traditional social order), as opposed to the supposed ills of *Gesellschaft* (the artificial and mechanical order of an industrial and urban society). Conservatives had sided with the old South. Democrats—including the endless throng of Germans who had emigrated to the United States to escape from poverty and from the attention of noblemen, bureaucrats, and recruiting sergeants—had sympathized with the North and with a U.S. constitution that permitted newcomers to the United States to get ahead.

Later on, during the 1930s and the 1940s, social democrats and British Labourites such as Clement Attlee and Ernest Bevin had been sympathetic to the United States as a pioneer of the New Deal, a free country, and the Arsenal of Democracy. The most strident anti-Americans had been the Nazis and, later on, the "soft" Left of the 1970s and 1980s, both of whom carried a related romantic legacy. Dr. Goebbels had denounced the United States as a warmongering, yet decadent, pluto-democracy, a land of hypocrisy, racial mongrelization, and exploitation. To the New Left, the United States was a nation characterized by self-righteousness and materialism, by racial and economic exploitation, by a record of robbery and repression in the Third World, and by its willingness to risk the destruction of humanity. Modern German schoolbooks often carried a similar message: The United States

was a land where "individualism tends to degenerate into brutal ego-
tism, freedom into lack of discipline, mobility into rootlessness . . . democracy into uniformity and mediocrity."[14]

The psychology of anti-Americanism in many ways resembled that
of the earlier anti-Semitism. Under the Nazi dispensation, Jews were
caught in a doublebind. If they were rich, they were exploiters; if they
were poor, they were a charge on the land. If they called for peace, they
corrupted the nation through pacifism; if they called for the defense of
the Fatherland, they were warmongers. The Americans now found
themselves in a similar predicament. When they strengthened their
forces in Europe, they were provoking war; if they considered with-
drawing forces from Europe, they were abandoning their allies. If they
invested funds abroad, they were guilty of exploitation; if they ab-
stained from putting money overseas, they were boycotting the Third
World. If they paid low wages, they debased the workers; if they paid
high wages, they corrupted the masses through consumerism, and so
on *ad infinitum*.

Neglected, on the other hand, were those features that made the
United States unique in the world: its scientific creativity, its generosity
in support of churches and charitable organizations; its extraordinary
willingness to receive and to grant citizenship to immigrants from all
over the world on a scale unparalleled anywhere else on the globe; and
the Americans' extraordinary success in evoking loyalty to the Constitution, the Bill of Rights, and to the country at large by its huge and
heterogeneous population.[15] (European misconceptions regarding the
United States were not improved by the failure of European scholars to
rectify the extraordinary imbalance between the impressive contribution made by American academicians to the study of European culture
and history on the one hand and by the scanty output of European
scholarship regarding the United States on the other.)

In Western Europe, especially in the FRG, anti-Americanism was
apt to accompany a new and diffuse form of nationalism linked to pacifism, or at least to a desire to disengage from the Atlantic Alliance, an
alliance that would only invite nuclear annihilation in the event of war.
Opinion of course varied widely, but overall, the Germans were more
inclined than the French to view the proposed deployment of U.S. medium-range ballistic missiles as the main threat to their own country.[16]
Germans, alone in Western Europe, had to cope with the problems of a
divided country. If only the Americans would depart, said the Greens,
the "German problem" might more easily be resolved. The new mé-
lange of nationalism, neutralism, and anti-Americanism was, of course,
not unique to Germany. British pacifists at times would hearken back

to Splendid Isolationism of the Victorian variety and French neutralists to their country's former grandeur. But in Germany alone, neutralism increasingly became linked to the demand for German reunification, for a change in the existing balance in Europe. The Nazi slogan, *Ein Volk, ein Reich, ein Führer*, might conceivably become a call for *Ein Volk, ein Reich, ein Frieden* (one nation, one Reich, one peace) or, as a Berlin taxi driver put, it, *vom Grossdeutschen zum Gründeutschen Reich* (from the Greater to the Greener German Reich).

The new nationalism had many roots. It owed something to the Vietnam war—interpreted widely, though inaccurately, as an exercise in U.S. imperialism. The Vietnam war, moreover, had evil effects of an indirect kind. The war had led to a massive transfer of experienced junior officers and sergeants from Western Europe to Southeast Asia. The U.S. Army in Germany became widely beset by drug abuse, indiscipline, and violence, for the military proved unable to isolate its young men from the wider problems affecting American society. As increasing numbers of black soldiers enlisted in the forces, Germans began to complain that "Harlem had come to the Fatherland." There was a frightening increase among American soldiers of crime and public drunkenness, leading to ugly clashes between soldiers and German civilians. Inflation thereafter reduced the U.S. soldier's purchasing power; all too often, G.I. Joe ceased to be respected and turned into an object of German pity, contempt, or hatred. By the early 1980s, the U.S. Army had at last rebuilt its discipline and efficiency. But the long interregnum had left a legacy of distrust—not merely among German leftists—but also among many ordinary citizens.

There was also the unexpected legacy of German success. The Federal Republic had attained extraordinary, and originally quite unanticipated, triumphs in the constitutional and economic spheres. The FRG was unquestionably the most successful state in German history. A young man or woman born anytime after 1949, the year in which the Federal Republic was established, could not appreciate the miseries of the immediate post–World War II years or West Germany's incredible achievement in resettling about 12 million refugees from the lost lands beyond the Oder-Neisse line and another 3 million from Soviet-occupied East Germany. International migration also affected public opinion in other ways. There was less firsthand news of the citizens' lot in East Germany as the Berlin Wall and the fortified border of East Germany caused the stream of refugees largely to dry up. Personal links between the FRG and the United States also diminished, as the United States, having changed its immigration laws, had ceased to attract large numbers of newcomers from Western Europe. (Between 1950 and

1969, nearly 800,000 had gone to the United States; by 1970, the number of emigrants had diminished to just over 10,000 a year. Between 1945 and 1965, 80,000 Dutchmen came to the United States; after 1968, their number had dropped to less than 1,000 a year.)

West Germans had come to take for granted the prosperity secured for so many years within the Atlantic Alliance. But there were many other strains. The Reichswehr of old had cooperated with the Red Army; Lenin, in turn, had been an admirer of the Germans' military efficiency. Long before World War II, conservative theoreticians had sought for a "third way" between Western capitalism and Soviet communism, and this tradition continued after World War II. Kurt Schumacher, founding father of the post–World War II Social Democratic party in West Germany, had stood for an all-German national solution; Konrad Adenauer for an unreserved commitment to the West. *Ostpolitik* had been an attempt to transcend the East-West division in Europe. Right-wing parties of the traditional kind, such as the National Democratic party, were indeed unable to make much of an impact on the German electorate. But national-pacifism, represented by academicians such as Helmut Diwald, increasingly gained intellectual respectability.[17]

The Germans more than any of their neighbors also suffered from a wider sense of malaise that went with *Angst* (anxiety) and a dread of nuclear catastrophe. Both superpowers were already overarmed. For many Germans, NATO came to be viewed as an American-designed instrument for manipulating Western Europe to Washington's advantage, even though the initiative for NATO had, after all, derived from Europeans against considerable resistance from highly placed Americans opposed to such a fundamental departure from traditional U.S. policy.[18]

Overall there was in Europe, especially in West Germany—the Western European front-line state—a sense of menace from the Soviet Union and a dread that no European associated with the United States. Insofar as Germany was concerned, the country remained not only divided between East and West, but the frontiers of the two German states (unlike those between West Germany and Austria) were drawn in as arbitrary a fashion as those of a nineteenth-century African colony in the heyday of imperialism, taking no account of existing historical or religious traditions.

Even in West Germany itself, the *Länder* had been reconstituted as newly hyphenated entities: Nordrhein-Westfalen or Rheinland-Pfalz. West Germany stayed a country without a true center. Bonn simply was the main seat of politics and administration with Protestant Hamburg and Catholic Munich vying for the status of West Germany's cultural and economic capital. Many of Germany's traditional cultural landmarks had disappeared. The radical Right in Wilhelminian Germany used to inveigh against *Junker und Juden*. In post–World War II Germany, both groups, having contributed much to German civilization, had practically disappeared—with consequences difficult to overestimate. Germany had long yielded scientific primacy to the United States. In place of traditional culture, Germans—even anti-Americans of the radical variety—had substituted American culture. Germany might be a great economic power, but spiritually the country seemed in disarray.

What of the future? The peace movement in a sense reflected both the success and failure of Western policies in general. For over three decades, NATO has secured to Western Europe freedom from invasion and a prosperity unthinkable in 1945. During the same period the prestige of the USSR as a revolutionary model worthy of emulation was shattered beyond repair. The Greens and their allies had inherited a long-standing peace and a welfare state whose existence had all too easily become accepted as a matter of course. The Western alliance by the 1980s had failed to inspire the same moral commitment as hitherto among the young. The 1953 election had entailed a historic resolve—firmly placing the FRG in the Western orbit. The 1983 election—on the face of it—reaffirmed the electorate's decision. The Christian Democrats received an absolute majority in the Bundestag. The Greens, on the other hand, obtained 5.6 percent of the vote—not in itself an impressive result, but one that provided them at long last with parliamentary representation and parliamentary legitimacy. Margaret Thatcher's smashing electoral victory in Great Britain in June 1983 possessed the same ambivalent quality. On the one hand, she gained an overwhelming parliamentary majority committed to NATO and a strong foreign policy. On the other hand, something like 28 percent of the British electorate voted for the Labour Party, ill-led and divided but committed for the first time to nuclear disarmament.

Fortunately for NATO, the neutralists' long-term prospects may not be as good as they seemed early in 1983. They are divided among themselves and they do not seem to have the capacity to develop a lasting and cohesive alliance. There are, moreover, strong countervailing trends. The 1983 German and British elections were only two of several contests since 1978 that had swept conservative-minded governments into office. Conservatives won national elections in Austria, Denmark, Norway, Belgium, and the Netherlands and local elections in France. The European socialist governments—especially those in Italy and France—were no less vigorous in their support of NATO. Contrary to a widely held stereotype in the United States, the European defense effort was already substantial and continued to grow. (By 1983, 90 percent of NATO's land forces were European, as were 75 percent of NATO's naval and air forces.)[19] Given patience, skill, and resolve, as well as the determination of that Western European majority that does not wish to succumb to Soviet pressure, the Western alliance will surely survive what has become the most serious challenge yet experienced in its history.

Notes

1. Cited in *Informationen zur Politischen Bildung: Frieden und Sicherheit* 190, no. 2 (1982): 12.
2. See, for instance, a poll of freshmen and sophomores at UCLA on the subject of nuclear war, *Psychology Today*, November 1982, p. 11.
3. I Samuel 22:2.
4. END Coordinating Committee, "An Open Letter to the Soviet Peace Committee, January 1983," *New Statesman*, January 21, 1983, pp. 12–15.
5. N. Lenin, Leon Trotzki, and Karl Liebknecht, *Gegen den Militärismus; Gegen den Pazifismus; Für die Bewaffnung des Proletariats* (Berlin: Verlag Junge Garde, 1921).
6. Yuri Andropov, Speech on the fiftieth anniversary of the founding of the KGB (Soviet secret police), December 20, 1967, in "Fifty Years Guarding the Security of the Soviet Motherland," *Izbrannye rechi i stat'i* (Selected speeches and articles) (Moscow, 1979), p. 114; see also Rolf Geyer, "Das sowjetische Friedenskonzept . . . ," *Politische Studien*, no. 33 (1982): 52.
7. For a more detailed appraisal, see Jeffrey G. Barlow, "Moscow and the Peace Offensive," *The Backgrounder* (Heritage Foundation), no. 184 (1982); and Count Hans Huyn, *The Soviet Peace Offensive*, Heritage Lectures no. 17 (Washington, D.C.: Heritage Foundation, 1982).
8. *Yearbook on International Communist Affairs, 1983* (Stanford: Hoover Institution Press, 1983), pp. xxi–xxii.
9. *Izvestiya*, June 21, 1981, cited in Barlow, "Moscow and the Peace Offensive," p. 21.
10. *Die Mannschaft: Kameradschaft der Frontdichter Frontsoldaten wollen den Frieden*, introduction by Hanns Oberlindober (Berlin: Satariverlag, 1937).
11. As Wolf Biermann, a Marxist opposed to the DDR put it, "I walked through a crowd of 300,000 people . . . The program was directed by the head of the DKP [the West German Communist Party]; strong-arm squads of the DKP

were guarding the stage . . . I get annoyed as hypocrisy infects the peace movement like syphilis and as so many people join it who only want disarmament in the West and who believe that the same armaments in the East serve the cause of peace." (Cited in Hans-Peter Schwartz, "Die Rückkehr der Schwärmer: Fragen an die Christen in der sogenannten Friedensbewegung," *Die Politische Meinung*, no. 205 [November–December 1982]: 21–22.)

12. Gert Bastian, "Warum ich die 'Nachrüstung' ablehne, Schreiben an Bundesverteidigungsminister," in Gert Bastian, *Atomtod oder Europäische Sicherheitsgemeinschaft* (Cologne: Pahl-Rugenstein, 1981), pp. 17–24.

13. Helmut Diwald, "Deutschland—was ist es?" in Wolfgang Venohr, ed., *Die deutsche Einheit kommt bestimmt* (Bergisch Gladbach: Gustav Lübbe Verlag, 1982), pp. 17–35.

14. Roswitha Sieper, *The Student's Companion to the USA* (Munich: Hueber, 1975), p. 117. Ernest A. Menze, *Land der begrenzten Möglichkeiten* (Heidelberg: Quelle & Meyer, 1975), is more temperate in tone, but nevertheless claims that the individual American wields no political power but constitutes, within the context of a democratic order, a danger for the power position of the ruling elite. U.S. governmental policy takes account of the ambivalence within the American character by inducing a superficial sense of contentment among Americans, thereby assuring its own position of power (p. 19). For anti-American stereotypes within the peace literature, see, for instance, Waldemar Kutte, *Hoffnung durch die Friedensbewegung* (Hamburg: the author, 1981), pp. 61–64; or, the travesty of U.S. history embodied in "Amerikas Weg zur Weltmacht Nv. 1," in *Komittee für Frieden und Abrüstung: Friedensdebatte in der Schweiz* (Bern: Das Komittee, 1982), pp. 69–79.

15. According to public opinion polls in 1982, 85 percent of American whites and 80 percent of blacks believed that their country had a special role to play in the world; 83 percent of the whites and 65 percent of the blacks considered themselves "extremely proud" to be Americans; 94 percent of the whites and 86 percent of the blacks opined that the United States was the best place in the world in which to live (*Public Opinion*, June–July 1981, pp. 24–32). Western European intellectuals were either ignorant of such findings or prone to dismiss them as evidence of a "false consciousness" to be ultimately corrected by a chosen vanguard of intellectuals.

16. *Nouvel Observateur*, November 13, 1981, cited in Willifred von Bredow, "Die Friedensbewegung in Frankreich und der Bundesrepublik Deutschland," in *Beiträge zur Konfliktforschung*, no. 3 (1982): 53–64. Thirty-three percent of the German but only 19 percent of the French respondents considered the stationing of U.S. rockets in Western Europe the main threat.

17. David Gress. "What the West Should Know About German Neutralism," *Commentary*, January 1983, pp. 26–31. For a detailed statistical and sociological analysis, see David Kramer, "The Generation Gap in the Federal Republic of Germany and Alternative Ideologies," in *The Federal Republic of*

Germany and the United States . . . 1983 (New York: Lehrman Institute Seminar Series, 1983).

18. See, for instance, Nicholas Henderson, *The Birth of NATO* (London: Weidenfeld & Nicolson, 1982).

19. Richard R. Burt, "Europe Pullout Isn't Deserved or Desirable," *Wall Street Journal,* March 28, 1983.

8

It's Time
to Change the
Atlantic Alliance

Melvyn Krauss

Public opinion polls indicate that West Europeans continue
to share the same values with Americans and have no illusions concerning the Soviet threat or what life is like under a communist government. At the same time, an unmistakable and disturbing
trend toward neutralism, pacifism, and accommodation of the Soviet
Union exists today in Western Europe.

No doubt this seeming paradox, which has troubled most observers
of the European scene in recent years, has complex roots. There are the
traditional economic, political, and cultural tensions between the
United States and Western Europe. The growing power of the Soviet
Union appears to have demoralized a substantial segment of the European public. And the seemingly abrupt switch from the détente-
oriented rhetoric of previous administrations to the Reagan administration's tougher talk probably has been more unsettling than many
Americans realize.

But the European attitude can also be seen as a perfectly rational, if
short-sighted, calculation of economic self-interest. And U.S. policy,
rather than helping to rectify this calculus, is actually at the root of the
problem.

By paying a disproportionate share of the cost of defending the
Western world, the United States allows its allies to escape the defense

burden that trade with the Soviet bloc implies. The Soviets spend some portion of their gains from East-West trade on their military buildup and foreign adventures, which the West in turn must counter. East-West trade thus imposes a "defense feedback" cost on the West, which is borne more heavily by the United States than Western Europe and Japan. The result is that our allies' trade with the Soviets represents almost pure economic gain to them, while U.S. trade gains are offset by the need to pay for the increase in defense costs that Western trade with the Soviets induces.

Defense "free-riding" by the Europeans and Japanese thus has given the United States' allies a distorted framework for viewing their economic relations with the USSR. Our allies heavily discount the effect their policies have on enhancing Soviet economic and military might because they can pass much of their defense costs to the United States. The growing European willingness to accommodate the Soviet Union will not be altered by mere changes of governments, although a Reagan administration might naturally find it somewhat easier to deal with, say, a Kohl government or a Thatcher government than with their Social Democratic or Labour party alternatives. And the attitude of the United States' allies is not likely to be changed by continually hectoring them for more defense spending. The distortion can be removed only by changing the framework of the alliance. It is time that the Western Europeans began paying the true cost of an effective defense for themselves. And this will happen only if the United States makes it clear that it will no longer do so by declaring its intention to phase out U.S. forces in Europe over a period of years and by revoking its automatic commitment to come to the aid of any member of NATO in case of war. The European perception that the United States will intervene with so much force that an ensuing local conflict would rapidly bypass Europe, inflicting most of its costs on the USSR and the United States, has led the Europeans to irresponsible political behavior.

That is not to say the United States would not or should not come to the defense of Western Europe if it is threatened with military attack. But the commitment should not be automatic. The United States would not be turning its back on its allies, but redefining the relationship.

This will lead to a much stronger Western Europe. It will restore freedom of action to U.S. foreign policy. It will help revitalize the transatlantic relationship, with Western Europe less the junior and the United States less the senior partner. And it will remove the incentives for Western trade policies that the Soviets have become adept at exploiting.

A Legacy of World War II

Defense free-riding by West Europeans is a legacy of the early post–World War II period when defending U.S. allies against Soviet imperialism was necessary because of their ravaged economies. Today, however, it can no longer be justified. Both comparable (if not higher) West European and Japanese growth rates and the political rehabilitation of Japan and West Germany dictate that the allies assume a greater share of the defense burden. In 1981, for example, the United States spent 6.1 percent of its GNP on defense, while Japan spent 0.9 percent, Luxembourg 1.2 percent, Canada 1.7 percent, Belgium 3.3 percent, the Netherlands 3.4 percent, France 4.1 percent, West Germany 4.3 percent and Britain 5.4 percent. In contrast, the Soviet Union is estimated to spend at least 15 percent.[1]

Table 8.1

Defense Costs of NATO Member-States

Defense expenditures as percentage of GNP, 1980		*Military manpower per 1,000 population, 1981*	
United States	5.5	Greece	20.20
United Kingdom	5.1	Turkey	12.30
Greece	5.1	France	9.38
Turkey	4.2	United States	9.09
France	3.9	Spain	9.05
Portugal	3.8	Belgium	9.04
Netherlands	3.4	Norway	9.02
Belgium	3.3	Germany	8.03
Germany	3.2	Netherlands	7.25
Norway	2.9	Portugal	7.05
Italy	2.4	Italy	6.40
Denmark	2.4	Denmark	6.34
Spain	1.8*	United Kingdom	6.14
Canada	1.7	Canada	3.26
Luxembourg	1.0	Luxembourg	1.90
Iceland	—	Iceland	—

*1975; 1980 n.a.

SOURCE: Based on Werner Kaltefleiter, "The Free Rider Problem in Alliances," *Mont Pelerin Society 1982 General Meeting* (West Berlin: Institut für Wirtschaftspolitik an der Universität zu Köln, 1983).

The ratio of defense expenditure to GNP, of course, is only a crude and often inaccurate indicator of a country's defense efforts. West Germany imposes a military draft, for example, while Great Britain does not. As a result, the 1981 ratio of military manpower to population was 8.03 per thousand in West Germany and only 6.14 per thousand in Great Britain. Relative to the British, the West Germans are doing more than their ratio of defense expenditure to GNP indicates. Italy spends only 2.4 percent of its GNP on defense, and the ratio of military manpower to population is 6.4 per thousand. Yet Italy's willingness to accept long-range theater nuclear forces on its soil represents a contribution to the common defense effort not captured by the statistics.

The fact that the United States' allies spend—sometimes substantially—on their own defense in no way indicates the absence of defense free-riding, as European apologists and accommodationists argue. What defense free-riding means is that because Western Europe understates its demand for defense, its share of the common defense burden is less—and that of the United States more—than is warranted by the true value of Western defense to the Europeans. Technically, the extent of European defense free-riding can be measured by the excess of the marginal value that accrues to the West Europeans from the marginal unit of current Western defense over the price it pays for that defense multiplied by the total units of Western defense consumption. And while that amount may be difficult to estimate empirically, that should not be taken to mean that defense free-riding is either trivial or nonexistent.

Damage to the United States

Defense free-riding damages the United States in several ways. First, it represents a transfer of income from the United States to Western Europe that no longer can be justified in terms of the relative strength of the U.S. economy compared with Western Europe's. At a time when the Reagan administration is under considerable attack for its defense-spending proposals, it seems particularly inappropriate for the United States to pay defense costs the Europeans and Japanese should be paying for themselves.

Equally important but less recognized, defense free-riding has helped push Western Europe toward pacifism. For the West Europeans to continue to press the Americans into financing an important part of their defense costs, they must hide their true preferences for defense. West European pacifism can be interpreted as part of a classic free-rider strategy to induce the United States to continue subsidizing West European defense needs. Moreover, the target of West European defense free-riding is not limited to the United States; the Europeans attempt to free-ride on one another as well. Although all the allies want the benefit of the U.S. nuclear umbrella, they prefer to have the missiles physically located on their neighbors' soil rather than on their own. The Dutch want the missiles located in Germany, the Germans want them located in Italy, and so on.

It is no coincidence that the new pacifism in Western Europe is weakest in France, whose own national nuclear force shields the French not only from the Soviets but from the charge that they are free-riders regarding nuclear weapons on their soil. It is strongest in West Germany, where in the March 1983 federal elections the Social Democratic party, in effect, offered the electorate a nuclear free lunch—the benefit of the U.S. nuclear deterrent and no U.S. missiles in Germany. French foreign minister Claude Cheysson undoubtedly is correct in saying that the Europeans understand and desire the deterrent value of nuclear weapons much more than Americans think.[2] The new pacifists and the nuclear free-riders are one and the same.

Not only does defense free-riding encourage pacifism in Western Europe, but it has pushed the Europeans closer to the Soviet camp by giving them a distorted framework for dealing with the Soviets—a framework within which the enemy is treated as if it were a friend. The editors of the *Wall Street Journal*, for example, have noted the incongruity of Europeans' selling subsidized butter to the Soviets: "The Europeans are in effect taxing their citizens to transfer resources to an economy that devotes an unconscionable share of its resources to building SS-20's aimed at the citizens of Western Europe. This does violence not only to free trade but to common sense."[3] The fact, however, is that given U.S. tolerance of European defense free-riding, such policy makes perfect sense for the Europeans. They pass the defense cost of neutralizing the SS-20s on to the United States and use the savings to finance their welfare state programs. What does not make sense, however, is that the United States allows defense free-riding to continue.

In short, what many American see as European weakness toward the Soviets is really the United States' weakness toward its allies.

Subsidizing the Soviets

The Reagan administration's first response to European-subsidized credit and sales to the Soviets was one of accommodation of the allies on the grounds that a firmer response would exacerbate tensions within the Western alliance. But as I wrote at the time:

> Accommodating our allies so they, in turn, can accommodate the Russians will not solidify the alliance—the common wisdom and that of former Secretary of State Haig notwithstanding. Rather, it will induce Europeans to behave in ways that the administration can only be expected to find intolerable. A case of Europe receiving the wrong signals was when Secretary Haig persuaded the administration not to declare Poland in default on its loans to Western banks. The Europeans—particularly the West Germans—lobbied hard for the U.S. to turn the other cheek and go soft on the Poles. Our allies got the accommodationist message: Western Europe could freely follow its own policies of pursuing détente and paying tribute to the Soviet Union with little regard for the opinions of the United States whose power could be neutralized by appeals to Western unity. The result, it should be noted, has not been the strengthening of the alliance predicted by the accommodationists of the State Department, but a deterioration as an emboldened Europe now offers the Soviet Union subsidized credit to construct the controversial pipeline.[4]

The controversy over the Siberian gas pipeline was concerned more with subsidized East-West trade than East-West trade itself. The Europeans offered the Soviets subsidized credit to finance the pipeline—that is, the Soviets were tendered loans several percentage points below prevailing market rates of interest. The concessionary rates were equal to those given Third World countries. Many experts (such as Fred Hoffman of the Rand Corporation) believed that without the subsidized credit and government guarantees, the pipeline deal never would have gone through.

The pipeline subsidies added a new dimension to the dispute between Europe and the United States over Soviet trade. In addition to the normal gains the Soviets will make on the pipeline transaction, they have received an unrequited transfer of real resources from European taxpayers because of the subsidies. Both the pipeline transaction itself and the subsidy can be expected to come back to haunt the U.S. defense budget. French president François Mitterrand was right when he complained that the Reagan pipeline embargo was aimed more at the Europeans than the Soviets. It is one thing to trade with the common enemy, another to pay tribute to them.

The Reagan embargo to stop the subsidies was bitterly attacked both in Europe and the United States as an act of colossal hypocrisy. Was Reagan not using a double standard when he embargoed the European gas pipeline at approximately the same time that he lifted the Carter embargo on U.S. grain sales to the Soviets? Indeed, Secretary of State Haig argued that lifting the grain embargo was a major foreign policy mistake, precisely because it compromised the U.S. position with Europe on such East-West economic issues as the Polish debt and the gas pipeline.

One response to the Reagan critics was that lifting an embargo was not the same thing as giving a subsidy. That is, the Europeans were subsidizing the natural gas pipeline; the United States was not subsidizing grain sales to the Soviets. Subsidies on the pipeline were at the heart of the issue, it was argued, because propping up defunct economies in the communist world can only increase the West's external vulnerability and weaken its economies.

But this argument failed to win the day for several reasons. First, persistent pronouncements by the administration itself that the purpose of the embargo was to punish the Soviets for their behavior in Poland, even though it is obvious to most that turning the economic screw in Poland would in no way change the brutal dictatorship the Soviets had imposed there, muddled the administration's case. Second, U.S. grain farmers do receive subsidies, although the United States was not giving the Soviets subsidized credit to buy the grain. Third, the Europeans do not appreciate the distinction between subsidized and unsubsidized trade since subsidies are a pervasive way of doing business in the European welfare state. European governments routinely give extra-market subsidies to projects that cannot pass the test of the marketplace, but which they want to pursue either to hide unemployment (by putting workers in useless jobs) or to transfer income to a favored sector of the economy. Finally, the Europeans were interested more in propping up their own economies than in refusing to allow the Soviets to prop up theirs.

A far better response than subsidies by Reagan to his pipeline critics would have been defense free-riding. When the United States trades with the Soviet Union, the additional defense burden such trade imposes on Western European countries is minimal. But when the Western Europeans trade and overtrade (through subsidies) with the Soviets, they do put a substantial additional defense charge on the

United States because of defense free-riding. That is why it was not hypocritical for Reagan to embargo the pipeline at the same time that he allowed U.S. grain sales to the Soviets to go through. If the United States enriches the enemy through trade, at least it pays for the defense consequences of its actions. The Europeans do not.

When Reagan rescinded the embargo in November 1982, there were brave but unconvincing cries from the administration that the embargo had achieved a harmonization of allied trade policies toward the Eastern bloc. Only time will tell how much harmonization was achieved (and what its value might be). Many felt that the embargo did more to split the alliance than anything the Soviets could have done. Others argued that the debate over the pipeline was worthwhile in that it allowed the Reagan administration to make a statement that needed to be made.

Making a statement, however, is not the same thing as solving a problem. Neither embargoes nor sanctions against West European nations whose Soviet bloc trade policies displease Washington will achieve the United States' objective; namely, containment of East-West trade within the context of Atlantic solidarity. To do that, the distorted conceptual framework through which the Europeans view East-West trade must be normalized. This in turn requires that the Europeans pay for their own defense. Both rationalization of East-West trade and transatlantic harmony require that European defense free-riding be eliminated.

East-West Trade Cannot Be Free Trade

Though concerned primarily with subsidized trade with the Soviets, the controversy over the Siberian natural gas pipeline also raised certain fundamental questions regarding East-West trade, independent of its role in creating tensions within the Western alliance. Most important of these is whether the economists' predilection toward free trade should be applied to commerce with political enemies as well as friends—that is, whether free (unsubsidized) trade with the Soviet bloc is appropriate for Western nations even in a world where defense free-riding is eliminated.

Responses to this question range between two extremes. Fervent anticommunists, on the one hand, favor no trade because they seek to deny the Soviets the economic benefits and discount the economic gains that accrue from such trade to private Western interests. Fervent free marketeers, on the other hand, favor free trade with the Eastern bloc because they discount the effect free trade has on building up the enemy, focusing instead on the economic gains East-West trade bestows on the Western private sector. Neither extreme appears desirable as a basis for setting national trade policy with the communist countries.

The case against free trade with the Eastern bloc is based on the defense feedback effect. The standard international trade models that prescribe free trade as the best policy implicitly assume that the economic gains made by one trading partner have no adverse repercussions on the other. This assumption is not met, of course, when the two trading countries are political and military enemies. The economic gains made by the Soviets, because they fuel their military machine, impose a defense cost on the Western trading partner (in the absence of defense free-riding); hence, the collective interest in defense expenditure must be balanced against the private interest in profitable exchange to determine the optimal trade policy. The free market alone will not give the proper signals.

For example, the real cost to the United States of exported grain to the Soviets cannot be measured solely in terms of market price, as it can when trade is with a friendly or politically neutral country. Instead, measurement of the cost must take into account the military hardware produced by the Soviets with the resources freed from the development and production of agricultural machinery that the Soviets would be forced to make if they had to produce their own grain. The defense feedback cost of the grain sales then is the costs the United States has to bear to counter the increase in Soviet military hardware facilitated by the grain sales. If these costs are underestimated (as when cost is measured solely in terms of the market), too much East-West trade will take place and the collective interest in defense will not be adequately served. If they are overestimated, too little trade will occur and the private interest in profitable exchange will be shortchanged.

Which type of error—too little Soviet trade or too much—is likely to occur if defense free-riding is eliminated? Ironically, it can be convincingly argued that the United States would be likely to err on the side of too much trade and Western Europe on the side of too little. The reasons for this relate to differences in the economic structures of the United States and Western Europe. The United States has a tradition of a competitive market economy, modified to some extent by government regulation. The Europeans, on the other hand, believe more in state-directed economies, modified to some extent by the need to compete in world markets.

The tradition of a strong private sector and a relatively weak public one in the United States means that private companies that do substantial Soviet bloc business are likely to push for increased trade and ignore the defense feedback costs. Indeed, many argue that this is presently the case in the United States and that it trades too much with the Eastern bloc. Conversely, the existence of a strong public and a relatively weak private sector in Western Europe means that if Europe assumes the costs of its own defense, consciousness of the defense feedback costs of East-West trade will keep trade levels down. This implies that the collective interest in defense could be adequately served there once the allies assume the costs of their own defense. The Europeans, in other words, have the way if they have the will. And if defense free-riding were eliminated, they would have the will.

A Western Dilemma

Détente has created a serious dilemma for the Western alliance. By encouraging expanded East-West trade, it has created tensions between the allies because of defense free-riding. On the other hand, tensions within the alliance can be expected to increase if the United States presses Europe and Japan to shoulder their fair share of the common defense burden. U.S. relations with the allies, then, are likely to remain stormy.

Stormy or not, the United States should press for a redistribution of the costs of defending the West, not to punish the allies but to relieve the burgeoning U.S. defense budget while giving Europeans the proper framework for dealings with the Soviets. One way to do this would be for Washington to set up a timetable for withdrawal of the 340,000 American soldiers, sailors, and airmen now deployed in Europe, as well as the 56,000 American troops in Japan. U.S. troops could be phased out in a manner allowing substitute allied troops or an equivalent deterrent capability to be phased in. This would put the ball squarely in the allies' court, and I, for one, believe they would not fumble it—if only because the West European world view, particularly vis-à-vis the Soviet Union, can be expected to change dramatically once defense free-riding is eliminated.

It is no secret that the free world is losing confidence in NATO's ability to counter the Soviet threat because, as presently constituted, it is politically moribund. By pulling its troops out of Europe, the United States would not be turning its back on the West Europeans, as some critics argue. Rather it would be indicating that the United States is seeking a redefined transatlantic partnership where each partner's economic and political status and its military contributions are balanced. In the short run, this undoubtedly would involve some harsh trade-offs within Europe between welfare state goods and military expenditures. But in the longer view, the trade-offs would be worth it because they would put Europe on an equal footing with the United States in defending the Western values and institutions both suscribe to.

Michel Tatu has written of the likely effect of these common values if the United States did pull its troops out of Europe.

> Every government and every society seeks security not in order to become part of one or another system and thus as an end in itself, but because security will permit the government or the society to maintain its identity and its values. Just as a shipwrecked person who has lost one plank will not let himself drown but will look for another plank, so there is no reason to suppose that the European governments, not abandoned by America but simply invited to take charge progressively of their own defense, will immediately give up the values in whose name they so long attached themselves to America.
>
> Must one believe that the European attachment to liberalism and democracy is valid only so long as the United States is willing to guarantee these values? Or is it rather the contrary, that the alliance with America springs from the Europeans' own attachment to these values. The argument that Europe would turn herself into another Finland lacks dignity as well as cogency.[5]

As true as this may be, the Finlandization argument has proved an effective tool for those on both sides of the Atlantic who prefer the status quo of a militarily dependent and subsidized Europe to the alternative of European military independence and self-support. And a tool that serves powerful interests rather than a plausible theory is precisely what the Finlandization argument amounts to. Michel Tatu is right when he argues that "the 'Finlandization' argument resembles more a stratagem (remain in Europe, otherwise you will lose it) than a reality." It is the glue that keeps the present Western alliance in place. No one dares breach it; otherwise, it is said, the Soviets will have all of Western Europe without firing a shot.

The State Department must be viewed as a principal player in this game to keep Western Europe militarily dependent on and subsidized by the United States. When I argued in the *Wall Street Journal* that the United States should adopt a Fortress America strategy to counter Finlandization arguments and end European defense free-riding, Richard R. Burt, assistant secretary of state for European affairs, responded:

The Soviet Union remains the preponderant military power in
Europe. The Soviet Union also continues to employ its military
power to achieve political objectives, including the intimidation
of Western Europe. In such circumstances, the withdrawal of
American troops and of the American security guarantee would
have the reverse effect from that Professor Krauss suggests. American withdrawal would leave European leaders with no realistic
means to provide for their national security except through accommodation with the dominant regional power, the USSR.
American withdrawal would, as a result, depress, not stimulate,
European defense efforts, while driving the U.S. into increasing
international isolation.[6]

Is it that the assistant secretary has been completely duped by the
Finlandization strategists or, as seems more likely, that the institution
he serves—the U.S. State Department—is a prime Finlandization strategist itself?

When Assistant Secretary Burt argues that a U.S. withdrawal from
Europe would depress European defense efforts from present levels, he
assumes to know what European defense efforts would be in the absence of U.S. subsidization. How does he know this? Economists pos-
tulate that in market economies, the demand for particular goods can
be judged only by market behavior. But defense is a public good, not a
private one. What the Europeans demand in the way of defense expenditure when the United States pays the bills in no way indicates what
they would demand in the absence of U.S. contributions. Indeed, as
argued above, public goods theory predicts that Europe presently understates its demand for defense precisely to get the United States to
pay more.

Secretary Burt's prediction that U.S. withdrawal from Europe
would depress European defense efforts from present levels not only
contradicts the theory of public goods, it contradicts the theory of alliances as well. For any individual member, joining an alliance imposes
political costs if only because it forces the member to adjust its own
policies to those of the group. For a country to enter an alliance, of
course, the benefits of membership must be greater than the costs.
What benefit other than cut-rate defense does NATO bestow on its
European members to justify the political costs that NATO membership implies? I can think of none. Therefore, if the Europeans really did
not want the present level of defense the United States provides them,
their present membership in NATO would be senseless. Revealed preference makes a much better case than does Secretary Burt.

There are several other reasons why the State Department argument that a U.S. pullout would reduce present European defense efforts should not be taken at face value. First and foremost, European military dependence on the United States means greater U.S. control over European military capabilites. This is particularly important in the area of nuclear armaments. The State Department continues to oppose the proliferation of nuclear weapons. U.S. subsidization of European defense needs thus reflects the desire by the State Department for the United States to maintain its post–World War II nuclear superiority *over its allies.*

A Europe that paid its own way and was militarily independent of the United States would, of course, need its own nuclear force. Could it be that a "nuclear Germany" or a European defense force is as frightening to the United States as it is to the Soviet Union? It should not be. The Soviet fear of a nuclear Germany explains both why the Soviet Union is against a properly orchestrated devolution of U.S. power in Western Europe (a nuclear Germany would replace a nuclear United States on the borders of the Soviet empire), and why Secretary Burt's Finlandization arguments about a European collapse and isolation of the United States can be taken with a grain of salt. If a U.S. pullout from Europe would be so damaging to this country, why are the Soviets opposed?

In the final analysis, the Finlandization of Europe is a phony issue. The real one—whatever one's views—is whether the European allies, particularly West Germany, are to become full nuclear partners with the United States in confronting the Soviet menace.

Second, from a bureaucratic point of view—particularly its traditional rivalry vis-à-vis the Defense Department—the Department of State has a vested institutional interest in preserving global arrangements that maximize international *political* considerations and minimize international *military-strategic* ones. If Western Europe were militarily independent, the major issues between the United States and Europe would be military and strategic coordination. This would, at the same time, enhance the importance of the Defense Department and downplay the role of State. On the other hand, the status quo is convenient for the State Department precisely because it amplifies the political aspect of U.S.-European relations to the detriment of the military one.

One example illustrates this point. In recent months the placing of U.S. missiles in Western Europe to counter the Soviet SS-20s has become a major political issue between the United States and Europe. The State Department has played an important role in trying to resolve the missile problem. If, however, the Europeans were themselves responsible for countering the SS-20s, the State Department's role would be negligible, and that of U.S.-European military coordination magnified. In other words, it is not simply that State Department policymakers blindly worship the status quo that leads them to be Finlandization scaremongers, but that there is an institutional imperative for doing so.[7]

Conclusion

Just as the Bretton Woods international monetary system was changed when it broke down under the strain of changing economic realities, it is now time to change the international military system that resulted from World War II. West European military dependence on and subsidization by the United States is no longer warranted or desirable. It has led to the "new neutralism" and "new pacificism" in Europe, which, though dangerous mostly to the West Europeans themselves, are also dangerous to the United States. European military immaturity has led to European political irresponsibility. It will soon be forty years since World War II ended. The time for change is now.

Notes

1. International Institute for Strategic Studies, *The Military Balance, 1982* (London, 1982).
2. Claude Cheysson, "French Defense Policy and the U.S.," *Wall Street Journal*, February 25, 1983.
3. "Pipeline Deja Vu," editorial, *Wall Street Journal*, November 16, 1982.
4. Melvyn B. Krauss, "The Siberian Pipeline and Europe's Welfare States," *Wall Street Journal*, July 19, 1982.
5. Michel Tatu, "The Devolution of Power: A Dream?" *Foreign Affairs*, July 1975, p. 680.
6. Richard R. Burt, "European Pullout Isn't Deserved or Desirable," *Wall Street Journal*, March 28, 1983.
7. I thank Bruce Bueno de Mesquita for bringing this argument to my attention.

9

Remaking the Community of the Americas

Robert Wesson

The greater the disarray in relations between the United States and its Latin neighbors, the more necessary it becomes to bring the nations of North and Latin America into a closer economic and political community. The United States cannot cease to be a world power, but it can act more effectively on the world stage if it forges special relations within the Americas.

Latin America is important for many reasons. It is a relatively reliable source of many materials, including petroleum, and a market for one-fifth of U.S. exports. Its economies are generally complementary to the U.S. economy, and for nearly all countries the United States is the greatest single market, supplier, and source of investment. Communications, transportation, and travel from all of the hemispheric nations go more toward the United States than Europe, much less Asia. Miami and New York are the Meccas of the Americas.

No less important, the Western Hemisphere forms something of a cultural community. Television programs imported by Latin America are overwhelmingly from within the hemisphere, from the United States or Mexico. Whatever the differences between the United States and Latin America, they belong culturally to the West (except for a relatively small Amerindian group). The Spanish and Portuguese cultures are close to the European mainstream; and if the Latin nations are alien to Texans or Minnesotans, they are far less so than those of Asia or Africa. The United States itself is becoming increasingly a Latin American nation, with about 20 million persons of Hispanic background, some 8 percent of the population. This is the fastest growing of the important minorities, and it tends to preserve its cultural endowment more than most ethnic sectors. It will certainly become much more influential in coming years.

There has been, moreover, a sense of community in the hemisphere ever since the colonies of Spain and Portugal separated from their colonial rulers a few decades after the British colonies of North America did so. The Monroe Doctrine of 1823 expresses the apartness of the new nations. Little was done for many years to formalize hemispheric bonds, but since 1889 the Pan American Union (later the Organization of American States) has promoted trade and cultural exchanges. Latin Americans have often been irritated by the United States and sometimes angered by interventions; conflict and bad feelings have been frequent between the United States and its neighbors to the south. But the feeling that they all had something in common, as against European powers, has been pervasive in somewhat the same way people feel themselves members of a family even though they may resent the paternalism of a parent. For the United States, likewise, Latin America has occupied a special position, unlike other parts of what has come to be called the Third World. In the postwar period, this relationship took the shape of the Organization of American States, formed in 1948 and theoretically a rather close league for mutual security with broad powers of decision by qualified majorities.

The hemisphere has also something of a shared political tradition. The Latin nations established after the breakup of the Spanish empire looked to the United States as their political model, and they adopted constitutions patterned after that of the successful young republic of North America. Latin America, despite its mostly dictatorial record, is exceptional in the world for its respect for the democratic ideal. Government by election, with civil liberties and constitutional procedures, has almost always and everywhere been accepted as the proper way to manage states. Even the dictators have generally paid formal obeisance to democratic norms, and military regimes vow to return to them in due course. Latin America is the only region of the Third World in which there is much promise for the spread of democratic government.

The political outlook for Latin America is also relatively bright because its economic prospects are much better than those of Africa and the bulk of Asia. Although such countries as Haiti, Honduras, El Salvador, and Bolivia are very poor, in general the American continents are relatively uncrowded and well endowed with agricultural and mineral resources. Per capita GNP runs from three to ten times higher than that of most African and Asian countries. There is no good reason that Brazil, Argentina, Uruguay, and conceivably Mexico should not be able to join the ranks of the industrial nations within a fairly brief time.

Latin America is also the most promising region for the exercise of leadership by the United States, the area in which its power may most effectively be employed for the benefit of both the United States and its partners. The Latin Americans are ambivalent in their feelings toward their great northern neighbor, admiration and respect being mixed with envy and resentment, but they take it for granted that the United States is the inevitable hemispheric leader. There have been only slight challenges to that role; Argentina early in this century saw itself as spokesman for the Latins against the growing dominance of the United States, and in recent years Brazil has much more mildly cultivated its position as regional power. Most Latin Americans willingly accept the role—even the dominance—of the United States as long as it does not infringe their independence and dignity. Latin America is consequently the area in which the United States has the best hopes of contributing to economic development and cultivating ideals of freedom and democratic government.

The Challenge in Latin America

It is imperative that we pay more attention to Latin America because the region's serious political and economic problems represent a grave challenge for the United States. Failure to respond effectively would mean a serious setback for the influence and security of the United States and its ideals. Success in coping with the threat of disorder, on the contrary, would much improve both the position of the United States and the prospects for world order.

The 1981–1983 recession accentuated the economic problems of Latin America, but the roots of these economic problems run much deeper. The symptoms are unemployment (in many countries a third to half of the work force lacks regular full-time employment), inflation (hyperinflation of 100 percent or more in Argentina, Brazil, Peru, and other countries), stagnant or declining production (the region as a whole showed negative growth in 1981–1983 after averaging a strong 6 percent annually in 1970–1980), declining standards of living for increasing populations, huge deficits on foreign accounts, and, most notorious of all, outrageous dollar debts.

As Colombian president Belisario Betancur frankly told President
Reagan on December 3, 1982:

> Mr. President, you are visiting Latin America at a time when it is
> experiencing its worst crisis of the last 50 years. At the end of
> 1982, our countries have seen their per capita income drop, un-
> employment and underemployment has reached 30 percent in
> some areas and foreign debt has reached $700 million [sic], mean-
> ing that of $100 million derived from exports, 60 percent will be
> used to service that debt. Each Latin American child is born ow-
> ing $300. [Radio Bogotá, December 3, 1982; in FBIS, Latin
> America, December 6, 1982, p. F-1.]

The foreign debts of Latin America, which totaled around $300
billion at the end of 1982, continue to rise rapidly. For Argentina, Brazil, Mexico, Venezuela, and Chile, payments due in 1983 were higher,
for some much higher, than the total value of expected exports. Causes
of excessive indebtedness included high petroleum import prices during 1979–1981 for most countries; weak prices for agricultural and
raw material exports; inflationary expectations that encouraged borrowing, followed by a leveling off of inflation; weak economic policies,
including grandiose expansion plans; capital export; excessive imports;
the effort to support unrealistic exchange rates; and governmental
waste and corruption, supported by foreign borrowing. The lure of
easy returns from high interest rates and upfront fees led international
bankers to lend huge amounts with extraordinary carelessness. The
governments of lending nations, especially that of the United States,
which desired high levels of lending for foreign policy purposes, encouraged openhandedness. There was no necessary connection with
need; the very fact that Mexico and Venezuela were flooded with
petrodollars encouraged them and lenders to add tens of billions in
loans to the flood.

As long as exports were rising rapidly, there was no problem. But
when both exports and the supply of petrodollars contracted, bankers
began pulling back. Borrowing, however, had become an addiction,
requiring ever more capital inflow. Semiwithdrawal, the restriction of
new loans to little more than what was required to meet payments on
the old, was inevitably very painful. The results of the foreign debt
crunch, combined with recession, were severe: national currencies lost
value, private payments could not be made, and prices of imported
goods and raw materials and equipment rose (if obtainable at all).

There followed loss of confidence, disinvestment, capital flight, unemployment, and declining standards of living.

The remedy prescribed by the International Monetary Fund is austerity, which inevitably causes short-term pain while promising future economic health and growth. It means accepting or accentuating the unpleasant consequences of financial strain: restricting imports; reducing government deficits in the face of lowered receipts and increased needs, by eliminating or cutting back social services and other nonessential expenditures; ending price subsidies; and accepting high unemployment.

Such austerity measures almost inevitably lead to political instability and radicalism. It is remarkable that Latin America has thus far not seen much more leftist-revolutionary ferment, but the potential for it is ever increasing. As the debt problem grows and foreign banks and the International Monetary Fund are seen as responsible for distress, there are obvious dangers of default, loss of economic and political freedom, and a sharp turn away by most countries of Latin America from their basically Western orientation. From Mexico to Argentina, the crisis may well get out of control and confront the United States with a major political threat.

Even before the ripening of the current economic crisis, Latin America was politically unstable. Democratic governments have regularly failed to manage the economy and keep order, and they have often been replaced by military regimes. It was just such conditions that led the generals to take charge in Brazil in 1964, in Argentina in 1966 and again in 1976, in Peru in 1968, in Uruguay and Chile in 1973. But the military have been no more successful in administering nations than civilians, despite the supposed independence of the former from fickle currents of opinion and political favor. Military governments, in turn, have been overtaken by economic troubles and have felt pressed to permit elections and restore more or less democratic rule. New democratic governments, such as those inaugurated in 1979–1980 in Ecuador and Peru, soon find themselves beset by turmoil, violence, disorderly politics, and economic decline.

Latin America has been unable to find a satisfactory form of government. Its societies are too divided to permit major decision making by ballot; yet authoritarian regimes also lack a firm foundation. The poor are too many, the middle classes and the rich too few, for basic political agreement. The cultured are too alien from the illiterate; and the masters are often of a different race from the peons. Such societies could function fairly tranquilly in the past when traditions held up irrational structures. But the strains of modernization have torn apart the poorly integrated societies of Latin America; modernization and development have sometimes seemed, as in Argentina, almost equivalent to excessive tensions and disruption.

The U.S. Nonresponse

The United States has actively and regularly engaged in Latin American affairs since the 1898 war against Spain, which made the United States a Caribbean power. Activism developed into interventionism in several countries; Nicaragua, Haiti, and the Dominican Republic were subjected to decades-long occupations in the first third of this century. Cuba and Panama became semidependencies, and generally the fiat of Washington became more and more influential over Latin America, reaching a zenith of influence at the end of the Second World War.

But influence was predicated on the relative stability of Latin America and its apparent immunity to radical or ideological disturbance. U.S. policy was casual, uncoordinated, and unplanned, based mostly on a sense of indubitable natural superiority in the hemisphere. It was mostly a series of responses to good business opportunities and reactions to ward off sundry threats to U.S. economic interests. And while the United States asserted itself fairly emphatically in the neighborhood, it did not take Latin America very seriously. Americans considered it rather a backyard, which might be untidy but could usually be ignored.

The basic goals of U.S. policy were economic access (for investment and exports), a reasonable degree of stability, and exclusion of hostile powers. As long as these were achieved—and they usually were with minimal effort—the United States neglected its neighbors. Only exceptional events, such as the Mexican Revolution of 1910–1917 or the threat of Nazi subversion in the late 1930s, moved the United States to take much notice.

World War II, in which nearly all the republics joined, raised hemispheric cooperation under U.S. leadership to its zenith. But since 1945 the course has been rather steadily downward. The United States took little note of its ebbing influence, however, until Fidel Castro raised a new threat from his "liberated territory of the Americas." In 1961, Washington launched the Alliance for Progress, the most ambitious undertaking of the United States in Latin America, as the democratic answer to the leftist threat; and at the time U.S. influence was still sufficient to lead almost all Latin American nations to break off diplomatic and economic relations with Cuba. However, the effort to reshape Latin American societies through the Alliance for Progress failed completely.

Numerous military takeovers, from Brazil in 1964 to Chile and Uruguay in 1973, accomplished by force what the nonviolent Alliance for Progress had failed to accomplish and fairly well liquidated the radical leftist threat in South America. The influence of the United States continued generally to decrease, as the United States turned its attention to Vietnam. The U.S. share of the republics' trade and of foreign investment in them gradually shrank. The Organization of American States, which had seemed a reliable instrument of the State Department when founded in 1948, became something like a forum for denouncing or making demands on the United States. Latin American delegations, once to be counted almost automatically on the U.S. side in United Nations voting, lined up more often with the so-called nonaligned nations. By 1983, Cuba, Grenada, Nicaragua, and Suriname (fortunately small to very small countries) were considered international adversaries of the United States.

There is generally a concerted U.S. response only when a crisis erupts in violence, as is currently the case in Central America, and the response, although energetic in its way, seems decidedly ineffective. It is not clear that hundreds of millions of dollars of military and economic aid to Central America, mostly to tiny El Salvador, have had any positive result. Somewhat similarly, the United States took note of Latin America's debt problems only when major countries teetered toward default. The crisis was handled only by hasty efforts to find money for new loans to permit payments to continue in due form and to avoid collapse of the afflicted economies. The bankers' austerity prescriptions are sufficient to cause major political problems in such countries as Mexico and Brazil but entirely insufficient to generate hard currency to meet the payment obligations. The crunch has been postponed but not solved.

The inadequacy of the U.S. approach to Latin America is also obvious in trade relations. The Latins need to export in order to buy U.S. goods and in order to make debt payments. But as soon as a new export finds acceptance in the U.S. market, domestic producers protest and press for a tariff or at least a quota to prevent serious penetration. Manufactured goods arouse especial resistance, but markets for raw materials are limited, and most export growth must be in manufactures. If a Latin American nation adopts subsidies to promote its exports, particularly when trying to break into new markets, U.S. laws impose countervailing duties. For example, Peru's fledgling democracy, which it is strongly in the U.S. interest to encourage, was jolted in November 1982 by new duties on Peruvian textiles. President Belaunde Terry, one of the Latin leaders most dedicated to the political ideals favored by the United States, was compelled to cancel a state visit to Washington, and Lima resounded to anti-U.S. riots.

The necessity of protecting the American consumer against lowered prices also extends to agricultural products whenever they are competitive with U.S. products. For example, the United States bars Argentine beef on specious sanitary grounds, and in October 1982 pressure from tanners forced the cancellation of free trade in hides between Argentina and the United States. When the Colombians learned to grow flowers efficiently and beautifully, the industry, employing over 100,000 persons, was threatened with exclusion from its only really big potential market. Latin Americans naturally conclude that the United States would like to keep them as suppliers of noncompetitive raw materials and to frustrate their efforts to industrialize and modernize their economics.

Protectionism is the greatest cause of friction between most Latin American countries and the United States—something almost unperceived by the U.S. public but vitally important to the smaller economies of Latin America. It is mostly for economic reasons that relations in the hemisphere have deteriorated to their lowest level in the fifty years since Franklin Roosevelt inaugurated the Good Neighbor policy.

It is clearly time for the United States to formulate broad and long-range purposes in relation to the hemispheric community, not only to redress the losses of the past but to build for a more productive future. The capacity of the United States is still very large. It can do much if it is willing to set aside petty interests and, instead of reacting spasmodically to irritations or threats, act more positively for the welfare of the hemisphere.

Positive Approaches to Latin America

The dangerous decay of hemispheric relations can hardly be reversed unless the United States displays much tact, sensitivity, restraint, and willingness to forgo immediate and narrow advantages. It must take into account the often brittle nationalistic feelings and irritability generated by inequality between the United States and its partners, especially the smaller nations, such as those of Central America, plus the distrust of past generations. Local distractions must not be allowed to harm the general cause, and policymakers should bear in mind that all

Latin Americans judge the United States on the basis of its actions toward every Latin American nation, not just their own.

A fundamental principle in dealing with hemispheric neighbors is that coercion or threat of coercion of any kind is undesirable. A wise administration should seek to influence behavior by use of incentives, the only punishment being withholding them, preferably quietly. Not only force but economic sanctions are usually counterproductive.

The most important potential incentive for Latin American cooperation with the United States is one that would have a substantial net benefit for the U.S. economy—namely, to slash barriers to the importation of Latin American products of all kinds, if not eliminate them entirely. A small effort in this direction was made in the Caribbean Basin Initiative, enunciated by President Reagan in February 1982. He proposed twelve years' free access to the U.S. market for goods from Central America and the Caribbean (except textiles and a few other products), along with facilities to expedite investment in the area. This positive proposal was very well received by almost everyone except producers who feared Caribbean Basin competition.

If freer access to the U.S. market was a good idea for twelve years, however, it would be a better idea for an indefinite period to encourage longer-range planning. There was no valid reason to exclude any particular class of goods from the Caribbean Basin Initiative. Unhappily, the product lines most readily undertaken by less developed countries, whose main economic advantage is cheap labor, are likely to compete with labor-intensive industries in the United States, such as the textile industry. But it would ultimately benefit the United States to move away from industries in which it has a comparative disadvantage (or to push them to higher mechanization, specialization, and quality production), and consumers would gain more in lower prices than producers would lose from the competition of imports.

Most important, if the Caribbean Basin Initiative is a good idea for that area, it should be extended to a wider area—namely, all of Latin America. Theoretically, it should be applied to the whole world, but this is not practical. China, for example, could flood the U.S. market as Latin American countries cannot. Spreading the benefits too widely would excessively dilute them, and there are sound reasons, as stated at the outset, for special treatment of the hemispheric group.

Reduction of trade barriers should be made without asking for counterconcessions, which would detract from the political and psychological value. Barriers to Latin American products should be eliminated entirely, but partial reduction—or even a pledge to impose no new barriers—would be far better than the current policy of irregular protectionism. While the U.S. market should preferably be opened to all friendly Latin American countries, trade concessions limited to democratic countries might be an incentive to political reform. Trade liberalization by the United States would also encourage Latin American countries to liberalize their own practices and conceivably could lead toward a hemispheric free-trade area.

Along with lowering trade barriers, a Latin American initiative should, like the Caribbean Basin Initiative, offer incentives for investment. It also must tackle the debt problem. There is no prospect that capital obligations, which totaled over $400 billion in mid-1983, can be repaid (barring a great deal of dollar inflation), and interest is payable only by new borrowing. Even if there were a much larger expansion of Latin American exports than can be expected for the foreseeable future, it would be highly undesirable to try to keep Latin American economies permanently burdened by large continuing payments in dollars. Even partially keeping up interest charges amounting to a major fraction of total export receipts would deprive Latin American economies of capital and eventually generate a strong and possibly disastrous political reaction. More lending, the bankers' answer, is not a long-term solution. Funds that should contribute to development are continually pre-empted by the need to stave off default, while the outstanding burden grows ever greater.

There ultimately must be some form of write-off of most of the outstanding debt, with the provision that new loans are completely at the risk of the lenders. In this case, the banks will ensure that the money is used for productive purposes that will provide for ultimate repayment. Halting the giveaway loans would be beneficial to the U.S. economy in the long run and to the Latin American economies, which need productive capital but are not really helped by handouts to cover deficits or to sustain artificial exchange rates.

Such measures would discomfit the Latin American Left, but it would be hard for anyone to object to them. By doing what Latin Americans of both Left and Right clamor for, they would tend to reorient Latin American economies toward that of the United States, making it more rewarding to cooperate with it. They would promote economic freedom and indirectly political freedom and democracy whether or not directly applied to that end. A secondary but important benefit of freer movement of goods would be that it would lessen pressures for movement of people and so ease the illegal immigration problem, in which the Latin Americans predominate. It should also make it easier to tackle such hemispheric problems as the traffic in illegal drugs—estimated at $1–6 billion yearly from Colombia alone. Most of all, it would foster the sense of a democratically inclined cooperative community in this hemisphere.

Most of the influence of the United States is economic, and economic approaches should do more for political development than political ones. Foreign policy, however, should seek explicitly the goals implicit in the economic program, and this means support for human rights and democratic governments. The United States, while not seeking to impose any particular institutions, may quite legitimately oppose the violence and hypocrisy, the force and fraud, that are usually if not always inherent in dictatorship. There should be no preaching to independent governments on the human rights (or any other) issue, but the United States should make clear its concern and the expectation that the members of the hemispheric club observe certain standards of civilized behavior.

How far to support dictatorial governments has been a perennial problem of U.S. foreign policy. While it is certainly necessary to carry on normal relations with them, it is not necessary to embrace them, even if they proclaim their (often more rhetorical than real) anticommunism. Dictatorships such as those in Chile or Paraguay are by no means so enveloping as those of communist countries or some others, like that of Qaddafi in Libya, but there is some justification for applying higher standards within the New World. It is in any event hurtful to the democratic cause for the United States to show favor to dictatorships. Tyranny is tyranny; and friendly tyrants, however preferable to unfriendly ones, are embarrassing.

It is not to be expected that all dictatorships will suddenly be transformed into constitutional states in which rulers are chosen by the will of the masses. To try to bring about popular democracy rapidly in most Latin American countries would be to open the doors to chaos, economic troubles, and new dictatorship. But it is reasonable to expect military or other arbitrary rulers to move in the direction of allowing broader participation in politics. The Brazilian generals have been relaxing their rule and gradually opening the state to democratic politics since 1974. Most nondemocratic governments claim either to be democratic or to be preparing the way for an eventual return to democracy, and the United States could inoffensively do much to encourage them in this direction.

Latin American intellectuals are mostly hostile to the United States because they see it as the bulwark of an unjust social order. It is, however, in the U.S. interest to foster equity in both dictatorial and more democratic countries. Betterment of the condition of the masses is in everyone's interest. Indeed, it is in the immediate self-interest of rulers to ameliorate social inequities. Efraín Rios Montt in Guatemala seems to have demonstrated how combining attention to the welfare of the peasants with stern rule can achieve what repression alone could not—namely, depriving the guerrillas of popular support.

The ultimate basis for movement toward democracy is the reduction of inequality. A redistributive program, however, is sure to be damaging to the economy. Moreover, it is likely to be ineffective and is sure to arouse passionate opposition. Much more promising are measures to increase the productivity of people—improving education, expanding health services, and checking population growth. These should be the principal objectives of whatever foreign aid the United States may dispense in Latin America—an amount that should be only a small fraction of the tens of billions of dollars currently given out as "loans."

The United States must deal, however, not only with more or less friendly dictatorships, such as those of Argentina and Chile, but with unfriendly dictatorships, those of Cuba and its allies in the Caribbean area, and the guerrilla movements they support. These represent not only a security threat but a hindrance to the economic and political development of the area, and they are a major burden on U.S. relations with the rest of Latin America, which has more than thirty times their populations and production. The United States must also recognize that its policy toward Cuba has been notably unsuccessful in the past, and there is little reason to believe that more of the same remedies—chiefly embargoes and efforts to isolate the adversary—are likely to be more successful in the future. Latin America generally desires the reincorporation of Cuba and its allies in the hemispheric order, and U.S. policy should be directed to that end. It must be made clear to the Cubans that they have much more to gain from cooperation with the United States than with the Soviet Union. Whatever can be done to solidify U.S. relations with Latin America in general will make the Cuban problem in particular more manageable. More broadly, the United States should endeavor to conciliate the moderate Left by supporting democracy and making it clear that the anti-Americanism of the extremists is only hurtful to the peoples of Latin America.

The United States must also do whatever is possible to dampen or settle quarrels between neighboring Latin American countries, by discreet pressure or mediation. The territorial disputes between Argentina and Chile, Peru and Ecuador, Colombia and Venezuela, Venezuela and Guyana, and Guatemala and Belize are all burdensome; cooling them would help to ease the arms races, lower military costs, facilitate productive investment, and decrease military influence in the governments concerned. In this context, an effort should be made to revive and strengthen the Organization of American States, which was badly shaken by what many Latins saw as a U.S. betrayal in the Falklands war. With the growth of hemispheric cooperation, the organization should take on not only a defensive but also a political role as a forum for discussion of hemispheric problems.

If such a hemispheric policy could be fulfilled, it would directly benefit the United States in its relations with its neighbors. It would also greatly improve the United States' position in the world, its security, and its ability to meet political or economic challenges from overseas. This policy could also lead the way for collaboration of the industrialized countries with the Third World and for the progress of the poorer majority of mankind. It might help lay to rest the idea that there is any acceptable alternative to freedom and democracy.

10

The Pacific Basin

Ramon H. Myers

T he new prosperity of the Pacific Basin states owes much to the United States' foreign aid and strong military presence since World War II.[1] By the 1970s these states had experienced unprecedented economic advance, and unlike the West, stagflation had not yet marred their development (see Table 10.1). In fact, the Pacific Basin had become so transformed that one European observer remarked: "While the epicentre of our world is quickly shifting from the Atlantic to the Pacific, European leaders continued either to ignore this critical evolution or to pay lip-service to its consequences."[2]

But in the mid-1980s dark clouds were gathering over the Pacific Basin. The tide of trade protectionism was running strong in the West, and Japan had become the major target. Troubles between strong leaders and their opponents in some Basin states were threatening to undermine political stability and even economic growth itself. The role of the state loomed more powerful than ever before, threatening to stifle private enterprise, the engine of growth. Sino-American relations, which had dramatically improved in 1979–1980, stalled in

I want to thank Dr. Charlene Seifert and other friends at the Hoover Institution for reading this essay and making many useful comments.

Table 10.1

East Asian Growth and Inflation

(percentages)

	1968–1973	1974–1980	1980	1981[a]	1982[b]	1983[b]
Real GNP/GDP Growth (average annual compound)						
Semi-industrialized[c]	10.7	8.6	2.7	7.2	4.3	6.4
Hongkong	10.2	9.9	9.8	10.4	3.5	6.5
South Korea	10.8	7.7	−6.2	7.1	4.9	7.0
Malaysia	9.4	7.2	8.0	6.5	3.7	4.5
Singapore	13.0	8.9	10.2	9.9	5.0	6.5
Taiwan	11.0	9.8	6.6	5.5	4.0	6.5
Less developed[c]	6.9	6.5	7.2	5.6	3.6	4.7
Indonesia	8.2	7.1	9.6	7.6	4.0	5.4
Philippines	6.0	6.3	5.4	3.0	2.5	3.5
Thailand	6.7	7.6	5.8	7.6	4.8	6.0
China	8.4	6.3	7.0	3.0	4.0	4.5
Average Consumer-Price Inflation (average annual compound)						
Semi-industrialized[c]	7.7	11.2	19.6	17.2	7.0	8.0
Hongkong	9.5	8.2	15.5	15.4	11.0	12.0
South Korea	11.2	18.5	28.7	23.3	6.0	8.0
Malaysia	2.7	4.5	6.7	9.6	7.0	7.0

Singapore	5.6	3.5	8.5	8.2	6.0	7.0
Taiwan	5.1	8.1	19.0	16.4	5.0	7.0
Less developed[c]	10.4	12.6	17.7	11.8	9.0	9.0
Indonesia	13.6	16.3	18.5	12.3	10.0	11.0
Philippines	10.9	11.0	17.6	12.2	10.0	9.0
Thailand	4.5	9.0	19.7	12.7	6.0	7.0
China	n.a	n.a	7.5	2.5	4.0	5.0

[a]Estimated. [b]Projected. [c]Weighted by relative size of 1980 GNP/GDP.

SOURCE: Based on *Far Eastern Economic Review*, December 10, 1982, p. 68, which used International Monetary Fund, *International Financial Statistics*, national sources, and Crocker National Bank Economic Department data and projections.

1983. And the growth of Soviet military power appeared to be altering the military balance of power in the region.

Each of these dangers deserves to be examined in more detail because the future prosperity of the Pacific Basin depends so much on free trade and the private sector. Without them the resources for national security cannot be maintained.

Four Present Dangers

Protecting U.S. industry is part of Washington's daily agenda. As the trade imbalance with Japan skyrocketed from $4 billion in 1976 to $20 billion in 1982, industrial leaders and politicians formed coalitions to press for restrictive trade laws stipulating, for example, that foreign cars could be imported only if 90 percent of their parts were American made. The situation worsened so much in 1982 and 1983 that U.S. ambassador to Japan Mike Mansfield aptly described the trade problem with Japan as not "textiles, color television, automobiles and steel; now it's the whole spectrum of trade relations."[3]

The second danger is the expanding role of the state and the potential of this process to destabilize economic growth and disrupt the polity. In order to finance the building of new industry or infrastructure, several Basin states have relied heavily on foreign loans. In 1983, South Korea's external debt was $36 billion, and 49 percent of its annual export earnings went for annual interest payments. The Philippines' external debt stood at $16.6 billion, with 79 percent of its export earnings devoted to interest payments. Indonesia, too, might be in a similar predicament if revenues from oil exports fall because of a decline in prices.

Most Pacific Basin states have been in the red in recent years. With slower economic growth, revenues have failed to match outlays, and government borrowing has begun to crowd out private investors and pre-empt more domestic savings. Greater state bureaucratization encourages more corruption and the growth of state-protected privileges.

In some Basin states, popular protest mounted against strong-men regimes. In the Philippines, massive public demonstrations broke out against the Ferdinand Marcos government in September/October 1983 following the mysterious slaying of Benigno "Ninoy" Aquino at Manila airport on August 21, 1983. Communist guerrilla attacks also became more frequent in 1983, and Mindanao Moslem separatist forces continued to fight government troops. As this essay goes to press, the prospect of President Marcos remaining in power is uncertain; should he be forced to leave office, political stability in the Philippines would be most problematic. In South Korea, students and church-affiliated groups continue to express opposition to President Chun Doo-hwan with demonstrations and public criticism.

A third danger is the uncertainty over Sino-American relations. By mid-1983, many issues had produced sharp disagreements between Beijing and Washington, but both parties continue to negotiate and try to reach accord. Washington noted the talks between Moscow and Beijing with some concern. The Deng Xiaoping faction continued to press forward with modernization, but it is not clear how long Deng can remain in power to keep those policies on track. Peace prevails in the Taiwan Strait, but any U.S. effort to assist the Republic of China (ROC) on Taiwan to enhance its national security meets with violent objections from Beijing. Further, Beijing might link its unhappiness with the U.S.-Taiwan Relations Act to other matters of business with the United States, perhaps impairing U.S. strategic interests in the Pacific Basin.

Finally, there is the relentless growth of the Soviet military machine in East Asia and the Pacific, along with Soviet efforts to expand its political influence in Southwest and Southeast Asia. Soviet rhetoric has been shrill and bellicose. For example, in January 1983 a Soviet spokesman warned Japan that "for such a densely populated, insular country as Japan" a Soviet nuclear-missile strike "could spell a national disaster more serious than the one that befell it 37 years ago." Moscow directed a similar threat against Australia in early 1983. A Soviet military buildup in the region, if continued at the rate of the recent past, could significantly alter the long-standing balance of power.

What are the implications of these dangers for Pacific Basin peace and security? What strategies can the United States adopt and implement to neutralize these dangers?

Meeting the Danger of Protectionism

If the United States enacts protectionist policies against Japan, automobile and steel workers would benefit at the expense of importers and consumers. In fact, the harm done would far exceed the short-term benefits for the U.S. economy because new, interdependent economic relationships have evolved in the Pacific Basin during the past two decades that will adversely affect U.S. protectionist policies.

Americans tend to look at U.S.-Pacific Basin trade as a one-way relationship and not as a complex network of trading interdependencies. For example, between 1974 and 1981 at least 60 percent of the Pacific Basin states' exports went to the industrial markets of the world, including Japan. As Table 10.2 demonstrates, intraregional trade among Pacific Basin states has helped to provide them "with a thickening insulation from the economic vagaries of the rest of the world."[4]

Foreign trade as a percentage of GNP is very high for all Pacific Basin countries except China. A third or more of the foreign trade of each state is conducted with other Pacific Basin states, especially Japan. Trade with Japan ranges between 15 and 25 percent of the total trade of each country except for Indonesia (43 percent in 1980). Nearly half of the Basin countries traded more with Japan than with the United States in 1980.

This trade connection is important because of Japan's strong demand for primary and intermediate products. A prime example is Australia, which exports sizable quantities of minerals to Japan. Japan's

Table 10.2

Regional Trade Interdependencies in the Pacific Basin, 1981

	GNP (billions U.S. $)	Foreign Trade (percentage)			
		of GNP	with Japan	with U.S.	with other Pacific Basin states
Australia	154.3	34	21	17	17
Japan	1,065.0	33	—	22	22
New Zealand	20.3	60	14	15	31
China	265.0	5	26	10	4
Hongkong	24.2	160	14	19	24
Taiwan	46.0	100	19	29	14
Indonesia	65.8	55	43	17	16
South Korea	63.4	86	22	24	10
Malaysia	21.4*	114	23	16	28
Philippines	38.7	43	23	25	14
Singapore	10.6*	153	14	14	31
Thailand	36.0	56	19	14	23

*1980 data.

SOURCE: Based on *Far Eastern Economic Review*, December 10, 1982, p. 70.

share of Australian exports rose from 18.7 to 37.5 percent between 1962 and 1973; the value of these exports increased some 800 percent during the same period.[5]

Increasing, too, were exports of Japanese-manufactured goods and Japanese capital and technology to these same states. Japanese exports of machinery rose rapidly between 1965 and 1980, a trend that can be charted by machinery's increased share of total imports, especially in the newly industrializing countries (NICs) of Asia. Japanese overseas investment, increasing thirty times between 1964 and 1973, continued to grow rapidly in the late 1970s. Through their trade and investment relationship with Japan, Basin countries increased their capital stock and manufacturing for export. Because of this new dependency between Japan and many other Basin states, there is a much higher correlation of the growth rate of gross domestic product in these states and imports from Japan than imports from either the West or from other regions.[6]

Related to this new trade dependency in the Pacific Basin are some important shifts in the composition of key commodities exported by different groups of Basin states. First, the Asian NICs have already replaced Japan as the primary supplier of textile products for Western markets. Now, these same NICs are competing vigorously with Japan to export chemicals, steel, and machinery to the West. They are also striving to catch up with Japan in high-technology fields like electronics.

This new horizontal division of labor in the Pacific Basin and the complex triangular trade relationship among the United States, Japan, and other Basin states have important implications for trade and economic development as the United States begins to build protectionist trade barriers to exclude Japanese goods. First, any decline in Japanese export earnings would soon affect Japan's imports from other Basin states, thereby adversely affecting their export earnings and their capacity to buy goods from the United States. Second, protectionist legislation aimed at Japan might also extend to imports from other Basin countries, thereby reducing their export earnings. Such a development would quickly lead to a reduction in their imports from both Japan and the United States. The end result could very well be a series of mini–trade wars leading to the reduction of trade and a decline in economic welfare in the Pacific Basin and the United States—with dangerous effects on political stability and international security.

Protectionism will not solve the serious trade imbalance between the United States and Japan. Advocates of protectionism at home must realize that a strong U.S. dollar and the declining competitiveness of the steel and automobile industries have themselves created most of the high trade imbalance between the two countries since 1978.

Japan responded to protectionist threats by limiting car exports until 1984 to give U.S. automobile manufacturers more time to recover. Moreover Japanese business firms are beginning to invest in the United States, and Tokyo is reducing tariff barriers. If the U.S. economy continues to recover strongly, the new cooperative measures between U.S. labor unions and corporate management might increase efficiency and reduce unit cost sufficiently for many industries to regain their former competitive standing, but at a greatly reduced scale of operations. If these efforts fail, other policies besides protectionism must be found to re-industrialize the United States.

Coping with the Growth of the State

Soon after the U.S. government used its economic and military power to nurture the recovery and economic growth of the Pacific Basin, governments in this region began taking an active role in economic life: states regulated foreign exchange rates, promoted import-substitution industries, sponsored land reform, and supported public education. Some states did more than others, and some were more successful than others. Not surprisingly, by the late 1960s the results were mixed. In some states the interaction between the private and public sectors had produced greater productivity and higher output growth than in others. Taiwan and South Korea outperformed the Philippines and Indonesia, for example.

Greater state involvement occurred in the 1970s as deficit financing increased and new policies to regulate old policies spread. Here again the reasons were complex, and they differed considerably by country. The South Korean government began subsidizing urban consumers by imposing price ceilings on many farm crops. The Philippine government increased public expenditures for tourism, extended land reform, and created energy sources not dependent on imported petroleum. Other Pacific Basin governments also intervened in the private sector through price regulation, new laws, and more state-financed projects.

Therefore, when the world recession of 1981–82 reduced the export earnings of many Basin states, their external debt rose and budget deficits worsened. The private sector suffered as well: some banks collapsed and unemployment spread.

In response to these setbacks, prominent businessmen from several

Basin states met in Taiwan in December 1982 to discuss the creation of a regional economic cooperation group like the European Economic Community.[7] While nothing concrete materialized from this meeting, it represented the first private sector effort, following numerous government attempts in the past, to explore a more formalized arrangement in the Pacific Basin to regulate and increase trade.

Would the private sector truly benefit if greater state expansion at home merged with a new supranational bureaucratic agency to regulate trade and investment for the Pacific Basin region? Certainly not. Any regulatory international organization of this kind would very likely foster monopoly with its attendant inefficiency. Therefore the United States should be cautious about supporting the formation of a regional organization that seeks to promote a "more orderly and rational economic development of the Pacific Basin community."

What would greatly benefit the Pacific Basin is better production and distribution of information for governments and businessmen alike. Basin governments might not have financed many projects such as steel mills and shipbuilding concerns had responsible officials been aware of similar efforts being undertaken elsewhere in the region. Existing organizations like the Asian Economic Development Bank could expand the systematic collection and dissemination of economic information.

The recent world recession will very likely prove a blessing for many Basin states. Shortfalls in government revenues have already forced states to balance budgets and cut back on numerous, wasteful state-financed projects. Although many private enterprises that have long benefited from such state spending will be hurt, enough time might be gained for the private sector to marshal its resources and carry on dynamically. If the past few years of economic misery can delay the growth of the bureaucratic state for even a short while, a revitalized private sector could again forge ahead.

Revitalizing Sino-American Relations

As a result of thirty years of mismanagement, Communist China still remains poor and struggles to feed over a billion people. Beijing has yet to reform and substantially improve the country's inefficient economic system to accommodate economic growth rates that will catapult Communist China into the ranks of modernized states by the end of this century. China's political system is also chronically ill: the 39 million members of the Chinese Communist Party (CCP) are divided over how to apply Marxism-Leninism to China; many even doubt the truth of Marxist ideology. The majority of party members, young and uneducated, attained power and status during the Cultural Revolution. They control the many youth, women, labor, and security organizations and even most economic units. Many rank-and-file party members therefore oppose the new policies that began to flow from Beijing soon after Deng Xiaoping and his faction wrested control from the Maoists.

In spite of Deng's new leadership and policies, serious political and ideological cleavages still exist within the CCP. In 1982 many important provincial tribunals found local party members guilty of various crimes and punished them with expulsion from the party and sentences to labor-reform camps.[8] Beijing's leaders do not trust most of their provincial party cadres to carry out their orders; rather than risk a wholesale purge, they have selected limited areas and subjected party members to gradual, but intense, "rectification" lectures. This process will take a long time to complete, and there is no guarantee it will work.

This is the Communist China that strategists in Washington view as a counterweight to the Soviet Union. Given the current crises in Communist China and the awesome task of legitimizing CCP rule, what are the real, expected benefits for the United States from the Sino-American relationship that has evolved since normalization in 1979?

The relationship is showing signs of severe stress. Although foreign trade spurted between 1979 and 1981, it has now peaked and will probably grow slowly because the economic structures of the two countries are not complementary. Communist China has neither abundant raw materials nor low-priced, high-quality manufactured goods to sell American buyers. Communist China would certainly like to export textiles, but U.S. officials ration these imports by quota as they do for other Asian textile-exporting countries.

Voluntary Chinese immigration is still a major problem for the United States, but it has also become a Chinese problem. By granting political asylum to defecting tennis star Hu Na, the Department of Immigration and Naturalization has probably set a precedent for other Chinese performers, as well as for visiting students, to seek similar asylum. Communist China responded by canceling nine cultural exchanges, but these proved to be minor events for both sides. Friction over defection and immigration will continue to beset the relationship.

Research cooperation and scientific exchange are also in trouble. American social scientists want to conduct field research in Communist China for extended periods, but Beijing has denied their requests.

Some 10,000 Chinese students and scholars move freely in the United States, but Washington has not curbed their freedom of research. This state of affairs probably cannot last very long. If the United States demands that the exchange program be made more equal, Communist China is likely to reduce the number of students it allows to study abroad.

Although the Carter administration signed a number of agreements on transferring high technology to China, the Reagan administration has been more cautious in granting export licenses for such transfers. Further, China's leaders do not want to comply with the restrictions governing any U.S. export of nuclear technology, and that exchange agreement is now stalemated. But Defense Secretary Caspar Weinberger visited Beijing in early October 1983 to convince the Chinese Communists of the danger from Moscow and of the need to cooperate more closely with the United States on military matters. Weinberger promised the Chinese permission to buy U.S. military equipment and high technology products, such as computers, and to train Chinese officers in the United States. His trip signaled a new effort by the Reagan administration to revitalize Sino-American relations.

The problem of Taiwan has still not been solved to the satisfaction of the Chinese. Public statements from Beijing after the August 17, 1982, joint Sino-American communiqué on selling arms to Taiwan indicate that Beijing's leaders will never be satisfied until U.S. military sales to Taiwan cease. In early 1983 Foreign Minister Wu Xueqian told visiting Secretary of State George Shultz that the Taiwan issue still remained a "dark cloud" over Sino-American relations. The Shultz visit to Beijing did not seem to initiate any new momentum in the relationship. President Ronald Reagan is scheduled to visit Beijing in spring 1984, but it is doubtful whether he can convince China's leaders of the special nature of the U.S.-Taiwan relationship.

The Chinese also have complained about a U.S. federal court decision ordering the government of Communist China to pay a group of Americans $41.3 million for debts incurred by the Manchu Dynasty.[9]

China rarely sides with the United States on key international problems. China supported Argentina in the Falklands war, endorsed the PLO position on the Israeli invasion of Lebanon, disagreed with the United States on the future status of Namibia, and refused to condemn the Polish government for imposing martial law and outlawing Solidarity. Finally, in 1983 the Beijing press began to compare U.S. hegemonism with that of the Soviet Union.

Given the serious internal problems of Communist China and the many issues where it is at odds with the United States, what are the strategic interests that both countries share? Are these important enough to justify any major U.S. concessions or any concessions at all to Communist China in the future?

Many policy makers in Washington advance four strategic arguments for trying to improve Sino-American relations. First, China holds down some fifty to sixty Soviet divisions on its northern borders, thereby preventing Moscow from concentrating more troops and firepower on NATO's eastern flank. A closely connected reason is the existence of stations deep inside China for tracking Soviet missile test launches. Since joint Sino-American efforts are involved in this exercise, the United States will receive the intelligence information gathered. Second, Communist China allegedly exerts some influence on North Korea's leaders and therefore can possibly discourage any adventurism from Pyongyang that might upset the military balance of power on the Korean peninsula. Third, Communist China's close connections with Pol Pot's forces in Cambodia and its hostility toward Vietnam make it a useful counterweight against Vietnamese and Soviet imperialism in Southeast Asia. Fourth, Communist China can discourage Marxist-Leninist guerrilla activity in Southeast Asia and minimize the violence that otherwise might spread.

These arguments ignore the facts, however. The USSR possesses the nuclear weaponry to destroy Communist China's cities and perhaps China itself. Soviet troops are posted along its 4,000-mile border with China to prevent Chinese border encroachments and quell any disturbances—such as those in Turkestan when ethnic groups moved across the border into China for sanctuary. The powerful suspicions and distrust of both sides are unlikely to be dismissed so that both parties can withdraw their troops. A decision by China to reduce its border troops will result only from direct negotiations with the Soviets and is not likely to be influenced by any deal the United States can strike with Beijing's leaders. Short of establishing an alliance with Communist China (which China would probably reject) and making major concessions to keep those Soviet troops pinned down, the United States can probably do nothing to influence the negotiations between Beijing and Moscow.

A Sino-Soviet détente resulting in relations like those of the early 1950s is improbable in the foreseeable future. Differences between the Soviet Union and Communist China far outweigh their mutual interests. The Soviets are anxious to maintain their Hanoi connection because it allows them access to Camranh Bay and gives them a launching pad for their penetration of Southeast Asia. Beijing views Hanoi as a major threat to its southern flank; hence disagreement over Hanoi's actions is bound to separate both sides. The same is true of Afghanistan. The Soviets intend to stay in that country until they have installed a regime friendly to Moscow. Beijing wants the Soviets out because the troubles in that country spill over into Pakistan—Beijing's ally. Although trade between Moscow and Beijing will probably grow and the exchange of visitors will increase, any breakthrough in negotiations that will affect the United States is unlikely.

Admittedly, Beijing-Pyongyang ties are close, but North Korea's leaders have long cleverly played China and the Soviet Union off against each other. North Korea is also intensely nationalistic, and Beijing's influence over any decision made by Pyongyang on reunification by force or gradual means is likely to be only peripheral.

Sino-Vietnamese hostility is, like that between China and Russia, profound and centuries old. In order to weaken Vietnam, Communist China wants a divided Indochina peninsula—not one under Hanoi's rule—so it will continue to intervene in that region to prevent Vietnamese hegemony however Sino-American relations evolve.

Finally, since 1981 Beijing has stopped granting material aid to Southeast Asian guerrilla forces but still provides morale support. That will continue whatever the progress of Sino-American relations.

Viewing these four strategic arguments in this way—within the context of the enormous difficulties Beijing's leaders face in maintaining order at home and the current cooling in Sino-American relations—strongly indicates that there is little need for Washington to make concessions to improve relations. Such concessions will certainly not guarantee a convergence of Sino-American interests. Where strategic interests already converge, Communist China can be counted on to defend them regardless of U.S. policy actions.

Although Communist China is neither the United States' close ally nor a dependable friend, Washington must recognize that it is an emerging power with unique problems and national interests. China's historical enmity toward the Soviet Union and Vietnam is not likely to be softened either by a Sino-American détente or by a stalemate. Such a change in enmity could occur only if a powerful leader emerged in Communist China who could effectively control the country and confidently deal with its northern and southern neighbors from a position of strength. The United States cannot finesse or create that situation.

Therefore, normal discourse and trade between Communist China and the United States should be continued, and where strategic interests are shared, both states should find it possible to cooperate when necessary.

Such reasoning leads to the conclusion that the United States' *de facto* two-China state relationship can continue until leaders in Taipei and Beijing decide to begin negotiations. That will not occur until new policies in Communist China have produced results that give the ROC on Taiwan sufficient confidence to begin exploratory talks.

Achieving a Military Balance of Power in Asia

Communist parties in Asia now rule roughly 1.4 billion people, but only Vietnam has close ties with Moscow. Even so, since 1979 Soviet imperialism has become more expansive: Soviet troops are now in Afghanistan; the Soviet military buildup in the Pacific continues.

The relentless Soviet military expansion is worrisome because all of the Basin states except Communist China depend on access to the Persian Gulf for oil. Since all Basin states depend on shipping for their foreign trade, the sea-lanes must remain open even if a limited war breaks out in another geopolitical theater. Another complication is certain chokepoints in Pacific Basin waters where shipping might be halted. Finally, the threat of nuclear blackmail hangs heavy over the region because of the enormous increase in nuclear missiles in Siberia.

In the Pacific the Soviet blue-water fleet (including over 110 submarines) now docks at Camranh Bay and patrols the Indian Ocean. The aircraft carrier *Minsk* and the amphibious attack ship *Ivan-Rogov* give the fleet added firepower. A squadron of 25 MiG-21 fighters is stationed on the southernmost Kurile island. Large numbers of supersonic Backfire bombers and SS-20 missiles with nuclear warheads, which can reach every Asian state except perhaps Australia, are located in the Maritime Province of Siberia.

But Soviet military growth and imperial expansion have not been matched by effective diplomacy. Soviet-Japanese relations remain poor; Moscow refuses to discuss the return of the four Kurile islands just north of Japan. By sending a squadron of MiG fighters to those contested islands, Moscow only enraged the Japanese. Indonesia's expulsion of a Soviet diplomat in 1982 confirmed the fears of many ASEAN leaders that Soviet diplomats were spies under diplomatic cover. Soviet relations with China have yet to be improved, even though negotiations under way might bring that about. Relations between Moscow and Pyongyang are still cool. Because Soviet diplomacy in Asia has been so crude, even bungling at times, the Pacific Basin states need not worry about an alliance between the USSR and one of their number. They need only be concerned with matching the Soviet military buildup to maintain a balance of power without provoking new military escalations. How can this be done?

The United States cannot bring this about without the aid of its Pacific Basin friends. So far, only South Korea is successfully modernizing its military forces, with U.S. aid, but it lacks the capability to assist the United States. The ROC on Taiwan can only purchase the spare parts and jet fighter aircraft it requires to maintain its security. The ASEAN states have gradually increased their defense expenditures in recent years to reach the maximum level of what they can afford to spend without imposing too great a tax burden on society. Since U.S. naval forces must now patrol in the Indian Ocean, the critical need is for some augmentation of U.S. military forces to maintain the free movement of sea traffic. It remains for Japan to make a greater defense contribution in this area. A modest defense effort by Japan could provide just the margin needed to match the current Soviet military buildup without initiating another arms race.

Four conditions must be satisfied if Japan is to contribute more to Pacific Basin security. First, Japanese leaders are more likely to cooperate with the United States by contributing more to Pacific Basin security if they can obtain guarantees that Washington will not restrict Japanese imports. Second, Japan's defense contribution should not be so drastic as to frighten and anger other Basin states, which still remember World War II. Third, Japan's increased defense spending must be modest enough not to create a domestic budget crisis and stir a violent political reaction that might unseat the ruling Liberal Democratic party. Finally, the new defense posture Japan assumes must not be so threatening to the Soviets that they will respond with their own defense buildup.

These conditions can be satisfied only if there is an appropriate Japanese defense strategy within Japan's political and economic means to justify and promote. Such a defense strategy should be a system of surveillance and deterrence, not one of advanced attack and retaliation. How would this work in practice?

Japanese defense spending rose 7 percent per year between 1978 and 1983, but overall expenditures still are less than 1 percent of the GNP.[10] These expenditures have supported some 180,000 ground troops backed by 830 tanks, 560 personnel carriers, and large quantities of field weapons.[11] Little spending has gone for air and sea forces, which now amount to only 48 escort vessels, 14 submarines, 40 mine warfare vessels, 333 aircraft interceptors, and 39 support fighters. Japan's defense force is structured to fight on the ground in the event of a conventional armed attack, a most unlikely prospect in this age of modern warfare. This defense posture can neither contribute to Pacific Basin security nor provide a credible defense for Japan. Japan needs a different defense strategy—realistic yet affordable.

Such a strategy calls for gradually scaling back ground forces and slowly reallocating those resources to build a small, high-quality air and sea surveillance system to monitor the ocean surface up to 1,000 miles south of Tokyo and a reasonable distance around mainland Japan.[12] This system would consist of a half-dozen AWACS monitoring aircraft with aircraft always airborne and collecting information on all foreign air and sea vessels in Japan's sea perimeter. Augmenting this system would be an assortment of hydro-buoys for monitoring submarines and several squadrons of very advanced jet fighters with the speed and firepower to appear on the scene quickly and escort enemy sea- and aircraft away from Japanese waters and airspace.

This new system would be closely integrated with U.S. military forces and those of other allied powers so that powerful pressures could be brought to bear on any foreign aggressor who appeared to be massing naval power to threaten the Asian sea-lanes. It would be a flexible extension of Japan's current defense system toward greater reliance on naval and air forces. Another advantage would be that no nuclear weapons would be placed in Japan, an important domestic political consideration.

Japan would share these data on foreign naval and aircraft movements with its allies. This system would not threaten the Soviet Union, but it would send a firm signal to Soviet military authorities that their military activities and movements in the Pacific were being closely watched and any threatening concentration of forces would elicit a powerful counterattack. Such a defense system would go far to help maintain the military balance of power in the Pacific. And Tokyo could develop it within a decade without stressing Japan's political fabric and finance it with only modest annual increments. Only the political will to reallocate current resources within the military establishment must be found.

Recommendations

In international relations the fortuitous event so often intervenes and deflects trends in different directions, affecting multilateral relations, economic prosperity, and even security. The four main dangers of the mid-1980s that I have cited could worsen or ameliorate depending on the whims of certain leaders and their current strength or eroding support at home. Unlike the situation in the 1950s, U.S. power abroad is now sorely limited, and policy options for U.S. leaders are few. Washington should adopt prudent policies based on patience and a tough negotiating stance—and a clear vision of what it wishes to achieve—to deal with the dangers threatening the Pacific Basin states. The dangers outlined above are serious, but a clear U.S. strategy toward the Pacific Basin with bipartisan backing could neutralize them.

Part of the policy design for this strategy has already been suggested. The three parameters of this strategy are (1) a U.S. commitment to free trade in the pacific Basin; (2) U.S. assistance to Basin states on a bilateral basis—not through any new Pacific Basin bureaucratic organization; and (3) U.S. recognition that Japan—not Communist China—must be the pillar of any U.S.–Pacific Basin relationship aimed at enhancing economic prosperity and security in the region.

The United States must remain committed to free trade, free enterprise, and minimal state intervention in economic activity except to make competition workable, to ensure that resource allocation can take place to accommodate structural change, and to encourage technological change and innovation. By adhering to these principles, U.S. leaders should be able to argue the negative consequences for U.S. business if protectionist policies are implemented to exclude Japanese and other Basin State goods.

Directly associated with this broad commitment, the United States should not participate in any supranational, regional economic organization of Pacific Basin states that seeks to set up a preferred trading arrangement. This action would be self-defeating in the long run. U.S. policymakers and diplomats should point out the dangers inherent in creating such organizations.

Equally important, Washington should worry less about trying to finesse the Sino-American relationship and simply permit current ties to evolve as conditions within Communist China allow. Communist China and the United States do share some strategic interests, and Communist China's national self-interests strongly reinforce those shared concerns. The United States need make no further concessions to Communist China on Taiwan, textile trade quotas, or other issues that now separate the two sides. Washington should simply carry on normal exchanges and observe if Beijing's modernization policies succeed.

As for the Republic of China on Taiwan, that island-state will continue to have strategic and economic importance for the United States. By virtue of the Taiwan Relations Act, the United States can maintain bilateral relations with Taiwan and still guarantee that peace in the

Western Pacific is preserved. Perhaps in the near future, when President Chiang Ching-kuo has retired, a new president may break with the past and chart a new foreign policy. Such a policy might argue for the concept of a single Chinese civilization within which two different political-economic systems compete with each other, each with a different flag, constitution, and constituency. This new foreign policy might make possible the restoration of diplomatic ties with major Western states, thus ending the ROC's isolation from the world community, which now so endangers the ROC. Such a progressive development could then pave the way for eventual peaceful negotiations with the People's Republic of China.

Meanwhile, to ensure that the balance of military power is maintained in the region, the United States should encourage Japanese leaders to develop a defense strategy along the lines outlined above and allow Japan to buy new U.S. equipment needed for such a surveillance and deterrence system. But the United States should not grant export licenses to Japan to reproduce those weapons and later sell them to other parties.

This strategy calls for only a slight expansion of the Reagan administration's policies. Articulating this strategy clearly and implementing it forcefully will serve U.S. interests in the Pacific Basin, help to nurture economic prosperity and enhance regional security, and maintain existing friendships with the developing countries along the rim of Asia's landmass.

Notes

1. The Pacific Basin states are Japan, South Korea, the Republic of China on Taiwan, the ASEAN states (Philippines, Singapore, Malaysia, Thailand, and Indonesia), New Zealand, and Australia. Communist China is also a Pacific Basin state, but I exclude it from the congeries of pluralistic, free enterprise, open societies of the Pacific Basin just mentioned.

2. Quoted in Anthony Rowley, "The East Discovers Strength in Adversity," *Far Eastern Economic Review*, December 10, 1982, pp. 68–69.

3. John Woodruff, "Tough Year for U.S.-Japan Ties," *San Francisco Sunday Examiner and Chronicle*, February 6, 1983, p. A13.

4. Derek Davies, "Community Begins at Home," *Far Eastern Economic Review*, December 10, 1982, p. 67.

5. Miyohei Shinohara, *Industrial Growth, Trade, and Dynamic Patterns in the Japanese Economy* (Tokyo: University of Tokyo Press, 1982), pp. 121–22.

6. Kiyoshi Abe, "Economic Cooperation Among Asian Countries," *Asian Journal of Economics*, 1, no. 1 (January 1982): 18.

7. Thomas Chesser, "Club for the Clobbered," *Far Eastern Economic Review*, January 6, 1983, pp. 80–81.

8. For such examples see the evidence cited in *Foreign Broadcast Information Service*, November 3, 1982, p. K17; November 19, 1982, pp. K3–4; November 23, 1982, pp. W9–11; December 3, 1982, p. Q3; and December 29, 1982, p. K11.

9. Cited in *San Francisco Examiner*, February 10, 1983, p. A18.

10. If pensions for the Self-Defense Forces are included in the national defense budget, total defense spending amounts to 1.6 percent of GNP instead of 1 percent (see *Far Eastern Economic Review*, February 3, 1983, p. 47).

11. These figures are for the Japanese Self-Defense Force in 1980. See Research Institute for Peace and Security, *Asian Security, 1981* (Tokyo: Nikkei Business Publishing Company, 1981), p. 162.

12. I am indebted to Colonel David Holt, a 1982–83 National Fellows Program Associate at the Hoover Institution, for the idea of this new defense strategy and how it could be supported by new equipment and personnel and yet paid for, in part, by the savings obtained from reducing Japan's ground forces. Colonel Holt is currently preparing a detailed article about this new strategy.

11

U.S. Policy in the Middle East: Problems and Prospects

George Lenczowski

For many reasons, the Middle East has constituted a major focus of U.S. foreign policy since World War II. As a cradle of Christianity, Islam, and Judaism, the region has had profound cultural affinities with the West, reinforced, albeit tragically, through the Crusades in the Middle Ages and, later, through Western missionary and educational activities. In terms of strategic importance, the Middle East has hardly a peer in any region of the world, situated as it is at the junction of Europe, Asia, and Africa. Moreover, its strategic value is enhanced by the presence of vital international waterways and abundant oil reserves.

Since World War II, three major issues have compelled the United States to pay close attention to the region: the Soviet threat, oil, and Palestine. As early as 1940, Foreign Commissar Molotov in negotiations with the German ambassador in Moscow described the area south of the Baku-Batum line in the direction of the Persian Gulf and the Indian Ocean as "the center of the aspirations of the Soviet Union."[1] By 1945 the United States was obliged to take notice of these Soviet designs.

Similarly, Washington had little choice but to define its attitude toward the area's oil resources. Sir Henri Deterding's famous statement that World War I was won on "waves of oil" is even more pertinent with regard to World War II and the postwar world economy. Containing some two-thirds of the world's petroleum reserves, the Middle East soon emerged not only as chief supplier of petroleum to the United States' allies in Europe but also, from 1970 on, as a source of much-needed energy for the United States.

Palestine provided another reason for a continuing U.S. interest. Forceful implementation of the Zionist program for establishment of a Jewish national home in a country with an overwhelmingly Arab majority was bound to produce an explosive international dilemma. Again, because of domestic politics and the strategic importance of Palestine, the United States was drawn into the conflict, partly as a supporter of Jewish statehood and partly as a mediator and peacemaker.

U.S. Response to Soviet Challenges

Soviet threats to the territorial integrity and political independence of Middle Eastern states became manifest in the northern tier of states immediately after the end of World War II. The Soviets established puppet regimes in Iranian Azerbaijan and Kurdistan in late 1945 and violated the treaty-stipulated pledge to withdraw from Iranian territory within six months after the end of the war. Soviet policy toward Turkey was similarly threatening and heavy-handed. At the Big Three Potsdam Conference in 1945, Stalin asked for virtual Soviet control of the Turkish Straits. He followed this with a demand for cession to the USSR of two northeastern Turkish border districts.

Simultaneously, the Greek government, freshly returned to Athens from exile in London, was the target of guerrilla warfare conducted by Marxist bands aided by the communist regimes of Bulgaria, Yugoslavia, and Albania.

Feeling that the British, until then the paramount power in this region, were no longer capable of protecting Greece and Turkey, President Truman made a major policy statement, known as the Truman Doctrine, on March 12, 1947, in which he pledged economic aid and military advisory assistance to these two countries.[2] In a subsequent declaration, Secretary of State Dean Acheson extended this pledge to Iran. These acts laid the foundation of the policy of containment, directed at the Soviet Union and international communism, a policy initially articulated by George Kennan in an article in *Foreign Affairs*.[3]

Concern about Soviet expansion southward caused Secretary of State John Foster Dulles to promote an alliance of states situated close to the Soviet Union. The outcome, in 1955, was the Baghdad Pact, grouping three non-Arab states—Turkey, Iran, and Pakistan—Arab Iraq, Great Britain, and, as a nonsignatory associate, the United States.

The Suez war of 1956 and the subsequent Soviet political penetration of the Arab East led Washington to devise new means to combat Soviet advances. In the Eisenhower Doctrine, a policy statement of January 1957, the president pledged U.S. economic and military assistance to any country in the Middle East threatened by "international communism."[4] Like the Truman Doctrine ten years earlier, the Eisenhower declaration represented a policy of containment but went a step further by pledging the use of U.S. forces.

In 1958, by stretching the doctrine's interpretation, Washington justified the landing of U.S. troops in Lebanon to protect the government of President Camille Chamoun against armed rebellion by groups aided by the Egyptian-dominated and Soviet-influenced radical regime in Syria. Corresponding to this crisis, a new configuration began to emerge in the Arab world: the radical versus the moderate states. The first group followed the ideology of Egypt's Gamal Abdul Nasser; the second was led by Saudi Arabia. An ever closer relationship began to develop between Riyadh and Washington. At the same time the two Arab camps engaged in what became known as the Arab Cold War, a process of mutual hostility, occasionally, as in Yemen in the 1960s, punctuated by hot warfare. In this Cold War the radicals, as a rule, were on the offensive.[5] In 1958 a revolutionary coalition led by army officers overthrew the monarchy in Iraq, proclaimed neutrality, and, subsequently, withdrew the country from the Baghdad Pact. The pact was renamed the Central Treaty Organization (CENTO) and its headquarters was moved to Ankara. At the same time the other signatories of the pact pressed Washington to define with greater precision its commitment to the defense of the pact's member-states. The response took the form of three bilateral security pacts with CENTO's Asian members in 1959. These had the merit of specifying more directly the U.S. commitment to protect each of the three contracting parties than did a mere associational relationship with the CENTO collectivity.

In 1951, moreover, Turkey had become a full member of NATO. Turkey thus received U.S. unilateral, bilateral, and multilateral guarantees and emerged as the most steadfast member of the northern tier U.S.-sponsored security system.

Iran was next in importance in this system, as a direct neighbor of the Soviets, as a major oil producer, and as the most powerful riparian state in the Gulf region. The Shah's staunch opposition to communism, his realistic appraisal of the Soviet threat, and his drive for modernization made him particularly eligible for security guarantees from Washington's point of view. Moreover, Iran was the natural candidate to fill the vacuum created by the British decision to withdraw from the Gulf by 1971. This dovetailed with the Nixon Doctrine of 1969, which committed the United States to reducing its direct military involvement in various areas of the world and helping regional powers strengthen their defense through economic, technical, and military advisory assistance.[6] A major recipient of U.S. arms, in 1974–75 Iran effectively helped Sultan Qabus of Oman defeat the Marxist-inspired rebellion supported by South Yemen in the province of Dhofar in 1974–75.

The U.S. containment policy in the northern tier, conceived and pursued on a bipartisan basis from Truman to Nixon and Ford, was a success. The USSR was prevented from violating the sovereignty and integrity of its Moslem neighbors, and peace based on military and economic support from the industrial West prevailed in this region for over 35 years. So long as Washington assigned a high priority to the defense of this region, the system worked despite certain difficulties. When U.S. resolve began to waver and when new priorities appeared during the Carter administration, the carefully constructed security system was shaken. As a collective enterprise, it had collapsed by 1979.

The first cracks began to appear in the 1960s. In the case of Turkey, the difficulty centered on Cyprus and on divergent interpretations of U.S. commitments to Ankara held by Premier Ismet Inönü and President Lyndon Johnson. Ten years later, the U.S. arms embargo and the suspension of U.S. bases in Turkey following the Turkish invasion of Cyprus brought relations between the two allies to an all-time low. However, by 1978 saner counsels prevailed in the U.S. Congress, and the embargo was lifted. The alliance was preserved despite the strains, even though it had lost some of its earlier luster.

Pakistan's relations with the United States had, during that period, also suffered various reverses because Islamabad expected U.S. backing not only against the Soviet threat but also in its disputes with India. The traumatic separation of Bangladesh added to the growing bitterness between Islamabad and Washington. By the late 1970s, to all practical purposes Pakistan had suspended its participation in CENTO.

But the decisive events in the breakdown of the regional security system took place in Iran. While the growth of revolutionary opposition to the Shah's rule stemmed partly from the political and economic errors of the government and partly from the psychosocial makeup of the Iranian nation, vacillations in U.S. policy can be viewed as a catalyst of the revolution. This policy oscillated between the idealistic and, in terms of Iranian history, questionable insistence on democratic principles on the one hand and repeated assertions of a close alliance with the Shah on the other. While the right hand was supporting Iran's ruler, the left was undermining him.[7] Ultimately, instead of liberal democracy, Iran experienced a religious dictatorship whose massive violations of human rights far exceeded anything practiced under the monarchy.

With Iran's defection, the security system built up over three and a half decades ceased to exist. The results soon became apparent. Moscow felt fewer restraints in embarking on an aggressive policy toward Afghanistan. A communist coup in that country in April 1978 was followed by the Soviet invasion in December 1979. And, as is typical of any new revolutionary center, the Khomeini regime in Iran launched a radical, fundamentalist propaganda campaign, threatening simultaneously its socialist neighbor Iraq, conservative Saudi Arabia, and the status quo mini-states on the Arab side of the Gulf. At the same time the hostage crisis terminated U.S.-Iranian relations.

The U.S. response to these two challenges, the Soviet and the Iranian, differed. On January 22, 1980, in a major policy statement some twenty days after the Soviet invasion of Afghanistan, President Carter declared that the United States would resist any attack on the Persian Gulf region, with military force if necessary.[8] This Carter Doctrine was to be supplemented by the creation of a Rapid Deployment Force to be used in the Indian Ocean–Persian Gulf region.

In 1981, the Reagan administration inherited a sad state of affairs in the northern tier: Afghanistan under Soviet control; Iran in revolutionary turmoil and utterly hostile to the United States; Turkey deprived of its erstwhile regional friends and still smarting to a degree from memories of the arms embargo; and the Persian Gulf region shaken by the revolution in Iran and the fear of a spillover of the Iraqi-Iranian war.

The challenge to the administration could thus be narrowed to three major points: how to restore greater stability to this region; how to protect it from further Soviet encroachments; and how to revive a friendly relationship between the United States and the powers of the northern tier.

The concept of stability applies both to domestic conditions and to international relations. In the northern tier, Turkey has achieved a considerable degree of stability despite the tensions within its multiparty system and the military interventions in 1960, 1971, and 1980. In fact, the presence of the army as a watchdog over the country's political morals has, in spite of its authoritarian connotations, protected Turkey from the disintegration threatened by extremist forces. It would be imprudent for the United States to penalize Turkey for its deviations from ideal democratic standards. Furthermore, Turkish leaders have neither rejected a multiparty system as a long-run proposition nor repudiated their alliance with the West. To its credit, since 1980 the U.S. government has pursued a policy of friendly normalization with the existing military leadership.

At the other end of the spectrum stands Afghanistan, ostensibly occupied by the Soviet military and ruled by a Marxist puppet government. In reality, Afghans are not reconciled to their fate, and Soviet rule is challenged daily by nationalist and tribal guerrillas. The United States' sympathies have been on the side of the resistance groups, and the Carter administration applied certain economic sanctions to the Soviet Union in response to the Soviet aggression. Economic sanctions, however, are an unreliable policy tool. They are not effective if the goods denied to the target country can be replaced by other suppliers. Moreover, they constitute a double-edged instrument if they hurt the economy of the exporting state. Grain sales to Russia have fallen precisely into this category; hence the Reagan administration has lifted the ban while continuing to deny the Soviets selected products of high technology. Although probably not decisive in influencing Soviet behavior, the use of economic sanctions has served the dual purpose of morally aligning the United States with an Islamic victim of communist imperialism and of notifying the USSR that it cannot follow expansionist designs with impunity.

As for Iran, its revolutionary upheaval has placed it outside the Western orbit without subordinating it to Russia. But this is a fragile kind of neutrality, apt to be disrupted at any moment because of internal instability or international circumstances. From the U.S. point of view, Khomeini's experiment has been a negative and disturbing phenomenon in the region. Yet its eventual disappearance will not guarantee an automatic return to normalcy because much will depend on the political group and system that succeed it. Hence Washington's attitude in the 1980s could perhaps best be described as "wait and see." Although not unfriendly to Iraq in its quest for immunity from Khomeini-sponsored subversion, the United States has avoided any close identification with Baghdad. On the other hand, the Reagan administration has taken a quietly positive attitude toward the collective efforts, under Saudi aegis, of the Gulf states to promote greater cooperation among themselves to ward off both the Khomeini-inspired revolution and communist subversion.[9] Major changes in U.S. policies in this respect are unlikely in the 1980s.

The Soviet threat to the Middle East has not been limited to the northern tier. The USSR has lent political, economic, and military support to a number of Arab states, primarily those with revolutionary regimes. Its policies have had a checkered record of success and failure, the latter especially notable in Egypt under Sadat. The USSR probably attained its greatest advance in South Yemen in the 1970s, where a combination of native Marxist rule and a close relationship with Moscow (seconded by East Germany and Cuba) has produced something like a satellite state. The United States' response has been to establish closer ties with those neighboring states threatened by South Yemen's revolutionary dynamism—namely, the Yemen Arab Republic, Saudi Arabia, and Oman. In the case of Oman, the United States has secured base facilities on the strategic island of Masirah (which served as a staging point in the hostage rescue mission to Iran). This policy of support for the nonrevolutionary status quo in the Gulf and the Arabian Peninsula will probably continue throughout the 1980s.

Access to Oil

Safe access to oil at reasonable prices has been the second major motivation behind the United States' interest in the Middle East. The Western oil connection has passed through several phases. Initially, Britain with its Dutch and French partners dominated the scene. In 1928, U.S. companies first entered on the area by acquiring close to a quarter of the equity in the international Iraq Petroleum Company (IPC). However, the price of admission included a restrictive clause— the Red Line Agreement—which forbade them from seeking separate concessions in areas of the former Ottoman Empire. Fortunately for the promotion of U.S. interests, a major company, Standard Oil of California (not a partner in IPC) was not bound by any restraints. Free to expand, it secured a concession in 1933 in Saudi Arabia—a historic step that led to the Arabian-American Oil Company (Aramco) and inaugurated an era of U.S. predominance in Middle East oil. The U.S. presence was further enhanced by the out-of-court settlement repudiating the Red Line's restrictive clauses—a step that permitted such giants as Standard Oil of New Jersey (Exxon) and Socony Vacuum (Mobil) to enter the Middle East on a major scale. Construction of the Trans-

Arabian Pipeline (Tapline) linking the Gulf with the Mediterranean
was another major move. And the massive entry of U.S. companies
into the Iranian oil consortium following the so-called Mossadegh crisis in the 1950s marked the final major stride in the involvement of the
U.S. oil industry.

With a foot firmly in the door, the United States—through its private enterprise—developed a policy with three objectives: gaining
physical access to oil through exploration, production, and transportation; protecting the existing concessions by promoting a political climate conducive to their preservation; and ensuring that oil was
available at accessible prices beneficial to the producing and consuming
states alike.

The second of these objectives, protection of the concessions, was
decisive because it provided the framework within which the other two
objectives could be attained without major crises and confrontations.
Rather obviously, support for moderate political systems was in the interest of both the U.S. government and the concessionaire companies.
By the same token, any coup or revolution likely to put in power a
group hostile to the United States or a party favoring state-run economies constituted an overt or covert threat to U.S. oil interests in the
area.

During the 1940s and 1950s, an uneasy status quo prevailed. But
in 1960 the first crack appeared in the existing structure with the creation of the Organization of Petroleum Exporting Countries (OPEC).
This collective body (grown to embrace thirteen states from the Middle
East, Asia, Africa, and Latin America) began to challenge oil companies, first on the issue of prices and then on a number of related problems. OPEC's growth in the subsequent two decades occurred at a
time of growing demand in the consuming countries; in a seller's market, its power to influence price levels was steadily increasing. Although OPEC was frequently viewed as a cartel, it lacked the classic
cartel's ultimate power, that of enforcing production quotas, a necessity if prices were to be effectively controlled in a buyer's market.

In the postwar period, the United States' access to Middle East oil
was generally maintained. However, it suffered interruptions and disturbances in the physical, political, legal, and economic sectors, usually
in connection with regional political crises or local wars. Any outbreak
of war, among either the producing or the nonproducing countries,
was likely to affect physical access to oil: production facilities, refin-
eries, terminals, and pipelines could and did suffer damage and disruption. To cite a few examples, the Arab-Israeli wars of 1956 and 1967

brought about partial sabotage and cutoff of the pipelines and closing of the Suez Canal. Similarly, the Iraq-Iran war, which began in 1981, disrupted oil supplies from both countries due to substantial damage to their facilities. Thus, even without being a direct political target of hostility, an importing country such as the United States was apt to suffer the consequences of any regional military conflict.

The position of such a country was bound to worsen if, for one reason or another, it became subject to punitive sanctions. This was precisely the case of the United States during the October war of 1973. Arab oil ministers decided to divide consuming countries into three broad categories: friendly, neutral, and hostile. They designated the United States as the principal hostile state and subjected it to a total embargo of crude oil and oil-derived products. The United States' pro-Israeli policy, specifically President Nixon's decision to grant major financial assistance to Israel when it was at war, precipitated this decision.[10]

Shortages of oil caused by politically motivated production cuts and embargoes were bound to have economic consequences as well. By the end of 1973, OPEC had quadrupled the price of oil. In what had become a seller's market, OPEC continued its policy of price boosts throughout the 1970s, culminating in a price level of around $34 per barrel by 1980, compared with about $3 per barrel in January 1973. These steep increases further aggravated recessionary trends in many industrial countries while proving extremely onerous—near ruinous— to a number of poorer Third World importing countries.

In addition, important changes were taking place in the legal status of the oil companies. Their exclusive long-term concessions were gradually eroded or, in some cases, cancelled. The general trend was toward growing participation of the host governments in the equity of the concessions—varying from 25 to 51, to 60 and even 100 percent, depending on the host country. In some cases outright nationalizations occurred. By the end of the 1970s, the old pattern of concessions had been replaced by the new one of a host country's owning fully or partly its oil resources and its producing/refining facilities, and sometimes even sharing in downstream operations beyond its borders. As a result, foreign oil companies were transformed into service contractors running the operations for a fee and buying oil with or without a preferential status. These trends corresponded to the general assertion of nationalist and often socialist policies in the host countries. In 1982–1983, high oil prices, combined with lesser consumption due to the recession, conservation, and partial substitution of other forms of energy brought about a glut of oil on world markets and an eventual fall in prices. At the same time, OPEC, successful when demand was high and prices rising, experienced serious inner strains in a shrinking market. Due to disagreements regarding production prorationing and illegal price discounting, it was on the verge of disintegration.

In the short run, the price crisis of 1982–1983 was likely to cause economic disturbance in a number of producing countries whose development programs had to be curtailed, with consequent effects on the international banking system. In the long run, cheaper energy prices will benefit both the industrial and the poorer Third World countries, accelerate recovery from recession, and, in due course, stimulate larger production in the host countries.

By the mid-1970s, the United States had become a net importer of 45 percent of its oil supplies due to the depletion of its reserves and the shrinking of production from some 11.5 million barrels a day (mbd) in 1970 to 8.5 mbd in the late 1970s, despite the new discoveries in Alaska and elsewhere. This substantial dependence on foreign oil imports represented a long-range trend. Although, as noted earlier, this trend was disrupted in the early 1980s, it was unlikely that the low import level would become permanent. Rather, there were good reasons to expect a return to the historical pattern of growth once the U.S. economy resumed its upward movement. There are two possible ways to avoid excessive reliance on foreign oil; namely, discovery of new domestic reserves and development of alternate energy resources, such as coal, shale, solar, geothermal, and hydroelectric. Of these, coal represents the most easily available form, but it poses serious environmental problems, which, in an ecology-oriented age, cannot easily be brushed aside. Abundant reserves of shale exist in the Green River basin (Wyoming, Utah, Colorado), but their successful exploitation poses cost and ecological problems. To produce one barrel of oil requires the crushing of 1.5 to 2.0 tons of rock. Production of a million barrels a day—a volume that would make some difference in overall energy production—might mean destruction of a small mountain a day, together with ample use of the rather scarce water resources of the mountain states. The high costs of such an operation at a time of falling oil prices caused one major oil company to withdraw from the shale venture in the early 1980s.

All of this points to the wisdom that, while safeguarding certain alternatives through research, development, and taxation incentives, Washington should take steps to ensure that Middle East oil is available to fuel the U.S. industrial machine and provide adequate supplies for home use. Hence a rational oil policy must promote stability in the

Middle East and such working relationships with the area's producing and transit states as reduce to a minimum the possibilities of sudden disruptions.

The Question of Palestine

The question of Palestine—the third reason for the United States' special interest in the Middle East—can be defined as a set of political and strategic issues arising from the rival claims of two national groups, the Jewish and the Palestinian Arab, to the same land. Although Jewish identity is often described in religious terms, the notion of Jewish peoplehood has never faded away, and political Zionism, launched by Theodor Herzl in the last decade of the nineteenth century, gave Jewishness a definitely nationalist flavor. In his famous book *Judenstaat*, Herzl asked for a Jewish state. Nearly fifty years later, in 1942, a Zionist conference assembled in New York issued the Biltmore declaration calling for the whole of Palestine to become a Jewish state, although the terms of the British mandate for Palestine in 1922 had provided only for a Jewish national home *in* Palestine.[11] When the matter of Palestine came before the United Nations in 1947, the solution then adopted (and favored by Zionists) was that of partition. However, after the conquest of the Arab parts of Palestine (West Bank and Gaza Strip) in 1967, Israel's policy veered toward permanent control of the occupied land and, since the advent of the Begin government in 1977, incorporation of this territory under Israel's sovereignty has become the real objective of its policy.

By the same token, based on uninterrupted occupation of the land for thirteen centuries, the Palestinians—supported by the rest of the Arab world—laid claim to all of Palestine and, unsuccessfully, tried to deny even part of it to the Zionists. Following three Arab-Israeli wars (1948, 1956, and 1967), the Palestine Liberation Organization (PLO) reconfirmed this exclusive claim by declaring in its charter in 1968 that Palestine is "an indivisible territorial unit"; the Palestinian Arab people assert their right "to self-determination and sovereignty over it"; and "the liberation of Palestine will destroy the Zionist and imperialist presence."[12]

Thus claims to Palestine as a whole represent the extreme positions of the rival Jewish and Arab parties. In between lies the area of compromise and moderation expressed in the idea of the partition of Palestine and peaceful coexistence of the two peoples. Following the June war of 1967, the U.N. Security Council opted for such a compromise in its

Resolution 242 of November of that year. Its guiding principle was the exchange of territory for peace: Israel was to withdraw from occupied lands; in return the Arabs would renounce belligerency, and the Palestinian refugees would receive justice.[13]

Resolution 242 was not implemented; instead a protracted stalemate, an Egyptian-Israeli war of attrition, and an escalation of tension led to the October war of 1973. Then, four years later, in 1977, President Sadat of Egypt made a bold move. Egypt, he declared, was ready to live in peace with Israel provided Israel withdrew from Egyptian territory and the occupied lands in Palestine. Subsequent triangular negotiation involving Egypt, Israel, and the United States led to the Camp David agreement of September 1978[14] and by April 1979 to an Israeli-Egyptian peace treaty. The Camp David agreement provided that during a transition period of five years, "full autonomy" was to be granted to the Palestinians in the West Bank and Gaza. Then the final decision on sovereignty over these lands was to be reached. Subsequent negotiations between Egypt and Israel and the United States and Israel had not, by mid-1983, brought matters closer to a solution.

The U.S. role in the Arab-Israeli conflict can broadly be described as that of mediator and peacemaker. Three principles have guided successive administrations: (1) Washington insists on the right of Israel to exist within secure boundaries; (2) despite a tilt toward Israel in terms of military and economic assistance, it does not want to alienate the strategically located Arab world; (3) it supports Resolution 242 as a basis for peace.

Although the Camp David agreement had aimed at the achievement of these objectives, it was only partially successful and may have been counterproductive for several reasons.

First, the concrete result of Camp David was a separate Israeli-Egyptian peace. Such a peace was a long-standing objective of Israel—for the purpose of separating Egypt from other Arab countries—and it could have been attained through bilateral Israeli-Egyptian negotiations without the onus that attached to the United States through its sponsorship of such a plan.

Second, while the U.S. intention was to produce a comprehensive peace settlement, the text of the Camp David agreement lacks a clear and unambiguous linkage between the Egyptian-Israeli and the Palestinian parts of the agreement. This has allowed Israel to eliminate Egypt from the common Arab front while delaying indefinitely the solution of the Palestinian problem.

Third, the text of the Camp David agreement is silent on the issue of Jerusalem, a sensitive point with Arabs and Israelis alike and one with a very explosive potential in the long run.

Fourth, the Camp David text does not mention Israeli settlements in the occupied territories, which are illegal according to international law.[15] Politically, by radically restructuring the demography of the West Bank and Gaza, the proliferating settlements strengthen the Palestinian Arabs' mood of resistance and despair and threaten the entire peacemaking process. Verbal agreements between President Carter and Premier Begin on this issue were apparently so vague as to give rise to widely differing interpretations (five years of freeze according to Carter versus three months according to Begin).[16]

Fifth, the text does not define "full autonomy" for the Palestinians in the West Bank and Gaza, thus giving rise to widely varying interpretations. Israel's definition tends to be severely restrictive: autonomy means limited municipal self-government over such matters as sanitation, sewer systems, slaughterhouses, and the like. To Egypt, full autonomy has a definite connotation of real self-rule just short of complete sovereignty.

Sixth, the Camp David text is also imprecise on the issue of Israeli forces in the West Bank and Gaza. In a rather confusing sentence, it says: "A withdrawal of Israeli armed forces will take place and there will be a redeployment of the remaining Israeli forces into specified security locations."[17] The question is: Are Israeli forces to be withdrawn from the occupied territories or merely transferred from one place to another? What does the expression "the remaining Israeli forces" mean? What is the meaning of "security locations"—is Israel expected to continue security control of the West Bank and Gaza in spite of the provision for "full autonomy"?

One cannot help wondering at the Camp David text's omissions and imprecisions. The euphoria generated in the U.S. Congress upon its announcement is somewhat hard to understand. If its intention was to produce Israel's withdrawal from the occupied territories while ensuring a comprehensive peace and recognizing the right of Palestinians to a home of their own, it certainly fell short of expectations.

Furthermore, the general reaction in the Arab world was negative. The Arabs regarded Camp David as a clear Israeli diplomatic victory. At meetings in Baghdad in the fall of 1978 and the spring of 1979, the Arab League first censured Egypt and then suspended its membership and attacked the United States as the malevolent divider of the Arab world. In the fall of 1981, President Sadat paid with his life for isolating Egypt from the Arab mainstream.

With the advent of the Reagan administration, there was evidence of a desire to move the stalemated peace process in the Middle East from the dead center it had reached in the declining days of the preceding administration. (President Carter was so preoccupied with the forthcoming elections that he, to quote Zbigniew Brzezinski, insisted on not being "bothered" by the issue of Israeli settlements in the West Bank and Gaza, even though he had opposed them earlier in his presidency.)[18] Secretary of State Alexander Haig proposed a "strategic consensus" that would group together Israel, Egypt, Jordan, and Saudi Arabia, presumably on the basis of their common fear of Soviet expansionism. Had a solid peace based on justice been achieved as a precondition, such a strategic consensus might have been seriously considered. As things stood in 1981–1982, lack of progress in peacemaking virtually guaranteed the stillbirth of the consensus concept. With fresh memories of the Israeli forays into Lebanon in the late 1970s and the overflight of Saudi territory by Israeli aircraft to bomb the Iraqi nuclear facility near Baghdad, neither Saudi Arabia nor Jordan could be expected to respond positively to a U.S. proposal to cooperate with Israel. In spite of their anticommunist orientation, the governments and public in both countries considered Israel the prime threat to their security and territorial integrity, rather than a more remote Soviet Russia.

Israel's invasion of Lebanon in June 1982, and the attendant massive destruction of Beirut and subsequent massacres in the Palestinian refugee camps of Sabra and Shatila, further confirmed the moderate Arab states' refusal to consider seriously any strategic consensus concepts. Although they received U.S. arms (but fewer than they had requested), they were unwilling to reciprocate by cooperating strategically with Israel or granting any favored treatment to the United States.

With the resignation of Secretary Haig, U.S. policy took a decisively new turn. The new secretary of state, George Shultz, focused his attention on the Middle East promptly after his appointment, and by September 1, 1982, President Reagan had proposed a new peace initiative, which reiterated the idea of an Israeli withdrawal in return for peace, called for an immediate freeze on Israeli settlements, and asked for "self-government by the Palestinians of the West Bank and Gaza in association with Jordan."[19] Although falling short of the Palestinian goal of self-determination, the proposal clearly recognized the Arab character of the occupied territories and rejected the Israeli claim of sovereignty. Furthermore, the president's unequivocal insistence on an end to the proliferation of Jewish settlements constituted a corrective step to his previous ambiguity on this issue and thus tended to reassure the Arab world (he had once declared that the settlements were "not illegal," although he acknowledged that they were an obstacle to peace). Above all, Reagan appealed to Israel "to make clear that the security for which she yearns can only be achieved through genuine peace" and that such a peace must be based on Resolution 242.[20]

With this initiative, U.S. policymakers were no longer concerned with the strategic consensus; instead they forcefully articulated the traditional U.S. policy of opposing expansionism[21] and injected a new idea of Palestinian self-government in conjunction with Jordan. Israel summarily rejected Reagan's proposal the next day. On September 9, at a summit meeting in Fez, the Arab states adopted a Plan for Palestine that reaffirmed "the Palestinian people's right to self-determination" with Jerusalem as their capital but on other points did not differ substantially from the president's plan. The important point was that the Fez plan did not claim the whole of Palestine and did not demand the abolition of Israel as a state.[22] Broadly, it resembled the plan submitted by Crown Prince Fahd of Saudi Arabia in August 1981, which implicitly recognized the existence of Israel.[23] The three plans had something in common: by steering away from extreme positions, they had become reconcilable.

Thus, at least two steps forward had been taken: U.S. policy was clarified, and a broad area of agreement with the views of moderate Arab states was established. What remained was to ensure implementation of the president's initiative. Three main hurdles had to be overcome: Israel had to be induced to withdraw its troops from Lebanon, an act needed both as a demonstration of peaceful Israeli intentions and as evidence of U.S. credibility as an influential force for peace; Israel had to desist from further proliferation of settlements; and the PLO had to authorize King Hussein of Jordan to act on its behalf in the U.S.-proposed peace negotiations.

Intensive shuttle diplomacy by Secretary Shultz culminated in an agreement between Israel and Lebanon in May 1983. It called for an Israeli withdrawal from Lebanon, provided Syria and the PLO also withdrew their forces, and it stipulated joint Israeli-Lebanese patrols of southern Lebanon. Although full implementation of this agreement depended on further agreements, primarily with Soviet-backed and reluctant Syria, the first positive move had been made.

As for the freeze on settlements and the PLO-Jordanian accord, the United States faced parallel situations on both sides of the Israeli-Arab political line: each side had its extreme and its moderate wing. In Israel the extreme position was represented by Premier Begin and his Likudreligious coalition, while the Labor Party and the Peace Now movement (the latter small in numbers) leaned toward greater moderation without necessarily endorsing the U.S. proposals in their entirety. On the Arab side, moderates were represented by Egypt, Saudi Arabia, and Jordan as well as by certain elements in the PLO, including its chairman, Yasser Arafat. Opposed to moderation was the so-called Arab Rejectionist Front (Syria, Libya, South Yemen as the hard core) and the militant leaders of certain fedayeen organizations in the PLO. The latter were strong enough to dissuade Arafat, in April 1983, from giving approval to King Hussein to enter the peace process on the PLO's behalf. By this act, the Palestinian hawks have clearly played into the hands of Premier Begin, whose preference for territory and the demographic Judaization of the occupied lands rather than for freely negotiated peace had become a guiding principle of Israel's policy by the early 1980s.

Thus rebuked by both Israel and the PLO, the United States might well be tempted to renounce its ungrateful mediating tasks. The point is that international affairs are too complex and too multifaceted to allow any government, especially a superpower, to adopt such a hands-off policy. First of all, to abstain from its peacemaking role would require curtailment of U.S. involvement. But the United States *is* involved; it has been assisting Israel to the tune of about $2 billion a year and transferring some of its most advanced weapons to it. Similarly, to abstain from further action and let things run their natural course might result in accentuation of Arab radicalism, more revolutionary upheavals (some likely to topple friendly Arab governments), a revival of Soviet penetration, and a possible outbreak of a new war in the Middle East. Whether Washington likes it or not, it is destined to continue its involvement in Middle East political processes.

By what methods can the United States influence the course of events in the area? Conceptually, there are only three ways: to use force, to apply pressure (through a threat of action likely to hurt the other party), or to practice persuasion. In its relations with a variety of countries, the United States has employed all three methods at one time or another. So have Israel and other powers as well. No self-respecting government intent on preserving its sovereign freedom of action can *a priori* renounce the use of any of these methods. It is, of course, unlikely that Washington would use force against either Israel or any Arab state or the PLO, unless vital U.S. interests were violated or endangered. As for pressure, it was applied, however gingerly, to Israel on a number of occasions: during the Suez crisis by President Eisenhower, during the Ford presidency when U.S. policy was reassessed, and by the Reagan administration when delivery of aircraft and weapons systems was suspended or delayed. The last occurred despite Secretary Shultz's repeated assertions that the United States eschewed the use of sanctions and preferred to convince Israel that it had more to gain by pursuing the path of peace than by relying on force and territory to ensure its security.

In principle, the United States has clearly favored persuasion through negotiation to achieve its political objectives. But a certain imbalance has crept into the conduct of U.S. diplomacy. Washington has negotiated with perseverance with those elements in Israel that espouse an extreme position on a Palestinian homeland, that is, with the Begin government. But the United States has refused to negotiate with the PLO, which equally, through its charter, denies the legitimacy of Israel. This U.S. refusal is based on Secretary of State Henry Kissinger's pledge to Israel in 1975. That pledge was not a treaty ratified by the U.S. Senate. It constituted an innovation in the annals of diplomacy in that a major power renounced in advance one of the peaceful methods of conducting foreign policy. Neutral observers may, moreover, criticize Washington for a degree of hypocrisy in this matter: when the U.S. government needed the PLO, it did not hesitate to communicate with its leadership. This was notably the case when the United States sought PLO support to free the American hostages in Iran and to ensure safe evacuation of its embassy personnel in Lebanon in the wake of the assassination of the U.S. ambassador during the Lebanese civil war. The rather rigid U.S. posture regarding contacts with the PLO on the most important issue—that of the peace process—deserves to be reviewed. By refusing to talk to PLO leaders, Washington deprives itself of the opportunity to exert influence in the direction of moderation, a situation that is likely to benefit only the extremists on both sides.

Although the foregoing has separated the three motivations behind U.S. interest in the Middle East for analytical purposes, in reality a close interrelationship binds them together. Safeguarding the region from encroachment or absorption by Russia is the overriding consideration because without it the other two—oil and Palestine—would lose their relevance. Because oil is concentrated in the strategically vulnerable Gulf area, much attention has been focused on that region since 1970, the eve of the relinquishment of British dominance there. Formation of the United Arab Emirates, strengthening of the Saudi military establishment, acquisition of base facilities by the United States in Oman, use of AWACS aircraft in Saudi Arabia, proclamation of the Carter Doctrine, creation of the Gulf Cooperation Council, and steps toward the establishment of the Rapid Deployment Force attest to the importance attached to this subregion by the United States and the local powers alike. However, it would be erroneous to say that the Persian Gulf has replaced the subregion close to the Mediterranean as the principal focus of politics and strategy. Egypt, the most populous country and potentially the greatest military power in the Arab world; Israel with its abundant and sophisticated arms and its territorial ambitions in the area; Syria, a country with strong ideological motivations and close ties to the Soviets; and the PLO are located in this Mediterranean zone, and it is precisely in that zone that endemic conflicts have disturbed the peace. Of these the Arab-Israeli feud and the fate of Palestine are of paramount importance, having claimed an inordinate amount of attention from U.S. policymakers over the past three decades. Developments in this western zone have profoundly affected and will continue to affect the politics, strategy, and economics of the Gulf, as the oil embargo of 1973–1974 attests. In turn, availability of oil, a major consideration in the formulation of U.S. policies, has its wartime as well as peacetime connotations. Use of oil by the industrial and Third World countries, to be beneficial to consumers and producers alike, must be based on unimpeded access, secure transportation, political tranquility, and economic stability.

U.S. policies toward the region, as elsewhere, have always been an outcome of a decision-making process involving the executive and legislative branches of government, but the two have not always acted in perfect harmony. Moreover, U.S. presidents invariably pass through two stages in the formulation of their policies, the electoral stage and that of actual incumbency. Each dictates a somewhat different political strategy. The demands of the presidency with its emphasis on national interest compete with temptations of partisan politics and often, especially during the first two years of an administration, have prevailed.

Despite certain oscillations, presidential policies toward the Middle East have displayed a good deal of continuity since World War II. No president could with impunity disregard the Soviet menace or the danger to the region and U.S. interests caused by the Arab-Israeli conflict or oil and energy problems. Eisenhower, Johnson, Nixon, Ford, Carter, and Reagan all opposed acquisition of territory by force. All stressed the need for Israel to be secure as well as recognition, in one way or another, of the rights of the Palestinians. And all took steps to ensure the continuous flow of oil.

The challenge to all postwar presidents has been the Soviet threat in the area. While the USSR has never hesitated to use force against local powers—witness Azerbaijan in 1945 and Afghanistan since 1979—when it could do so with relative impunity, its main strategy has been to support anti-Western nationalism and to exploit any resentments that U.S. policies in the region have generated.

The policies of major powers sometimes pose the question whether promotion of their national interests (at least as perceived by their governments) accords with moral principles. Today, in an era of mass communications and increased popular awareness of international issues, it is mandatory that the relationship between power and morality be clarified as fully as possible. Fortunately, in spite of all the difficulties, it would appear that with reference to the Middle East, moral principle and the national interest of the United States have tended to be in harmony: support for a just peace based on the principle of national self-determination is both moral and in agreement with the traditions and realistic goals of U.S. policy in the region.

Notes

1. *Nazi-Soviet Relations, 1939–1941: Documents from the Archives of the German Foreign Office,* Department of State Publication 3023 (Washington, D.C., 1948), pp. 257 and 259.

2. Text in Ralph H. Magnus, *Documents on the Middle East* (Washington, D.C.: American Enterprise Institute for Public Policy Research, 1969), pp. 63–67.

3. "The Sources of Soviet Conduct" (by X), *Foreign Affairs*, July 1947.

4. Text in Magnus, *Documents*, pp. 86–93.

5. See Malcolm Kerr, *The Arab Cold War: A Study of Ideology in Politics, 1958–1967,* 2d ed. (London: Oxford University Press, 1967); and George Lenczowski, "The Arab Cold War," in Willard A. Beling, ed., *The Middle East: Quest for an American Policy* (Albany: State University of New York Press, 1973).

6. Melvin R. Laird et al., *The Nixon Doctrine* (Washington, D.C.: American Enterprise Institute for Public Policy Research, 1972).

7. In the abundant literature on the Iranian revolution, Michael Ledeen and William Lewis's *Debacle: The American Failure in Iran* (New York: Vintage Books, 1980) stands out as one of the most sober analyses. See especially chap. 3, "Carter and Iran," pp. 65–96.

8. Text in *New York Times*, January 24, 1980.

9. The instrument of this collective policy has been the Gulf Cooperation Council, established in Riyadh on February 4, 1981.

10. For a more detailed study of Arab oil policies, see George Lenczowski, *Middle East Oil in a Revolutionary Age* (Washington, D.C.: American Enterprise Institute for Public Policy Research, 1976).

11. Texts in J. C. Hurewitz, *Diplomacy in the Near and Middle East* (Princeton, N.J.: Van Nostrand, 1956), 2:106, 234.

12. Text of the charter adopted by the Palestine National Congress in Cairo, July 1–17, 1968, courtesy Arab Information Office in New York.

13. Text in Magnus, *Documents*, p. 205.

14. Text in *Middle East Journal (MEJ)*, Autumn 1978, pp. 471ff.

15. In particular Art. 49 of the Geneva Convention IV, 1949, which says: "The Occupying Power shall not deport or transfer parts of its own civilian population into the territory it occupies." For an extensive discussion of principles of occupation, see Morris Greenspan, *The Modern Law of Land Warfare* (Berkeley and Los Angeles: University of California Press, 1959), pp. 269ff.

16. For the post–Camp David difficulties, see Jimmy Carter, *Keeping Faith: Memoirs of a President* (New York: Bantam Books, 1982), pp. 408–9.

17. *MEJ*, Autumn 1978, p. 471ff.

18. Zbigniew Brzezinski, *Power and Principle: Memoirs of the National Security Adviser, 1977–1981* (New York: Farrar, Straus & Giroux, 1983), pp. 438, 442, 443.

19. Text in *Current History*, January 1983, p. 33.

20. Ibid.

21. See Secretary of State William Rogers's speech at the Galaxy Conference, December 9, 1969, in *New York Times*, December 11, 1969.

22. Text in *Current History*, January 1983, p. 33.

23. Ibid., January 1982, p. 4.

12

Africa: The Struggle Between East and West

Peter J. Duignan

A frica is important to Americans. It is a major continent of over 454 million people, with more than 50 votes in the United Nations. As a global power with global interests, the United States needs to have access to and influence within the area. Economically, it wants equal opportunities with other nations to bid for Africa's resources and to invest and trade. The United States and its allies will increasingly need the minerals of Africa. Diplomatically, the United States wants to retain some influence with African governments. Strategically, it needs to utilize the passageways, ports, and airfields of the continent and to protect its vessels in the sea-lanes around Africa. The route around that continent is of vital importance to the West: 70 percent of Western Europe's oil and 90 percent of its strategic minerals are shipped around the Cape of Good Hope. The Soviet navy now has the power to threaten supply lines in that area.

U.S. economic interests in the continent are not great: about 12 percent of its imports come from Africa and about 7.6 percent of its exports and only 4 percent of its foreign investment go there. Still, even if it does not need markets or investment opportunities in Africa, the United States needs African minerals and oil. In any case, it will be drawn into African affairs by virtue of Soviet interests in the region.

Conflicts abound in most of Africa. The Soviets know how to use tensions to their benefit—and there are all too many of these tensions—troubles occasioned by rapid urbanization; unemployment; governmental instability; ethnic conflicts; poverty; rising oil prices for some; falling oil prices and a general slump in the price of other raw materials for others. Africa's 45 black-governed nations face other difficulties: large foreign debts, protectionism and trade restrictions, declining foreign aid, and rising populations. A 1981 World Bank survey, *Accelerated Development in Sub-Saharan Africa: An Agenda for Action*, noted other major problems: corruption, inefficiency, national lassitude, excessive government control, ownership and spending patterns, and the neglect of agriculture. Although the Soviet Union and its clients can benefit from such widespread difficulties, they have done little to cause them or to help alleviate the economic problems. But they have encouraged liberation fronts and, for example, intervened in Ethiopia and Angola, creating civil wars and refugee problems.

Africa's chronic instability, its numerous civil wars and so-called liberation struggles, its valuable resources, and its many strategic locations suggest continued opportunities in the 1980s for great-power intervention. In fact, the cold war has never ended in Africa. Détente (or peaceful coexistence) applied to Europe, not to the Third World, where the struggle between capitalism and communism continues.

Soviet activity in Africa has increased since 1974 when the Portuguese empire in Africa collapsed. The Soviets learned that proxy wars paid off when the whole of Southern Africa was destabilized. As Nigerian scholar Oye Ogunbadejo has noted, the "USSR's policy choices for the 1980s will no longer be restricted to the defensive, reactive sphere; they are likely to allow for greater initiative and assertion . . . the Soviet Union [is] increasingly becoming a truly global superpower."[1] The Soviets are now able to project their power anywhere in the world because of their new air and naval forces and because of their use of allies and clients as surrogates under the guise of "proletarian internationalism." Because Soviet interests are global, the United States' interests must be global too—that is, U.S. policy toward a region like Africa must consider the full range of U.S. interests, not just U.S. regional interests in Africa. U.S. policies in Africa are therefore best understood from a global, not just a regional, perspective.

The United States has never had an overall strategic or conceptual approach to Africa and its problems. It has generally sought a regional orientation, but time and again it has been forced into global views— usually because of the fear of increased Soviet influence. But it has not been consistent, nor has it fully implemented either globalist or regionalist strategies. If the United States were fully committed to a global strategy in Africa, as the State Department claims, it should be supporting the Somalis more and encouraging guerrilla warfare by the dissident Ethiopian ethnic communities to force the dissolution of the country as well as to push the Soviets and Cubans out. Instead, Washington has restrained the Somalis and failed to aid the Eritreans, Gallas, or Tigres out of concern for regional peace.

Historically the United States has tacitly accepted African nationalism and the right of self-determination, so long as Soviet support for communist movements was indirect and masked behind "fronts." The United States wanted a free Africa, but not one dominated by or subservient to communism. When Soviet-Cuban influence became direct and massive in Angola (1975) and Ethiopia (1976), the United States became more concerned. Although the Reagan administration has introduced a globalist perspective in Southern African affairs (calling for the removal of Cuban troops and Soviet technicians), the United States is unlikely to continue in this vein unless significant reforms occur in South Africa. Reagan's policy of "constructive engagement" does not include the acceptance of apartheid now.

Many of the problems of the United States in Africa therefore revolve around Soviet involvement in "wars of liberation" and in keeping Marxist regimes in power. African nationalists and governments have turned to the Soviets for arms, training, and financial assistance when the West refused such aid. As a result, the Soviets in varying degrees dominate major political movements like the South-West African People's Organization (SWAPO) in Namibia, the African National Congress (ANC) in South Africa, the Popular Movement for the Liberation of Angola (MPLA), and the Front for the Liberation of Mozambique (FRELIMO).

The Politics of Subversion

Independent Africa has remained, and will continue to be, a field of international competition. In economics, the European Economic Community (EEC) is by far the most powerful contender. The EEC is Africa's most important trading partner; the United States, Japan, and the Soviet bloc trail far behind. France has also maintained a military presence in several of its former territories, a presence that the United States should encourage in its own self-interest.[2]

Soviet Imperialism

Africans must contend, in addition, with the influence of the Soviet Union. The Soviets have made themselves felt through their dealings with established non-Marxist governments, through the pressures exercised by orthodox communist parties (which are mostly weak and ineffectual), and through liberation movements—originally designed as "fronts" including some noncommunists—dedicated to bringing about "national democratic revolutions" as stepping-stones on the way to socialism. After the revolution, according to communist theoreticians, these fronts should gradually be transformed into Marxist-Leninist "vanguard parties" dedicated to the pursuit of scientific socialism, operated through "democratic centralism," and joined in a global struggle to bring about world revolution under Soviet leadership.

The new Soviet imperialism, as we have seen, has been sustained in Africa by the deployment of Cuban troops assisted by Soviet and East German advisers. Early in 1983, the total number of Cubans in Africa exceeded 40,000, nearly one-quarter of Cuba's armed forces (a far higher proportion than the proportion of Americans in Southeast Asia at the height of the Vietnam war). The Organization of African Unity has been in no position to deal with this new threat, any more than its members could cope with the "white menace" in South Africa. The Soviet offensive is supported by a combination of diplomacy and military force. Not only is the Soviet fleet impressively strong, but the Soviet air force can transport large numbers of troops complete with heavy equipment over thousands of miles. It also benefits from an international army of well-wishers (not necessarily communist) who applaud any move that weakens the West. As communist theoreticians see it, the new form of proletarian internationalism involved in military intervention would shift the international "correlation of forces" in favor of the Soviet camp and help it to disrupt strategically and economically the strength of "imperialism."

According to communist policymakers, the pursuit of revolution in Africa requires the transformation of progressive movements and fronts into disciplined cadre parties. This process began in Angola, Mozambique, and the People's Republic of the Congo; it is now under way in Ethiopia, across the Red Sea from Soviet-dominated South Yemen. The new parties are expected to accept Marxism-Leninism, perhaps as gradually as the Mongolian and Cuban ruling parties did earlier. At the same time, the new Marxist-Leninist states would "cement their solidarity" with the Soviet bloc.

Soviet political infiltration accompanies commercial, cultural, and, above all, military expansion. It seems clear that Soviet strategists are seeking control over the global "choke points" where maritime routes converge. Some U.S. strategists are skeptical of this interpretation, but I believe it makes sense from the Soviet standpoint. Why should the Soviets want to control the Horn of Africa if not for strategic reasons? Why support revolutionaries in Ethiopia and South Yemen when these countries have no valuable minerals and their foreign trade is insignificant? Why endanger détente by supporting revolution as far afield as South Africa and Afghanistan? The answer is clear—for strategic purposes.

The Soviets will therefore continue to combine the politics of subversion with a drive for strategic advantage. Fortunately, they face major problems in Africa. Given the diversity of the continent's ethnic composition and the relative weakness of the industrial proletariat in all African countries except South Africa, the Communists cannot succeed there as readily as their theoreticians assume. They also face other obstacles. These include the persistence of tribal modes of production in many parts of the continent, the dissension and lack of disciplined cadres within the new Marxist-Leninist ruling parties, and the inability of these parties to deal with the economic disasters engendered by domestic terror, wars, and civil strife. Above all, foreign intruders of whatever political conviction must cope with the extent and diversity of Africa; no single formula can cope with the problems of this entire continent.[3]

Trouble Spots

U.S. policies in Africa face their greatest difficulties in Northwest Africa, the Horn of Africa, and Southern Africa.[4]

Northwest Africa

Morocco has been fighting a secessionist group called the Polisario (Popular Front for the Liberation of Sakiet al-Hamra and Rio de Oro) since 1975 when the Spanish withdrew from their Saharan colony. The Polisario is a Marxist group supported by Algeria and Libya and armed by the Soviet Union. In recent months the Moroccans appear to have contained the war by building a mammoth dirt wall to keep out the Polisario.

Washington should continue to support and arm Morocco. Morocco has a relatively free press, permits opposition parties, and is ruled by a constitutional monarch. The United States should support King Hassan's opposition to the Polisario and ignore, for the time being, claims to self-determination from scattered and ethnically heterogeneous nomad communities that lack the wherewithal to set up a viable state.

The king's throne is by no means secure. Hassan is a traditionalist who depends on a religious and military elite; in effect, though, he governs alone and does not share power. The society is split between Arabic and Berber speakers, and the latter dominate the army. The royal family is criticized for corruption, inefficiency, and its ostentatious style of living while 60 percent of the population remains poverty-stricken. But the monarchy also has distinct assets, including the advantage of past association with the anticolonial cause. Hassan is a more skillful ruler than the former Shah of Iran, and his attempt to incorporate the northern part of the one-time Spanish Sahara is popular.

It is in the United States' interest that a moderate monarchy should continue to prevail and that a friendly, rather than a radical, power should control the Strait of Gibraltar. The United States has used Moroccan territory for air bases and communications; it may need to do so again. An unstable or unfriendly Morocco could hurt the interests of Israel, Egypt, and Zaïre. Moroccan troops have twice saved President Mobutu of Zaïre from losing cobalt- and copper-rich Shaba province; a 5,000-man Moroccan garrison keeps Zaïre in the Western camp. Morocco has been a moderate voice in Middle Eastern politics, and Hassan's support is necessary for U.S. efforts to make the peace treaty between Israel and Egypt (including the surrounding Arab states) work. U.S. support for Hassan can partially counter Libya's massive buildup of Soviet arms, which threatens NATO's control of the Mediterranean, and bring peace to the area. In the future, for example, the United States should not sell helicopters to Colonel Qaddafi of Libya while refusing such hardware to King Hassan, as it did during the Carter administration. Such policies do not bring peace; they act as powerful destabilizing factors.

The Horn of Africa

The Horn of Africa is strategically important, dominating the major maritime route through the Red Sea to the Suez Canal. Included in its area are the states of Djibouti, Somalia, and Ethiopia—the most important of the three. The United States' interests here are both regional—it wants peace in the area—and global—it does not want Soviet and Cuban control of the area.

Ethiopia is one of the most ancient and populous African states (30 million); militarily, it is more powerful than all of its African neighbors combined. It was subject to the rule of Emperor Haile Selassie until 1974, when he was overthrown by a radical military coup. The Dergue (ruling council) committed itself to a socialist system and terrorized Ethiopia's population. In 1977, Somalia attacked the Ethiopians in the Ogaden, a region the Somalis long claimed. Soviet airlifts and Cuban troops prevailed and pushed the Somalis back. Guerrilla warfare, however, continues in the Ogaden and in other parts of the state, particularly Eritrea and the south.

Somalia fell under Soviet influence after General Mohammed Said Barre staged a coup in 1969. The Soviets built up the Somali armed forces and constructed a modern port and airfield at Berbera. When the Somalis invaded the Ogaden in 1977, the Soviets had to choose between the Somalis and the Ethiopians. When they supported the Ethiopians, the Soviets lost Berbera but gained assets and influence in a strategically more important state.

By 1983, the Dergue had failed to rebuild the Ethiopian empire. In some outlying areas, the military junta's writ did not run at all; wide stretches had fallen into anarchy or were holding on to precarious forms of local independence. The army formed the country's main unifying force. Nevertheless, the growth of Soviet power in the Horn of Africa has far-reaching military implications. The junta and its ally may not control the Ethiopian hinterland in its entirety, but the Soviet naval buildup in the Red Sea and the Persian Gulf is accelerating. Soviet pilots have tested flight routes from the Gulf of Libya and Malta; Soviet aircraft operate from Aden in South Yemen and Massawa in Ethiopia, where the Soviets have established a major air base. Soviet naval units use facilities at Aden, at Socotra off South Yemen, and at Massawa, where their presence forms an ever-present threat to the vital Western oil route.

This expansion of Soviet power has placed the United States in a dilemma. Americans have no conceivable interest in encouraging a socialist Greater Somalia whose claims threaten both Ethiopia and Kenya. U.S. interests are best served by promoting peace and stability in Africa, an objective that cannot be attained if existing boundaries are challenged. During the 1980s, the United States should supply sufficient arms to Somalia to prevent Ethiopia from expanding its territory at Somalia's expense. Somalia, however, must be persuaded to give up its hopes for a Greater Somalia. On the other hand, it could be given grazing and watering rights in the Ogaden.

The United States should no longer permit itself to be driven onto the ideological defensive by the Communists, their proxies, and the humanitarian "conscience vote." Instead, the United States should speak with a stronger voice. Ethiopian rule has been brutal. The United States should oppose the bloody Ethiopian repression of the Somali in the Ogaden and of other minorities who are now being decimated, such as the Falasha. The United States should likewise help the Galla and the Eritreans, thus placing additional strain on Ethiopia while helping to improve U.S.-Arab relations. Ethiopian claims to Eritrea are comparatively recent, and they have neither ethnic nor religious foundation.

Above all, the United States can derive no advantage from strengthening the Soviet Union's hold on the southern shores of the Red Sea. Until such time as Ethiopia adopts a friendlier policy, the United States should encourage rebellious ethnic groups within the Ethiopian empire. Perhaps Ethiopia should be rebuilt as a multiethnic confederation that would grant full rights to the Moslems and pagans who, between them, outnumber the Amhara ruling group. As a long-term objective, the United States should seek the withdrawal of Cuban troops and Soviet advisers from the Horn of Africa. The permanent neutralization of the Horn would be in the interest of the West. Neutralization should enable Ethiopia and Somalia to decrease the swollen military budgets that consume a large share of their GNP. Furthermore, it would end the threat to the stability of Kenya and the Sudan that is fed by Somali ambition and Eritrean refugees. Primarily, neutralization would deny the Soviet Union one of the strategic prizes of Africa.

Zaïre

Given Zaïre's enormous potential wealth, its strategic position in the heart of Africa, and the current absence of an effective alternative to President Mobutu's authority, the United States has little choice but to support Mobutu no matter how poor his record. There is at present no evidence that any of his opponents would be less corrupt or inefficient. Zaïre is the major producer of two strategically important minerals: copper and cobalt. The latter is especially valuable to the United States for its use in superalloys for the aerospace, electronic, and machine-tool industries. Zaïre produces 50 percent of the free world's cobalt, and there are no adequate substitutes or alternative sources of supply. The 1980s will see the West increasingly dependent on such strategic minerals. It is not in the interest of the United States to promote the breakup of Zaïre through the spread of anarchy. By diplomacy and security aid, it must ensure the country's stability.

Reluctantly, therefore, the United States should continue to back Mobutu, hoping that a patient policy of persuasion, along with foreign experts to provide counsel to his government and businesses, may improve somewhat the performance of his regime. The United States, with Belgian and French aid, should retrain the Zaïrian army and police and educate a new class of efficient administrators to re-establish administrative control in the provinces. The transportation system must be rebuilt and the peasants guaranteed security so that agricultural production can be restored.

Nevertheless, Zaïre is unlikely to overcome its difficulties unless it adopts a more decentralized form of government. Given the erosion of Kinshasa's control over the outlying provinces, the inefficiency of the central civil service, and the lack of discipline in the army, Kinshasa would only be recognizing reality if it loosened its constitutional hold over the provinces in general. A loosely structured Zaïre would probably face the problems of the future with more success than a centralized Zaïre run as a despotism.

Angola and Mozambique

With the MPLA's victory in 1975, Angola moved into the international lime-light. Some American academics have called for U.S. recognition of the Marxist-Leninist regime at Luanda, as have liberal politicians who considered such recognition justified by both self-interest and equity. But it is not in the United States' interest, or in the interest of the Angolan people, to recognize the MPLA government. For the present, the MPLA is an anti-Western group that looks on the Soviet communist party as a model. According to its own statements, the MPLA is not simply a radical African nationalist group, as claimed by academics and even by such U.S. government agencies as the Agency for International Development. The MPLA, which in 1977 became a Marxist-Leninist vanguard party dedicated to the pursuit of "scientific socialism" and world revolution, does not seek to pursue a neutral foreign policy. The MPLA firmly sides with what it calls the "socialist camp" in the global struggle against the forces of world capitalism.

Operating as the self-styled "vanguard of the proletariat," uniting workers, peasants, and intellectuals in a country overwhelmingly dependent on backward farmers, the party believes in the Leninist principle of "democratic centralism" and looks to the transformation of Angola into a socialist state. The MPLA's influence is weak among dissident ethnic groups such as the Bakongo in the north and the Ovimbundu in the south. By 1979, almost half of the Central Committee were military professionals.

In 1983, some 15,000–20,000 Cubans were deployed in Angola. Without Soviet and Cuban assistance, the MPLA would not rule in Angola. Without a feeling of complete Cuban security from U.S. threats (a feeling engendered by U.S. forbearance), Fidel Castro would not have dared to deploy so large a portion of his forces overseas.

Admittedly, the MPLA permits the Gulf Oil Company to operate on Angolan soil, but this is only common sense—a substantial portion of Angola's revenue comes from Gulf Oil's operations. Similarly, the Soviet Union and its allies have consistently asked for and received Western credits and infusions of technology and managerial expertise. That does not mean that they are not communist governments or that Angola would not, in time of international tension, stop selling oil to the West. The Soviet Union itself, however, considers these commercial relations instruments in the international class struggle, which they intend to win. Going beyond Lenin's predictions (in my opinion), capitalists now compete among themselves for the privilege of selling on easy credit terms the very rope by which they will be hanged.

In terms of international morality and civil rights, Angola's record has been deplorable. It is a police state complete with re-education centers and German-trained secret police. There is widespread persecution of practicing Christians; whites have fled or been forced to leave. The MPLA is a minority party that rules through terror and Cuban troops; it represents only one-third of the people. The other two-thirds are represented by the National Front for the Liberation of Angola (FNLA) and the National Union for the Total Independence of Angola (UNITA), which holds large parts of the country. Free speech, a free press, and the right to vote—the same freedoms that the United States sought to establish in Zimbabwe through international embargo—are absent in Angola.

There is yet no sign of improvement. Food shortages are everywhere; the Benguela Railway has not operated since 1975 because of guerrilla activities; and exports, except oil from Cabinda, have dwindled. Angola has joined the long list of countries whose bright hopes in a revolution have been dispelled by post-revolutionary reality. The United States should not recognize the MPLA as the legal government of Angola but should arm and train the FNLA and UNITA to force the

MPLA to form a coalition government. It should also encourage the Cubans, East Germans, and Soviets to return to their homelands.

While FRELIMO, which controls Mozambique, has maintained somewhat more independence from the Soviet Union than has the MPLA, it is still a self-proclaimed Marxist-Leninist party and is an admitted member (as is the MPLA) of the international Marxist-Leninist movement. The United States should encourage FRELIMO to leave the Soviet camp, to refuse all facility or base rights to the Soviets, and to practice a form of détente with South Africa.

Southern Africa

Southern Africa is the richest, most developed part of Africa and is of major strategic importance to the United States.[5] The states of Southern Africa (South Africa, Namibia, Botswana, Swaziland, Lesotho, Zimbabwe, Zambia, and Mozambique) are wedded into a state system dominated economically, politically, and militarily by South Africa. U.S. policy in Southern Africa has been ambivalent and inconsistent, alternating between cooperation with South Africa and support for black nationalism and attacks on apartheid.

In spite of the United States' vital interests in South Africa, it has hesitated to promote these interests by allying with South Africa. Washington saw the costs as too high in terms of black African and world opinion. Fundamentally, the United States has been, and is, committed to forcing reform in South Africa, ending apartheid, and gaining independence for Namibia.

The Carter administration initially supported human rights issues in order to win black support but then muted its criticism when it realized the United States needed Pretoria's cooperation to settle the Rhodesian (Zimbabwe) and Namibian issues peacefully.

After President Reagan was inaugurated in 1981, the State Department argued for further concessions to South Africa in order to end the stalemate in Namibia. Washington announced a new policy of "constructive engagement" that had both regional and global ramifications: it sought peace in Southern Africa and it sought to force the Cubans out of Angola.

Constructive engagement, according to an administration spokesman appearing before the Subcommittee on Africa of the House of Representatives in 1982, has as its objectives: (1) fostering movement toward a system of government by consent of the governed and away from the racial policy of apartheid and political disenfranchisement of blacks; (2) continued access to the strategic minerals on which the

United States and other members of the Organization for Economic Cooperation and Development are dependent; (3) assuring the strategic security of the Cape sea route, through which pass vital U.S. oil and mineral supplies from the Middle East and South Africa; and (4) regional security in Southern Africa against the Soviet-Cuban threat.

There are five components to the U.S. approach to the Southern African region: (1) internationally recognized independence for Namibia; (2) internationally supported programs of economic development in all the developing countries of the region; (3) negotiations to force the withdrawal of Cuban troops from Angola; (4) détente between South Africa and the other states of the region; and (5) peaceful evolutionary change in South Africa away from apartheid and toward a system of government based on consent of the governed.

The United States has also been negotiating bilaterally with South Africa on Namibian independence. The major new element in the negotiations is the requirement by both Washington and Pretoria of withdrawal of Cuban forces from Angola. The United States believes this is necessary to get South Africa to give up Namibia and to initiate constructive changes within South Africa itself away from apartheid. This reflects the new global outlook of the Reagan administration, which sees Cuba as an integral part of the Soviet drive for world dominance.

President Reagan has indicated that his administration regards apartheid as repugnant to basic American values, but that as long as South Africa appears to be attempting to move away from its racist system of government, the United States should be helpful and encouraging. Constructive engagement therefore is dependent on reform within South Africa and the attainment of internationally recognized independence for Namibia.

Constructive engagement has produced few positive results. In my view, Washington will be unable to continue its present policy in the face of severe African hostility without registering more success. It appears, therefore, that constructive engagement has worked no better than President Carter's human rights approach, at least as regards Namibia, which is no nearer independence than it was before.

In South Africa, in spite of some reforms and new openings to Indians and Coloureds, there has been no new legislation to end discrimination since 1980. Furthermore, South Africa has increasingly militarized its relations with all its neighbors and attacked these countries with impunity and excessive force since 1981. The world is witnessing the Israelization of Southern Africa. Unfortunately, constructive engagement has had limited success, as have previous diplomatic efforts to get South Africa to reform significantly.

African leaders increasingly condemn U.S. efforts on the grounds that they are ineffective or that the United States practices a form of closet collaboration with Pretoria. Yet alternative plans promise no solution either. The sad truth is that external pressure has failed and will continue to fail to produce reform until the internal conditions for change develop. Only Pretoria can help the United States continue its policy of constructive engagement by making bold domestic reforms, by cooperating on Namibian independence, and by stopping attacks on its neighbors. If this is not done, then we will see a new U.S. policy— either distancing itself (or even disengaging) from South Africa or returning to diplomatic harangues and increased sanctions.

The international campaign against South Africa has generated great pressures for change. It has helped awaken black consciousness and has revived the liberation struggle. There is no evidence that the anti-apartheid movement will lessen its pressure to isolate South Africa and to reduce the amount of assistance South Africa receives. While international opinion cannot force significant changes or defeat South Africa—only internal subversion and external assaults can do that—it can isolate South Africa, deny it goods and services, and thus raise the costs of continuing the apartheid system.

Unreformed, South Africa will never again command the friendly respect that it enjoyed in the United States when Prime Minister Jan Smuts was at the helm in Pretoria (1939–1948). The U.S. commitment to racial equality and to human rights is now too strong to tolerate apartheid. South Africa will have to make more significant reforms and share power with blacks, Indians, and Coloureds before Americans will accept an alliance—and this is true no matter how important the Cape route is, how much the West needs South Africa's strategic minerals, or how strong the Soviet-Cuban presence becomes. South Africa's anticommunism, or its value as a military base during wartime, will not prove sufficient to overcome hatred of apartheid during a time of peace.

The United States and Africa, Today and Tomorrow

The West cannot prevent Soviet aggressiveness but should attempt to contain it. The West's best option is to shore up key states, assisting them to develop economically and to govern themselves. For the 1980s, however, the picture looks gloomy and full of violence—ethnic, regional, and ideological—that will further involve rival foreign powers. Indeed, the superpowers could conceivably join in a local conflict in Africa.

The Afro-Marxist and the military dictatorships will probably be economically worse off by 1990 than they were in 1980. The condition of the masses in many states in all likelihood will deteriorate steadily. African states have long been allied with other Third World countries in seeking to establish the New International Economic Order, which would radically alter the balance between rich nations (called, somewhat inexactly, "the North") and the multitude of poorer ones ("the South"). In 1974, they joined in pushing through the United Nations a resolution committing it to this new order. What the Third World countries want is "to alter their aid, trade, and investment relations with the industrialized countries of the North and gain for themselves a greater voice in the management of international, economic, and political affairs."[6] These goals are supposed to be achieved through preferential trade agreements, a fund to secure international commodity agreements, better access to industrial technology, and increases in aid.

The new order, however, has few prospects of success. Africa's major hope for development lies not only in industrialization, but above all in improved agriculture. If agricultural output is not increased, many states will experience further food shortages. The present African governments often support inefficient, high-cost, import-substitution industries; that is, local manufactures to take the place of foreign goods. Africa suffers from a fundamental and irrevocable scarcity of resources—from poor soils and a difficult climate. Yet black governments face heavy demands from their citizens for more material welfare. Too many of these governments insist on trying to do more, but they achieve little except further restriction of private enterprise and initiative due to their lack of trained, skilled, and dedicated personnel.

A self-reliant approach to development will work better than the present African form of socialism, which is heavily dependent on foreign aid. Self-reliance would mean accepting more realistic goals and a slower pace of development. An increased emphasis on private enterprise operating within a market economy would also make African politics less risky and violent. Ethnic rivalry for control of the state might diminish when the state is no longer seen, as it is currently, as the primary source of power, privilege, profits, and perquisites. A strategy of self-reliance would also encourage individuals in the pursuit of their own best interests. (The Ivory Coast, for example, relies mainly on private enterprise. Its economic performance far surpasses that of neighboring Guinea, which has placed its trust in a quasi-socialist economy.)

In all likelihood, however, the traditional approach of seeking foreign handouts while embracing state socialism will persist through the 1980s, resulting in slow and unbalanced economic growth or stagnation. The North is unlikely to give significantly more aid than it has given in the past; the South, unlike OPEC, has no means or strategy with which it can force additional concessions from the industrialized countries. The West will probably continue through the 1980s to provide cooperation and economic assistance. The Soviet Union gives primarily military aid, not economic assistance; for instance, the Soviets have done nothing to combat the widespread famine in Ethiopia, which looks to the West for shipments of food. Bilateral agreements with the United States and the EEC thus offer the most promise for Africa.

What of the future? The United States has been overly inclined to shape its foreign policy in Africa to win the approval of the Third World—the so-called uncommitted nations of Asia and Africa that supposedly will hold the world balance of power in the future. This view neglects the military realities of power and looks on the present struggle for world supremacy as an ideological beauty competition between East and West, a competition in which the panel of judges is made up of Asians and Africans. Nations are indeed influenced by ideas, but economic and strategic factors play an even larger part in world affairs. It is doubtful that the West would be justified in subordinating its interests to the real or imagined demands of neutralists. It is, in fact, only the strength of the West that has made it possible for Afro-Asian countries to afford the luxury of neutralism. Once the West weakens, these countries will be imperiled.

There can be no simple rule of thumb for U.S. foreign policy toward Africa as a whole. There are many African countries, and the United States needs many different African policies. The United States needs to be flexible and realistic and to avoid the view that U.S. policy must always be ideologically acceptable to others. Political and economic warfare against South Africa would not liberalize that republic or improve the lot of its black people. The United States should seek to cooperate with a reform-minded Pretoria insofar as collaboration is in its strategic interest. The West should seek to support moderate forms of government in Namibia rather than aid its declared enemies. Similarly, it should consider recognition of Angola only after all foreign troops—Cuban and East German—and Soviet military experts have left. This would force the MPLA to form a coalition government with the two guerrilla organizations that now oppose it from the bush. Such a withdrawal should be a necessary condition for diplomatic relations with the United States.

In a more general sense, the United States must become more realistic in the conduct of its African affairs and make it clear to African governments that certain of their policies are not in the best interests of the West. The United States will have to take sides on issues, not simply always back blacks against whites or radicals against conservatives.[7]

The West has yet to develop a coherent policy toward African development and security problems. The United States needs to focus its aid to shape events in countries that receive it; the United States should also aid countries directly rather than funnel funds through international bodies. Arms and security programs should be instruments of U.S. diplomacy in Africa. The Reagan administration has wisely revived the military assistance program.

The United States therefore must reinvigorate its African policy by devoting more aid and military assistance to Africa.[8] It should denounce Soviet-Cuban involvement in Africa for the instability it has caused, respond positively to requests for security assistance when the states requesting it act in their own and the United States' interests, praise the French for maintaining regional security, and do likewise. The United States must point out to the African nations that it is also in their interest to discourage Soviet domination and to develop policies that promote peace and economic development. In this way it can unequivocally demonstrate that the United States has common—not divisive—interests with Africa as a continent and with African states as independent governments.

Notes

1. Oye Ogunbadejo, "Soviet Policies in Africa," research paper (Ife, Nigeria: University of Ife, 1979), p. 40.

2. For an analysis of this issue, see F. Roy Willis, *The French Paradox: Understanding Contemporary France* (Stanford: Hoover Institution Press, 1982), chap. 4.

3. Thomas H. Henriksen, ed., *Communist Powers and Sub-Saharan Africa* (Stanford: Hoover Institution Press, 1981).

4. For detailed analyses of these areas, see L. H. Gann and Peter Duignan, *Africa*

South of the Sahara: The Challenge to Western Security (Stanford: Hoover Institution Press, 1981), *passim*.

5. On Southern Africa, see L. H. Gann and Peter Duignan, *Why South Africa Will Survive* (New York: St. Martin's Press, 1981).

6. For more extensive coverage of these issues, see Colin Legum, I. William Zartman, Steven Langdon, and Lynn K. Mytelka, eds., *Africa in the 1980s: A Continent in Crisis*, Council on Foreign Relations, 1980s Project (New York: McGraw-Hill, 1979).

7. Ibid., p. 13.

8. For an excellent analysis, see Chester A. Crocker and William H. Lewis, "Missing Opportunities in Africa," *Foreign Policy* 35 (Summer 1979): 142–61.

13
Soviet Foreign Policy

Robert Conquest

I

An understanding of the true nature of Soviet foreign policy is clearly central to our understanding of the world today. Yet there is no real agreement even about its most basic motivations among our public and our politicians.

We are all prone to parochial misconceptions about the deepest motivations underlying other political cultures. It requires a constant effort of the intellect and of the imagination to free us from the habit of making such unconscious assumptions about the present thoughts and future actions of the Soviet leaders. Western policymakers have often failed to grasp these basic differences, which are not so much of opinion as of motivation. In the USSR the present Marxist-Leninist ruling elements are actually unable to see the world in terms other than their own. It is not so much a matter of arguable beliefs, as of what is, by their whole experience, soaked into their bones.

We are all the products of our historical, social, and political origins; and theirs, quite alien to ours, are to be found first in the entire Russian background, but even more in the specific Leninist political and ideological experience. The ruling elite are the products of centuries of history, of personal and collective experiences, of indoctrination, and of psychological suitability to surviving those experiences and accepting that indoctrination.

First of all, at least since the fourteenth century, the whole of Russian history evolved on lines very different from those of the West. Even our "feudalism" was a matter of rights as well as obligations: in theirs only the rulers had rights and, in the words of the great Russian historian Klyuchevsky, "The State swelled up; the people shrank." Though there were other currents, the overwhelmingly dominant tradition has been that of the autocracy, bureaucracy, and serfdom of Central Russia.

The Russian revolutionary tradition was itself within the old despotic tradition. From the 1820s, revolutionaries spoke not of democracy or liberty, but of dictatorship to establish utopia. And even among the revolutionary sects, Lenin's Bolsheviks were noted for their extreme centralization, extreme ruthlessness, and extreme narrowness of mind. In 1912 they numbered less than 10,000 members; five years later they were in power. A very thin slice of the political spectrum had imposed its rule by force.

In Stalin's purges in the 1930s this thin slice of political Russia was sliced ten times thinner. Any remaining signs of humanism or the critical faculty were stamped out as half the already Stalinized party went to the execution cellars and the labor camps.

In addition to extravagant bloodletting, a major characteristic of the Purge was falsification and secrecy, what Pasternak called "the inhuman power of the lie." Among its products was the silencing, the atomizing of society. It was this atomization that left in Russia only one effective social mechanism: the Stalin apparat. And this was now thoroughly cleansed of the "critical" element and had become a complete, even instinctive, servant of despotism. In this aspect, the purges may be seen as destroying that part of the Party which Western attitudes had affected. The present Soviet leadership is derived from social strata which were never influenced by Europeanization.

Moreover the members of the present Politburo, both old and young, owe their careers to the Terror, when official statements formally decreed that all who did not adequately denounce others were themselves among the guilty.

The new Stalinist institutions were based on these principles and manned by these characters—possessed, by our standards, of an enormously odd and aberrant set of attitudes and motivations.

Such are the political and psychological origins of the generation that now rules the USSR. Over the years they recruited like-minded younger men as their aides. Even now, of the 40 top leaders only five had not taken their first step up the political ladder in Stalin's time— and only two of the dominating Politburo (six of them had been

Stalin's personal selection for his Central Committee). Even among the provincial secretaries, from whom a new generation of leaders traditionally comes, two-thirds were on their way up before the old dictator's death.

The principles with which the teaching of the Communist Party and their own experience equipped them may, for our purposes, be defined under four headings.

First, it is a way of seeing the world which is in the very strictest sense dogmatic; that is, it accepts the idea that a final world philosophy, political philosophy, and theory of society have been devised; and that the nature of the perfect human order which will prevail throughout the future is known and can be realized by theoretically prescribed methods. That is, it is a closed system of thought, and one which, being "true" in contrast to the falsehood of all others, implies a closed society. As a result, in Solzhenitsyn's words, "The primitive refusal to compromise is elevated into a theoretical principle and is regarded as the pinnacle of orthodoxy."

Second, this way of thinking implies that the political leaders, and political considerations generally, are on a higher and more comprehensive plane than all other elements in society and are empowered to make the final decision in all fields.

Third, it is based on a view of history, and of the world in general, that sees struggles and clashes as the only essential mode of political or any other action—on Lenin's principle *Kto–kogo?*—who–whom?—that is, that everything is struggle, in which there is a winner and a loser. And long practice in putting this principle into operation has generated an attitude so deeply ingrained as to be almost automatic.

Fourth, the dogma's claim is universal, applicable to the whole world. All other political orders—even "communist" ones which deviate in any significant way from that of the USSR (for example, Dubcek's Czechoslovakia or Mao's China)—are in principle illegitimate and should be destroyed when tactically convenient, just as deviant political or other views within the USSR are subject in principle to total suppression.

Such are the foundations, both theoretical and instinctual, of Soviet foreign policy.

II

Soviet foreign policy is in principle "forward," in accordance with the Leninist notions of "who–whom." a typical formulation, in the official *The Foreign Policy of the Soviet Union* (Moscow, 1979), is as follows:

> The Communist Party subordinates all its theoretical and practical activity in the sphere of international relations to the task of strengthening the positions of socialism, and the interests of further developing and deepening the world revolutionary process. Directed towards strengthening peace and the security of the peoples, imbued with a spirit of solidarity with revolutionary, progressive forces throughout the world, Soviet foreign policy constitutes one of the chief factors of the class struggle in the international arena.

"Class struggle in the international arena" means, of course, the struggle between the Soviet and pro-Soviet elements and the adherents of the Western and other political systems.

About 1965, a decision seems to have been made in the Kremlin to take on the West in armaments and on a world scale.

The expression "offensive against the positions of Imperialism" now began to appear regularly in the Soviet press. The first use of it seems to have been by Brezhnev in an address to the Congress of the Romanian Communist party on July 20, 1965, when he noted that "some years ago" the communist parties had already concluded that the relation of forces had shifted in their favor, and that in the meantime this had reached such a stage that "the progressive forces are now on the offensive." The call for this "offensive" was formalized in the manifesto of the communist parties in November (*Pravda*, November 28, 1965).

But the USSR, and the whole Soviet bloc, was economically far weaker than the United States and the West. Moreover, the Soviet economy was also, and permanently, years behind in technology. On any analysis, but especially a Marxist one, the case was hopeless.

The Kremlin decision was for steps to be taken to ensure that the West be persuaded not to translate its economic and technological superiority into military power.

So one of the major aspects of Soviet foreign policy has been, and is, the conduct of a campaign aimed at the public and the politicians of the Western countries, with the aim of weakening Western military strength and political determination.

Brezhnev and other Soviet leaders frequently warned that no form of détente with the West must in any way moderate the ideological struggle. As Walter Laqueur, director of the Institute of Contemporary History, notes, in the West

> Soviet insistence on the continuation of the ideological struggle is all too often not taken seriously; because the idea is alien to Western thought, people are inclined to think that Soviet pronouncements are merely a matter of lip-service to doctrine. In fact, however, "ideological struggle" is not something which concerns the philosophers. It is a synonym for political struggle, and political struggle, needless to say, means power, not only the power of ideas, but also some far more tangible things.

The method by which the Western mind was influenced included the avoidance of the more extreme acts of repression against the Soviet dissidents, who (as they unanimously agree) had no other defense than Western opinion. It included a certain superficial camouflage of Soviet expansionism. And it included negotiations for an asymmetrical reduction in those armaments in which the West had hitherto enjoyed superiority.

These measures were all put through at the minimum level thought adequate to persuade the West, or rather a sufficiency of people and politicians in the West, that there were serious prospects of the USSR's accepting a cooperative role in the world community.

As a result, Gromyko was already able to claim in his June 1968 speech to the Supreme Soviet that "during any acute situation *however far away* [my italics] it seems from our country, the Soviet Union's reaction is to be expected in all capitals of the world"; and to upgrade this, in his speech to the Party Congress in 1971, to "today there is no question of any significance which can be decided without the Soviet Union or in opposition to it"—yet such a claim by the West, in connection with Poland for example, is hotly rejected as grossly illegitimate.

The success, or even the partial success, of such a policy implied the presence in the West of politically powerful elements susceptible to a fairly crude form of deception—above all about the historical imperatives which dictate Soviet policy.

A delusive picture of Soviet attitudes is fairly common nowadays even among those who particularly concern themselves with the study of Soviet matters; or rather, this is the case in the United States, though very rare among their British and French equivalents. It seems to be due to several causes. First, parochialism—the assumption, often unconscious, that others are not very different from ourselves, or are bound to become increasingly like us (as though the Western culture were a norm to which all others naturally drift if not otherwise prevented). Second, the supposed systematic knowledge given by "political science" of a certain type, by which abstract political systems are substituted for the real and individual Soviet Union, or it is treated on the international scene as no more than another Great Power in a chess player's symmetry with the United States. Third, one should not perhaps underestimate the power of mere wishful thinking, however sophisticatedly expressed: for the reality of the Soviet presence on the world scene is highly unpalatable to anyone wishing for a reasonably cooperative international order. Fourth, in some cases at any rate, one seems to find the equivalent of Albert Camus' comment about Frenchmen who took an unrealistically favorable view of the Soviet Union, "It is not so much that they like the Russians as that they heartily detest part of the French": that is to say, factious hostility to one's own government or culture induces tempering of the wind to the unshorn wolf outside.

Such were the bases, or some of the bases, for the Soviet "political warfare" effort against and within the West, without which the rest of the Soviet program would have been abortive, and which continues to be one of the main elements of Soviet foreign policy.

III

The effectiveness of Soviet action in the "political warfare" field is, of course, greatly increased by the minimal possibilities given to the West to contest the ideological struggle in the USSR itself. Professor Robert F. Byrnes has noted, as an important element in the domestic foundation of Soviet foreign policy, that

> ... the ignorance to be found among even educated citizens of Moscow of events within the Soviet Union and of Soviet policy elsewhere is overwhelming, and constitutes, again, a chronic handicap to the Soviet government. No Soviet citizen I met was at all well informed about the Soviet budget, the size of the Soviet armed forces, the number of Soviet troops in various Eastern European countries and the problems those countries face, or about Soviet policies with regard to SALT, the Middle East, Africa, or the other areas of critical concern throughout the world. Indeed, the misinformation poured upon the Soviet people by all the media makes one yearn for old-fashioned ignorance. [*Survey*, vol. 23, no. 4.]

This "internal front" is nevertheless a crucial element in Soviet foreign policy. For it is easy enough to see that if a "siege mentality" prevails in a given major power, this in itself is enough to produce a state of continued international tension and a danger of war. The view taken in Europe, leading eventually to the Helsinki Agreement, was that the way to get such a mentality to develop into something more peaceable was by the beginnings (gradual as they might be) of a freer movement of people and ideas.

As a result, on August 1, 1975, the United States and its European allies, the neutral European states, and the Soviet Union and its allies, signed the Final Act of the Helsinki Conference "to improve and intensify their relations and to contribute in Europe to peace, security, justice and co-operation as well as to rapprochement among themselves and with other States of the world . . ." The signatories committed themselves to the view that respect for human rights and fundamental freedoms "is an essential factor for the peace, justice and well-being necessary to ensure the development of friendly relations and co-operation among themselves as among all States."

This was in fact a serious attempt to go to the real sources of tension. We and our allies were by no means insisting on instant changes. The agreement was in terms of "gradually to simplify and to administer flexibly the procedure for exit and entry," "to ease regulations," "gradually to lower," "gradually to increase." In fact there has been no sign of even the most modest improvement in the USSR, let alone, for example, such things as "improvement of the dissemination, on their territory, of newspapers and printed publications, periodical and nonperiodical, from the other participating states." Does this mean that, having failed to secure fulfillment ("solemnly" guaranteed) of their undertakings in this field, we should now abandon the idea?

The human rights issue is central, on any but a very short view, to our relations with the Soviet Union. When all is said, the basic motivations of the government which disposes of the largest armaments in the world, and has shown itself consistently hostile in principle to all that we stand for, are the basic element of the problem. When the Soviet Union represses democrats, Christians, and others, it is not only our sympathies that are engaged, but our interests too. For the way in which the Kremlin treats those advancing Western ideas when they are in its power—that is within the Soviet Union—is a wholly clear indication of the way in which they would treat the rest of us if they had the opportunity. That is, the "ideological" warfare against bearers of Western ideas inside the USSR is one and the same as its campaign against the West.

IV

The actual ideology of Marxism-Leninism itself constitutes an important element in the projection of Soviet foreign policy aims.

It is true that Marxism is dead among thinking minds in the Soviet empire itself, moribund in France, aging in the rest of Western Europe, and only to be found in the other advanced countries in the lower levels of an insulated academe. In the more vulnerable targets of Soviet policy, among immature intelligentsias seeking (like the Russian intelligentsia before them) utopias with which to replace repressive or imperfect regimes in the local tradition, the appeal is far greater—providing, moreover, a supposed recipe for a new order (with themselves in charge) which will bring their countries to modern levels in double-quick time.

More important yet, this is combined with the notion of the Leninist-style party: the monolithic machine devised organizationally and ideologically to fight on regardless of losses or qualms until the taking of power; and the monopoly of power and its perquisites thereafter. Moreover, while fifty years ago the more backward countries looked to Western democracy as the advanced system, Leninism has provided the most archaic despotic attitudes with a cloak of "modernity."

This has served the Kremlin well, particularly in areas where it was able to exert direct organizational influence—as, through the totally pro-Soviet Portuguese Communist Party, on the small and inchoate group of intellectuals who came to form the present regime in Angola, or through the indoctrination of a handful of semiliterate officers in Ethiopia.

Training in organizational tactics has, of course, been backed up by actual military and paramilitary training, on a secret basis, in the USSR, Czechoslovakia, Bulgaria, and North Korea, a further major element of Soviet strength in countries where other political tendencies have less experience in such matters.

V

A major aspect of Soviet foreign policy is to be found in the enormous, disproportionate investment in arms which constitutes the material basis of Soviet expansion and the main crux of Soviet-Western relations and negotiations. To put it briefly, the USSR—a poorer country, with far smaller margins—invests in armaments approximately double the proportion of its gross national product that is done by the United States or any other Western country. Moreover, owing to military pay rates and other factors, the USSR is able to obtain from this a much higher proportional effective result than is possible in the West. (So that the argument about armament investment in monetary terms—themselves often misunderstood—is to a large degree a red herring: the important thing is to compare the actual armies and armaments, not what they supposedly "cost.")

The creation or rather the maintenance and extension of vast armed forces is, in fact, one of the main concerns of Soviet foreign policy. As the Head of the Army's Political Department, A. A. Epishev (Deputy Secret Police Minister under Stalin), has said: "Socialism's military might objectively assists the successful development of the revolutionary liberation movements."

The immense investment in arms is, of course, a *product* of Soviet basic attitudes, rather than a causative element in itself. It may nevertheless be noted that such military programs have their own momentum. The huge resources put into the blue-water fleet could not easily be diverted into other channels (under Soviet conditions far less easily than the fairly smooth change in postwar America or Britain in the mid-1940s, which had no parallel in the USSR).

But more important is the mistaken notion of an "arms race," in the sense that the Soviet armament drive is thought by certain commentators in the West to be related to the occasional bursts of rearmament which have been undertaken by the United States and its allies, first at the time of the Korean War, then as a result of the Cuban crisis, and finally at the present time.

In fact the gross Soviet arms effort has, since the late 1940s, proceeded at the maximum feasible rate, only varying a little through different Politburo views of internal economic and social constraints, but not at all in reaction to the ups and downs of Western military investment.

This armament, needless to say, constitutes a key element in the whole Soviet ability to project their power throughout the world.

VI

When it comes to the particular actions open to the Soviet Union, these will, of course, depend upon unforeseeable events in the various areas of the world. Certain probable trends may, however, be adumbrated.

In areas where the West is vulnerable, a forward policy of advance and consolidation is likely.

Among these is Central America and the Caribbean. It is true that, from a purely military point of view, the USSR and its allies are at an apparent disadvantage. However, since important political and public opinion in the United States tends largely to nullify the objective American advantages, the prospects may yet be promising for the extension of the Soviet *place d'armes* in the area.

In Southern Africa prospects of peaceful interracial settlement, which once looked good in Namibia and Zimbabwe, are now very poor. Thus, the prospect is of the gradual buildup of a guerrilla war against the South African regime—even if some sort of settlement is achieved after all in Namibia. Though Angola is under reasonably close Soviet control, Zimbabwe and Mozambique are not. Nevertheless their leaderships are, from the Soviet point of view, reasonably proof against moderation. At the same time, in South Africa itself, the main body of black opinion may still be moderate, but the (entirely Soviet-oriented) Communist Party of South Africa's power over the African National Congress clearly provides very strong leverage for initiating a guerrilla war, while the speed of change in the white Nationalist government, which might have had results in different circumstances, appears quite inadequate as things are.

We are therefore likely to see a steady and careful buildup of a belt of guerrilla fighting right across the continent, which may (as in the Zimbabwe case) take some years to become really effective; and which on a purely military view will have small chance of real success in the foreseeable future; but which with Soviet control over at least part of the movement, and of part of their base area states, will put Moscow in a strong position locally, and on the international scale will win popularity in the Third World, and present the West with a choice of rather unsatisfactory options.

In Europe, the main handicap Moscow has to take into account is the presence of American troops and missiles, and the evident intention of both American parties to honor their commitment to European defense. Except in the extreme case of a general collapse of the American position elsewhere, and of American morale at home, there would be little advantage for the Soviets in a military attack. As they have been doing for the past forty years, they must continue to use their weaponry to bring political pressure on the European allies and encourage all movements tending to disrupt or disarm the West. Any Soviet political progress depends, therefore, on matters they can influence but which are outside their direct control, and their resource is to keep up the pressures and hope for political advantage. It should be added that Western European tendencies to accommodate them are heavily dependent on whether or not they are able to maintain their position in Eastern Europe without major clashes with the local populations.

In the Middle East, the position is so complicated and unpredictable that present Soviet intention seems to be to await events, while supporting their few remaining clients to the best of their ability.

That this area is, in principle, one of the main traditional targets of Russian expansion is, of course, true—"the direction of the Persian Gulf" was specifically claimed by the USSR in the negotiations with Hitler in 1940. Moreover, though there are elements in the Soviet land forces which seem to regard the new-style overseas adventures as beyond the country's real interests, all military and political trends are united in favoring a forward Middle East policy. And the attraction of controlling an important part of the Western fuel necessities need hardly be stressed.

The arguments against too aggressive a policy in the area are, however, of some force. First, the comparative lack of success of, and the investment of military resources in, the Afghan operation. Second, the apparent, or possible, firmness of the West, and in particular the United States, in the defense of its interests in the area, as compared with its political weakness in Central America and Southern Africa (though a Soviet planner could indeed note that political weakness in areas where American military strength can easily be brought to bear, and political firmness in an area where it is difficult for the United States to act, is a prescription ideally suited to Soviet interests). But third, there is the unpredictability of the whole area. So that, with all the belief in, and planning for, a future Soviet preponderance from the Caucasus to the Horn of Africa, there are reasons (for the time being at least) for fairly careful Soviet conduct.

In the Far East, the maintenance of the Soviet political and military base in Indochina must be the primary object of immediate concern. But more fundamentally, the problem is to neutralize Mainland China as an anti-Soviet force and to prevent the military re-emergence of Japan. With Japan, the only feasible tactics at present are the same as those being used against Western Europe—a combination of implicit threats with soothing assurance. With China there are two possibilities—reconciliation with or overthrow of the Chinese communist regime. Both have been considered—and as to the latter, the Soviet Union seems twice in the past twenty years to have been close to considering armed attack on the People's Republic—which, apart from the inevitable disastrously adverse effects in the world at large, might probably have been undertaken. Moreover, though the Soviet General Staff seems confident of a successful blitzkrieg taking over northern China, further prospects seem to have been less promising; and after the Afghan experience may be less attractive yet. At the same time, any true reconciliation seems excluded by the Soviet principle that all "socialist" states must accept the Soviet model or be in heresy and schism, and by the Chinese understanding (often more clear-minded than that of Westerners) of Soviet aims. The best Moscow can hope for is probably an easing of tension.

These brief sketches of the general possibilities in various regions can go no further than suggest the main thrust of Soviet tactics, given the current position and likely developments. An important addendum must be that Soviet policy, though consistently expansionist in principle, seeks targets of opportunity as they present themselves, and only a prophet could predict precisely what crisis will arise, and where, which might provide them with an entry.

VII

If we are to sum up, we might first go back to late 1946, when the then Secretary of State, James F. Byrnes, had to announce to a high staff meeting of the State Department that the immediate postwar policies of the United States of trying to placate the Soviet Union had proved futile, that its hostility and obduracy were inherent, and that the United States must recognize that it had a long-term adversary to cope with. What has changed since then? Many things, but not Soviet long-term intentions.

From the point of view of the West, it is true, as Engels commented of an earlier time, that "as soon as Russia has an internal development, and with that, internal party struggles, the attainment of a constitutional form under which these party struggles may be fought without violent convulsions . . . the traditional Russian policy of conquest is a thing of the past"—and that is not yet. In the meantime, various evolutions and revolutions are possible. But for the immediate future Russia is stuck with a group of rulers who are faced by a society tending in every respect away from their concepts, but who are in possession of an immensely powerful instrument for blocking social and political change. In foreign affairs we have the unpleasant problem of an inept Soviet oligarchy, with huge military resources, answerable to none and possessed of a surly hostility to all other forms of political life.

It is sometimes said that the Soviet order has already changed in an absolutely essential fashion: that it is no longer the vehicle of an irreconcilable Leninist dogma. If this were true, it would be of great importance. To accept it as true if it were not true, on the other hand, would mean that we were basing our foreign policy on a major fallacy. One would think, therefore, that those who believe that such a change has taken place would offer evidence of some sort that this has indeed occurred.

Such evidence might include showing that the state and party institutions which are the vehicle of the Leninist dictatorship have changed. Here we are on safe ground: no such change has taken place. Then it might be shown that there was a tendency to pluralism in the thought of the Soviet rulers, and hence to tolerance of other ideas: no sign of such a change has appeared, either in the conduct of the Soviet rulers towards unorthodox ideas within the Soviet Union or in their attitudes to political and other views they regard as heretical or wrong in the outside world. Finally, a tendency to reconciliation with other orders might be expected to manifest itself in the acceptance of a lower level of armament than that now in being and the avoidance of a "forward" foreign policy in various parts of the world: this too does not sound like a very reliable description of what is actually going on.

The central problem for Moscow seems to be this: the maintenance of the present political system will mean the gradual deterioration of the USSR into second-class power. In principle, the rulers must either accept this or change their system. Neither option seems plausible. But a third possibility remains—to embark on an expansionist foreign policy. This seems to have been the choice made in the mid-sixties, with the enormous investment not so much in the strategic missile force, which could according to certain arguments be considered a necessary match for that of the United States, but also in a huge navy, whose sole role is to export Soviet influence and apply Soviet pressure in hitherto virgin territory.

The sensible choice, *from a Western point of view,* would have been to make some attempt to modernize the political and economic system, to introduce the principle of consensual pluralism. The pressures pushing the Kremlin in this direction are obviously powerful, but, as things are at present, not nearly as powerful as the built-in strength and inertia of the Party machine and the Party mind. Until the third path, that of expansion, is blocked, there is little question of even the beginnings of the evolution of the USSR into a peaceful inhabitant, in principle, of a world community.

The evolution of the Soviet state into something approaching true civic culture is not a short-term prospect. But, let us repeat, if the West pursues the correct policies, it should be the single direction that lies open. And such an evolution is essential in the long run if world peace is to be maintained and a cooperative world order is to be created.

Above all, the representatives of the West must constantly bear in mind that it is impossible to conduct a sensible foreign policy if one makes baseless assumptions about the most profound motivations of the other political cultures and psychologies that at present share the globe with our own. Such misunderstandings are endemic in circles in the West concerned with international politics or with instructing the public mind about their nature. This is a situation which it is hardly enough to call unsatisfactory: it is potentially disastrous. Alexander Herzen wrote over a century ago: "Let Europe know her neighbor. So far she only fears him. Let her find out what it is she fears."

14

Soviet Military Power

H. Joachim Maître

Rarely in history has a nation so passively accepted such a radical change in the military balance. If we are to remedy it, we must first recognize the fact that we have placed ourselves at a significant disadvantage voluntarily. Henry Kissinger[1]

The restoration of strategic parity is only possible by investing large resources and by an essential change in the psychological atmosphere in the West. There must be a readiness to make certain limited economic sacrifices and, most important, an understanding of the seriousness of the situation . . . When examining the general trend of events since 1945 there has been a relentless expansion of the Soviet sphere of influence. Andrei Sakharov[2]

The U.S.S.R. wishes to live in peace with all countries, including the United States. It does not nurture aggressive plans, does not impose the arms race on anyone, does not impose its social order on anyone . . . The Soviet Union will continue to do everything possible to uphold peace on earth.
Yuri Andropov[3]

For the first time in postwar history, at the Strategic Arms Reduction Talks (START) and the Euromissile talks with the Soviet Union, the United States is negotiating from a position of acute weakness. At the Intermediate-range Nuclear Forces (INF) negotiations, in particular, the Soviet government has insisted that the United States not be allowed to modernize NATO's nuclear forces and in fact is claiming veto power over NATO armament. The West is paying the price for two decades of its own unilateral restraint, during which it responded to the Soviet arms buildup with its own arms build-down. The challenge confronting the West, the world's leading economic center, is to rebuild its military forces or risk eventual defeat at the hands of the Soviet Union, a second-rate economic power.

By the end of the Carter administration, the Soviet Union had established a decisive lead over the United States as a military power, having surpassed the United States in all measures of nuclear armaments, except numbers of warheads. After more than a decade of efforts by Washington to achieve an effective agreement on strategic arms control, Moscow had upgraded and enlarged its nuclear arsenal from a position of inferiority to one of superiority. By 1980, the Soviet Union possessed roughly 40 percent more strategic missiles than the United States. Since then the lead has widened in both numbers and throw-weights (payloads). The Soviet SS-18 intercontinental ballistic missile (ICBM) has a throw-weight ten times that of the U.S. Minuteman ICBM. The SS-18's 25-megaton warhead has 2,000 times the destructive power of the Hiroshima bomb.[4] Today, the Soviet Union could destroy 90 percent of American ICBMs in a first-strike strategic assault with only one-fifth to one-third of its own ICBMs.[5]

No record of the Soviet Union's strategic arms buildup over the past twenty years could be complete without taking into account the analytic and prophetic talents of then secretary of defense Robert S. McNamara, who in 1965 urged American restraint: "The Soviets have decided that they have lost the quantitative race . . . there is no indication that the Soviets are seeking to develop a strategic nuclear force as large as ours."[6]

The Soviet buildup of land-based strategic forces during the 1960s and 1970s was complemented by similar efforts and achievements in sea-based strategic forces and nuclear and conventional naval forces. By early 1980, the United States had lost its traditional superiority in naval power over the Soviet Union, which now has the world's largest and most modern surface navy, the largest fleet of attack submarines, and the largest fleet of strategic submarines equipped with ballistic missiles. For the first time in naval history, the Red Navy is deploying aircraft carriers in two oceans and is expected to launch its first nuclear-powered full-size attack carrier in 1984, thus acquiring the capacity necessary for projecting Soviet naval power globally.

During the crucial years of Soviet naval buildup from 1968 to 1980, the U.S. Navy was forced to halve its number of ships, from roughly 1,000 units to 453; "the Soviets built, we mothballed."[7] The American build-down was exacerbated by the self-destruction of the Canadian Navy under the auspices of Prime Minister Pierre Trudeau. According to a 1983 parliamentary committee report, Canada's navy, once the world's third largest, now cannot defend Canada's coastline or fulfill other commitments to NATO.[8]

Yet the Soviet buildup most directly affecting U.S. ties to Western Europe—and designed to split NATO—occurred in intermediate-range nuclear weapons and short-range (battlefield) nuclear forces. By 1983, the Soviet Union had in service 351 SS-20 reloadable launchers and 39 rocket regiments. The Soviet Union's new SS-21 short-range missile, produced at the rate of four per month, is adding to the massive threat facing NATO in Central Europe. Yet, despite the overwhelming USSR nuclear arsenals, which threaten to dismantle NATO politically, McNamara, a notorious strategist of failure, still recommends to a Western world under Soviet siege that nuclear weapons—serving "no military purpose whatsoever"—should not remain an element of NATO defense and that NATO should not even use them in response to a nuclear attack.[9]

Encouraged by such advocates of unilateral disarmament in the West, the Soviet Union continues the buildup of its military machine. New generations of strategic bombers, submarines, and ground-, sea-, and air-launched cruise missiles will augment Soviet strategic options in 1984 and thereafter. Despite grave economic problems, the Soviet Union continues to allocate an estimated 15 percent of its GNP to the military buildup.[10] Is all of this "to uphold peace on earth"?

A realistic assessment of Moscow's arms policies is the first step toward organizing a coherent defense, but we must realize from the beginning that the buildup of arms and arms doctrines is a consequence, and not a cause, of particular state policies. The nature of the state and the ambitions of its rulers determine the direction and pace of armament, the kinds and numbers of weapons, and military tactics. The Soviet Union is no exception to this universal rule, although the very existence of the Soviet Union depends on armed force to an exceptional degree.

According to Mao Zedong, Marxist-Leninist theoretician and accomplished practitioner of totalitarian power, political power grows out of the barrel of a gun. No Soviet leader has contradicted Chairman Mao's dictum. On the contrary, Soviet-style communism since World

War II—aside from relying on brute force solely for its continued rule at home—has rigorously pursued policies of armed conquest and oppression abroad. In addition, the Soviets have systematically violated international conventions and treaties that they have signed. Their actions offer an objective measure by which to judge actual Soviet intentions.

1. The Red Army was used to quell yearnings for freedom and to prevent political change in East Germany (1953), in Hungary (1956), and in Czechoslovakia (1968).

2. In 1979, the Red Army invaded Afghanistan, where 120,000 Soviet troops remain as an occupation force.

3. Through the 1970s, the Soviets instigated violence and armed uprisings in Angola, Mozambique, and Ethiopia, thereafter using Cuban proxies to keep oppressive Marxist regimes in power.

4. The Soviets are stoking unrest and armed insurrection in Central America, and they continue to provide materiel support for a massive military buildup in Nicaragua.

5. The Soviet Union forced the suspension of Solidarity and imposed martial law in Poland.

6. The Soviet Union continues to violate the 1974 Threshold Test Ban Treaty by exploding underground nuclear weapons with yields in excess of 150 kilotons.

7. The Soviet Union is violating and circumventing provisions of the 1972 Anti-Ballistic Missile Treaty, thus gaining advantages in missile defense capabilities.

8. In the 1960s and early 1970s, the Soviet Union masterminded, financed, and fueled North Vietnam's armed aggression into South Vietnam, Laos, and Cambodia and supports North Vietnamese rule in neighboring countries and encourages subversion in Thailand and Malaysia.

9. Since the mid-1960s, the Soviet Union has embarked on a massive military buildup and has achieved superiority in strategic and conventional forces.

Between 1945 and 1983, the worldwide geostrategic balance has been profoundly altered to the detriment of the free world. At the end of World War II, the United States was sole owner of the atomic bomb and the world's only superpower, with the USSR a distant challenger.

When NATO was founded in 1949 in response to the aggressive and expansionist foreign policy of the Soviet Union, the United States was not only the undisputed leader of the West, but was also uncontested as a world power. Its might was based on three solid foundations: military hegemony rooted in a monopoly of nuclear weapons, economic supremacy, and unrivaled financial power.

By 1950, the Soviet Union had exploded its first atomic bomb and continued with determination on the road to superpower status, while the remaining foundations of American global might also began to erode. A decisive shift in America's military supremacy was triggered by the 1962 Cuban missile crisis, when the United States, by forcing the Soviet Union to withdraw its newly landed missiles from Cuba, seemingly administered a serious setback to Soviet superpower ambitions. Yet, in a conciliatory gesture toward the humiliated adversary, the United States withdrew all of its 100 Thor and Jupiter intermediate-range, land-based missiles from Turkey, Italy, and Great Britain, while the Soviet Union kept its 450 SS-4 (1,900-km range) and SS-5 (4,100-km range) in its Western military districts. Furthermore, the Cuban setback caused the demise of Soviet premier Nikita Khrushchev, a moderate, and the rise to power of Leonid Brezhnev, ideologically and militarily a hawk.

The geostrategic East-West balance in the mid-1960s, at the onset of the Brezhnev era, can be summed up as follows: (1) the Warsaw Pact was significantly superior to NATO in conventional forces and nuclear intermediate-range missiles; (2) this Warsaw Pact superiority was matched by NATO's lead in battlefield nuclear weapons plus U.S. strength in nuclear strategic forces; (3) worldwide, the West was still ahead, mainly in naval forces and strategic nuclear arms, but the Soviet Union was no longer just a formidable conventional power. Under Brezhnev, the Soviet Union's military buildup resulted in indisputable superpower status.

Although Soviet intermediate-range missiles were able to cover a large number of European cities and several military soft targets throughout the 1960s and early 1970s, America's unquestioned strategic superiority seemed to be an adequate deterrence to the Soviet forces. In the mid-1970s, however, the Soviet Union had achieved approximate strategic parity with the United States through the introduction of a family of highly accurate multiple independently targeted re-entry vehicles (MIRVed), missiles equipped with several warheads, each capable of hitting different targets; and the Soviets showed no willingness to reduce the level of this intermediate-range nuclear force.

They did the opposite. In 1974, they started deployment of the supersonic Backfire intermediate-range bomber (4,000-km range), and three years later their SS-20 appeared on U.S. high-altitude films. The mobile SS-20 Pioneer, with three MIRVed warheads and hard-target accuracy, represented a huge qualitative leap over the preceding generation and vastly improved the Soviet Union's Western Europe attack options.

It is in this context that the 1979 NATO decision to start deployment of 108 Pershing II ballistic missiles (1,900-km range) and 464 Tomahawk ground-launched cruise missiles (2,500-km range) at the end of 1983 must be seen. Deployment is not, as claimed by both Soviet propaganda and Western "peace" movements, an attempt to acquire a new war-winning capability, nor does it represent a sinister new twist in the arms race. Rather, NATO's theater nuclear force modernization program presupposes that mutual deterrence can be achieved only if a balance exists between both forces. That balance has been lost to the East's advantage and has to be regained, preferably by negotiated reductions.

The justification for INF deployment was made at both the military and political levels. Politically, there was a need to demonstrate Western resolve to the Soviets by providing a firm response to the SS-20 threat. Militarily, deployment was also meant to reassure Europeans that the U.S. commitment to the defense of Europe would be strengthened. As was to be expected, given Western Europe's poor record in taking tough stances toward the Soviet Union, certain governments, notably those in Brussels and the Hague, soon began to waffle in the face of well-organized and militant peace movements. West Germany, NATO's key member on the continent, displayed its bitter division both in the Bundestag and in the streets. While Chancellor Helmut Kohl, a Christian Democrat, has supported the zero-option strategy proposed by NATO, whereby the Soviets would have to scrap all of their SS-20s in exchange for no Pershing II and cruise missile deployment, the Social Democrats, now in opposition under the uncertain leadership of Jochen Vogel, showed increasing inclination to compete with the anti-American and anti-nuclear Green Party in opposing deployment of modernized Euromissiles. The Soviet Union's capable propaganda machine has found dependable spokesmen for the Soviet viewpoint in Egon Bahr, the Social Democrats' specialist for questions of arms control, and in Oskar Lafontaine, another Social Democrat.[11]

The massive Soviet arms buildup accelerated with the advance of soft "détente." During the 1970s, the Soviet arms industry introduced four new types of ICBMs, two new breeds of tanks, a new generation of tactical aircraft, and the world's largest fleet of attack helicopters. In 1979 alone, when the Kremlin's interpretation of détente reached its peak with the invasion of Afghanistan, the Soviet Union produced 3,000 main battle tanks, 1,800 combat aircraft, 4,000 armored troop carriers, and 250 ICBMs.

In contrast, a series of unilateral defense decisions by President Carter gravely affected the West's security. He canceled the B-1 strategic bomber and slowed down all other U.S. strategic programs: the MX missile, the Trident submarine, and various cruise missiles. He imposed a 5.5 percent ceiling on salary increases intended to augment the quality and morale of the all-volunteer armed forces. He vetoed the Navy's newest nuclear carrier, the CVN-71 *Theodore Roosevelt*, and stopped production of the Enhanced Radiation Warhead after having convinced then German chancellor Helmut Schmidt to request this revolutionary tank-breaking weapon, so vital to a Western Europe threatened by the Warsaw Pact's overwhelming superiority in armor. Furthermore, President Carter had pushed a SALT II agreement blatantly unfavorable to the West and entered into European disarmament talks with the Soviets in October 1980, thus jeopardizing deployment of the new Euromissiles in Western Europe.

As a result of Soviet resolve and Carter's lack thereof, (1) the USSR was close to achieving breakthrough superiority in Central Europe; (2) NATO would have to use nuclear weapons to stop a conventional assault; (3) the Soviets had built up a lead in tactical nuclear weapons, thus limiting Western options; (4) the Soviets had expanded their fleet of strategic transport aircraft and surface ships, enabling them to land troops more quickly in Asia and Africa than could the West; and (5) the USSR had punctured the American nuclear umbrella by achieving at least parity in long-range nuclear delivery systems.

With Carter's defeat in November 1980, the decade of "détente" ended, a strange and one-sided relaxation of tension during which Western nations had attempted to build cooperation and understanding with Soviet bloc states by means of cheap credit and advanced technology, while the Kremlin expanded its influence and military might at the expense of Western interests. After the buildup of Soviet satrapies in Ethiopia, Angola, Nicaragua, and Mozambique, it could no longer be argued seriously in the West that the main thrust of Soviet foreign policy was toward the defense of a *cordon sanitaire* rather than an ideological imperialist crusade. The liberal assumption that Soviet leaders are basically similar to politicians in other countries had proven to be a major fallacy in Western assessments of Soviet intentions.

Enter President Reagan. His previous pronouncements on major foreign policy and national security problem areas had shown him to be free of illusions regarding communist ideology. In June 1977, he commented on:

Soviet Expansionism and American Idealism. "The Soviet Union has a global objective. That fact alone makes our idealism vulnerable. We Americans would dearly love to let everyone live in peace and harmony. This may be described as a global objective, . . . but it is no substitute for coherent global *policy* in the face of real challenges."

Soviet Arms Buildup. "Despite its huge arms buildup in the past few years, the Soviet Union does not want to fight a war if it can be avoided. Instead, the Soviet buildup seems to be designed primarily for political leverage—to achieve their aims indirectly . . . they want to accomplish the gradual encirclement of the West and reduction of its strategic and economic influence."

Détente. "Détente between the United States and the Soviet Union may actually have improved the climate for Soviet promotion of proxy wars . . . We saw détente as a relaxation of tensions . . . They saw it otherwise. Détente, to the Soviet Union, became . . . a victory for the USSR and a growing sign of Western weakness."

The West and the World. "Perhaps the most important reality facing us today is the shrinking global influence of the West . . . throughout the West, it seems to have engendered in the Western public at large that sense of fatalistic indifference which . . . living by the side of a volcano induces in the local population. That indifference presents the Western world with its greatest challenge in ages. I am talking not only of Western loss of natural resources and materials, though that is occurring, but beyond it to the decline of the Western concepts of political responsibility and individual freedom."[12]

If candidate Reagan had not seemed inclined to accept the West's shrinking global influence and cultural decline, President Reagan appeared determined to resist and reverse the trend, starting with the shoring up of the West's eroded defenses. No prophetic talent was required to predict that President Reagan's stress on defense spending and his apparent no-nonsense approach to Soviet expansionism were bound to create friction within the Atlantic Alliance, particularly with those European partners still enmeshed in the illusion of "détente."

The NATO defense doctrines of Flexible Response and Forward Defense pretend preparedness for all eventualities. With Forward Defense, NATO will meet the invaders along the frontier between East and West Germany. Under Flexible Response, NATO will block aggression from the East with whatever means are necessary and suitable. Given the imbalance in quantity and quality of troops, as well as equipment and ordnance, between the Warsaw Pact and NATO armies in Europe, extensive war-gaming and battlefield projections indicate that in the event of a conventional assault from the East, NATO will have to use tactical nuclear weapons after the first 24 hours to protect the West's troops from annihilation.

Both Flexible Response and Forward Defense have thus far been considered vital for the continued existence of West Germany and Western Europe in a future war. Without Forward Defense, West Germany will inevitably be turned into a vast battlefield. Without Flexible Response, namely, the use of nuclear weapons against overwhelming conventional forces, West Germany and its neighbors to the west would inevitably fall under Soviet rule.

Over the past twenty years, U.S. strategy for a possible war in Europe has been as follows. The Pact forces attack with conventional weapons, and NATO troops defend themselves. If they hold, the war is over. If they are losing—as they probably would be, given the Soviets' strength in conventional arms—they resort to tactical, battlefield nuclear weapons. If that step stops the Pact, the war is over. If NATO is still losing, the United States will attack the USSR with strategic nuclear weapons. Every U.S. president has pledged to do so since nuclear weapons became part of the U.S. arsenal. Approval of the West German government is not required.

Year after year, during Reforger ("return of forces to Germany") exercises stretching over several months, the U.S. Air Force airlifts 10,000 combat troops to Germany and back to the United States. Western Europe has come to rely on the rapid availability of U.S. supplies and reinforcements for its defense in case of war. West Germany, in particular, places great emphasis and trust on repeated U.S. assurances that a minimum of six combat divisions will be airlifted to Germany within ten days after an act of aggression from the East. Few within NATO wish to acknowledge, however, that the United States has neither the divisions nor the strategic airlift capabilities to make those assurances hold. And given the Warsaw Pact's blitzkrieg doctrine, those crucial ten days will not be available. In any case, West European defense planners seem united in their urgent demand that the United States reintroduce the draft to boost its manpower reserves.

Since its inception in 1949, NATO has lived with the reality of being quantitatively inferior in conventional forces to its potential adversary. Initially, this disadvantage was of minor importance because the United States, NATO's only superpower, was then, and remained for nearly twenty years, superior in tactical and strategic nuclear weapons. Since the Soviet Union has counterbalanced the levels of tactical and strategic nuclear forces, and has achieved a significant lead in medium-range nuclear systems, NATO's numerical inferiority in conventional forces has attained a new dimension, particularly since the conventional force imbalance has shifted even further to NATO's disadvantage.

NATO's strategists now stress that the credibility of NATO's deterrent could be undermined by a conventional surprise attack from the East. The imbalance in conventional forces would require an early first use of nuclear weapons to compensate for the deficiencies in NATO's conventional forces. This situation, which was demonstrated by agitated debates in Western Europe following the 1979 double-track decision to modernize NATO's theater nuclear forces if the Soviet Union refused to cut the number of SS-20 intermediate-range missiles, creates uncertainty, insecurity, and sensitivity to strong pressure among the NATO partners. It is claimed that strengthening NATO's conventional force capability and the deterrent role of its conventional forces have now become urgent and unavoidable requirements.

The "conventional option," defined as the capability to halt and repel conventional Soviet aggression, is as old as NATO. As early as 1952, at the NATO summit in Lisbon, a proposal was made for the conventional defense of Europe based on a recommendation of 96 divisions and 9,000 tactical aircraft. In 1983, NATO had at its disposal 26 divisions and 1,800 tactical aircraft. From these numbers alone, it is evident that contemporary NATO is far from the conventional option envisaged in the 1950s.

In the democracies constituting NATO, budget and personnel for defense purposes can be modified upward only within moderate limits for the foreseeable future. Therefore, the sole conventional key for improving NATO's defense capabilities is technology, space, and time, specifically, an array of advanced new weapons systems with new munitions to be used in a framework of an updated NATO Forward Defense strategy.

Until 1983, NATO had planned in the event of Soviet aggression to destroy the first enemy echelon by conventional defensive means at the border separating the two Germanys. The aggressor's staging areas, through which the second and third echelons would be brought forward, were not threatened by NATO's conventional forces. To destroy a Soviet breakthrough group consisting of 600 tanks, 500 armored personnel carriers, 50 artillery batteries, 200 surface-to-air missiles, and 300 trucks would require about 5,500 aircraft sorties to deliver 33,000 tons of gravity bombs. With NATO's newest generation of weapons and precision-guided munitions, its new all-weather, long-range tactical strike aircraft, and submunitions delivered in a standoff manner, the Soviet breakthrough group could be destroyed with either 3,000 tons of "dumb" (gravity) bombs delivered in 600 sorties or with a limited quantity of "smart" (electronically guided, laser-guided, or heat-seeking) weapons delivered in less than 100 sorties.

According to NATO analysts, one ton of advanced technology submunitions can achieve the same effectiveness as a small nuclear weapon of 2–3 kilotons. Thus, a widened "conventional option" is alleged to possess an enhanced deterrent effect.

Investigating the contemporary fashionable thesis that NATO might be able to protect Western Europe without resorting to nuclear weapons (provided more money is spent on conventional weapons), the *London Economist* claims to have found "real substance." The gap between today's weak conventional NATO system of defense and a more reliable version is considered "not huge." For an additional 1 percent of GNP annually in national defense expenditures, conventional defenses can allegedly be sufficiently strengthened to enable NATO to hold the Pact's attacking forces for more than a month.[13]

The *Economist*'s calculations of a NATO nonnuclear defense budget, however, fail to take into account the Pact's and NATO's present operational doctrines. The Pact's strategy is based on the need to disperse its forces, precisely because of NATO's battlefield nuclear weapons. Without the need to disperse, the Pact would be able to attack in a concentrated and massed armor fashion. To block such an attack with conventional forces would require NATO expenditures far beyond the modest increase envisaged by the *Economist*.

Moreover, it is doubtful that even a defense budget increase of 1 percent of GNP can be attained by NATO's European member-nations. While periods of peace always produce tendencies to reduce defense spending and hence force levels, Western Europe seems to have opted for delegating its defense to others. Eagerly joined by Canada—whose atrophied navy now has neither the ships nor the manpower to protect Canada's shores let alone Atlantic sea-lanes—Western Europe has gone far down the road to denmarkization. Like Denmark, most of Western Europe has decided there is no need to spend more money on defense since its stronger allies will be forced to defend it anyway.

Since the early 1970s, systematic and rapid improvement in Soviet-built tactical aircraft has alarmed NATO. The introduction of Sukhoi Su-24 Fencer all-weather fighter bombers and Mikoyan MiG-25 Foxhound air-superiority fighters into the forward areas of Warsaw Pact countries has given the Soviets new attack capabilities against targets deep inside NATO territory, as far west as Wales. The Fencer also signals the arrival in the Pact's central region of a new family of ordnance for all-weather aircraft delivery, including AS-10 and AS-14 laser-guided missiles, and a new anti-radiation homing missile with a range of 150 nautical miles. Air cover for the Fencer is now provided by the newest version of the famous MiG-25 Foxbat, the Foxhound, equipped with an advanced look-down/shoot-down radar system. Thus, the elimination of U.S. forward based systems—the 150 General Dynamics F-111E and F-111F heavy fighter bombers deployed at the Royal Air Forces bases at Upper Heyford and Lakenheath, respectively—through conventional tactical air power is a realistic threat to NATO.

The Warsaw Pact's air forces have undergone extensive modernization since 1974, with the upgrading to modern Flogger, Fitter, and Fencer combat aircraft. Because of these modernization programs, NATO's technological lead has been decreasing, and its numerical lead has been lost. From 1979 to 1983, the USSR produced three fighter aircraft per day (Saturdays and Sundays included). As a consequence, the total force structure of NATO versus Warsaw Pact air power now stands at one to two plus, with the gap widening in favor of the Warsaw Pact states.

By 1975, Soviet airpower was configured for essentially defensive/counter-air missions. Today, the Warsaw Pact deploys in its frontal aviation units dual-capable forces oriented toward offensive, ground-attack/interdiction and air-superiority missions.

While production and deployment of inventory aircraft with major performance improvements (such as range and payload plus all-weather capability) continue in the USSR at twice the U.S. aircraft production rate, the Soviet Union is also beginning mass-production of four new aircraft designs: the Sukhoi Su-25 ground-attack plane, with the first two squadrons already operational in Afghanistan; the Sukhoi Su-27 air-superiority fighter, considered the Soviet equivalent of the American Grumman F-14 Tomcat and McDonnell Douglas F-15C Eagle; the Mikoyan MiG-29 interceptor, with a maximum speed of Mach 2.8, which is equipped with track-while-scan, long-range weapons radar, and AA-9 standoff missiles; and the Ram-P long-range fighter bomber with strategic potential. Without exception, these new aircraft designs underline the radical trend from defensive to offensive air operations, including advanced electronic countermeasures in operational aircraft, such as the Fitter H and the Flogger D.

NATO analysts claim that the Soviets and their allies could attack NATO forces in the central region with concentrated airpower containing as many as 2,500 aircraft. This claim is supported by military intelligence. Exercises of such magnitude, involving air-to-ground missile and electronic countermeasure simulation, have been conducted within Warsaw Pact territory. More important, the claim has been verified by Viktor Suvorov, a former regimental tank commander in the Red Army and staff officer at the Red Army's Tactical School who defected to the West.

According to Suvorov, the Warsaw Pact's strategic offensive plan against NATO is divided into five stages. The first stage or initial strike lasts for a half-hour and involves all available rocket formations. Targets are command posts and command centers, lines of communication and communication centers, airfields and antiaircraft rocket emplacements, rocket bases and stores for nuclear weapons, and radar positions to achieve the offensive breaks in enemy defenses that must be made for the waves of aircraft constituting the second stage—a mass air attack, lasting between 90 and 120 minutes. The surprise and mass assault will utilize nuclear weapons throughout.[14]

Suvorov's scenario should put to rest NATO's increased reliance on the "conventional option," that is, the use of improved conventional defense capabilities through high-technology conventional arms and munitions to block a conventional attack from the East. Such an attack is demonstrably not a primary option in the Warsaw Pact's war planning; on the contrary, a conventional attack seems the least likely option because it would invite the risk of stalemate or even defeat, given NATO's avowals of intent to use nuclear weapons rather than accept defeat. "On balance, the weight of evidence supports the probability that the Soviets would open a war with a theater-wide nuclear strike and thus challenges the scenarios on which the NATO defense is predicated."[15]

While the defense debate in the West is preoccupied with the hypothetical threat of tens of thousands of T-72 and T-80 Soviet tanks pouring across the West German border and reaching the Rhine within 48 hours,[16] more realistic views exist and find expression in the nonconformist press. Retired French general Pierre Gallois, who in the 1960s formulated Charles de Gaulle's strategy of an independent French nuclear deterrent, is explicit: "The next war won't start with a tank invasion of Germany . . . The next war will begin with a Soviet surprise simultaneous attack with highly accurate low-yield nuclear weapons against all the military targets in Western Europe, with minimum casualties of civilians and U.S. personnel. The Soviet tanks will be used only for mopping up and occupation."[17]

Recent Soviet military developments and warfare doctrines suggest that the Warsaw Pact is systematically modifying and improving its capabilities to fight a version of war for which NATO is least prepared. At the same time, NATO is urged from within to close the huge gap that has developed in conventional forces vis-à-vis the Warsaw Pact, when it is obvious that such a move would (1) meet with lip service only from most European allies, (2) play into the hands of Soviet planners contemplating a surgical first strike with nuclear arms, (3) fool public opinion in the West by misrepresenting Soviet war planning, and (4) make strategic and tactical sense only if NATO radically altered its defense posture and operational doctrine.

When NATO was created in 1949, the Soviet Union was a European power. Through three decades, NATO has worked well in countering the Soviet threat in Europe. But over those thirty years, the Soviet Union has become a global power, expanding into Africa, Asia, Central America, and into the five oceans, actively threatening NATO members at their jugular: the sources of raw materials. Yet, NATO's European members, plus Japan and Canada, have deftly left the defense of the sea-lanes, that is, of their own economies, to the United States. In return for protective services received, they have not relieved the United States of certain responsibilities for the defense of Western Europe in Europe, such as filling the gap left by American conventional forces transferred to troublespots elsewhere on the globe. Western Europe's refusal to redefine its commitment to NATO by upgrading its contribution and honoring other U.S. global military obligations is best summed up by Manfred Woerner, West Germany's defense minister and staunch defender of NATO: "For the Federal Republic of Germany, deployment of forces outside the NATO area is out of the question . . . Any withdrawal of forces earmarked for the defense of Europe would increase the present disadvantage of NATO in the East-West force ratio . . . A reduction of the American presence in Europe would clearly be contrary to American global interests."[18]

In explaining why NATO doesn't work, Ronald C. Nairn states a truism carefully circumvented by political NATO: "The core reason for the unworkability of NATO is this: For better or worse only a superpower can 'balance' another superpower. And in a real alliance, a superpower cannot behave as a superpower."[19]

Given the Soviet Union's new capabilities for projecting military power globally, the original concept for NATO's posture has outlived itself. NATO will have to expand its area, widen its scope, or risk self-destruction. The "Should the U.S. Pull out of NATO?" debate, started anew by Ronald Nairn[20] and taken up by Paul Seabury,[21] Melvyn Krauss,[22] and Earl Ravenal,[23] can no longer be seen by Europeans as merely a revival of discredited isolationism. Rather, it is proof that the Soviet Union—by establishing itself as a superpower, challenging the United States worldwide, and thus forcing a re-evaluation of traditional commitments and priorities in the United States—might be inching closer to reaching the dominant aim of Soviet foreign policy after World War II: the removal of American military presence from Western Europe and Soviet hegemony over all of Europe without firing a single shot.

The Soviet SS-20s, aside from threatening all of Western Europe, are primarily tools of political blackmail, produced and deployed to decouple the United States from Europe. It is mainly up to Western Europe to reject the *pax Sovietica* looming over the horizon. Only will is required. The resources have always been there.

Notes

1. Henry Kissinger before the Senate Foreign Relations Committee, July 31, 1979.

2. Andrei Sakharov, "The Danger of Thermonuclear War," *Foreign Affairs* 61 (1982–83): 1007, 1014.

3. Text of Soviet statement on relations with the United States, *New York Times*, September 29, 1983.

4. International Institute for Strategic Studies, *The Military Balance, 1980/81* (London, 1980).

5. According to Paul Nitze, as quoted in Richard Nixon, *The Real War* (New York: Warner Books, 1980), p. 159.

6. Quoted in ibid., p. 156.

7. Ibid., p. 193.

8. *London Daily Telegraph*, June 21, 1983.

9. *International Herald Tribune* (Zurich), September 15, 1983.

10. U.S. Department of Defense, *Soviet Military Power*, 2nd ed. (Washington, D.C., March 1983).

11. Oskar Lafontaine, *Angst vor den Freunden: Die Atomwaffenstrategie der Supermächte zerstört die Bündnisse* (Hamburg: Spiegel-Buch, Rowohlt Verlag, 1983).

12. Ronald Reagan, *United States Foreign Policy and World Realities* (Stanford: Hoover Institution Press, 1977), pp. 4–8.

13. "Without the Bomb," *London Economist*, July 31, 1982.

14. Viktor Suvorov, *Inside the Soviet Army* (London: Hamish Hamilton, 1982).

15. Graham D. Vernon, "Soviet Options for War in Europe: Nuclear or Conventional?" *Strategic Review* (Washington, D.C.: United States Strategic Institute, Winter 1979), p. 56.

16. Robert Close, *Europe Without Defense? 48 Hours That Could Change the Face of the World* (New York: Pergamon Press, 1979).

17. John Train, "The Soviet Wedge in Geneva," *Wall Street Journal*, September 28, 1983.

18. Manfred Woerner, "The Security of the Federal Republic of Germany in the 1980s," in *Germany: Keystone to European Security*, AEI Foreign Policy and Defense Review Publications (Washington, D.C.: American Enterprise Institute, 1983), pp. 45–46.

19. Ronald C. Nairn, "Why NATO Doesn't Work," *Wall Street Journal*, March 26, 1982.

20. Ronald C. Nairn, "Should the U.S. Pull out of NATO?" *Wall Street Journal*, December 15, 1981.

21. Paul Seabury, "NATO: Thinking the Unmentionable," *Wall Street Journal*, December 24, 1981.

22. Melvyn B. Krauss, "It's Time to Change the Atlantic Alliance," *Wall Street Journal*, March 3, 1983; see also Chapter 8 above.

23. Earl C. Ravenal, "The Case for a Withdrawal of Our Forces," *New York Times Magazine*, March 6, 1983.

15
Eastern Europe: Between the Soviet Union and the West

Milorad M. Drachkovitch

World peace is still determined by what happened at the heart of Europe. The failure to comprehend that adequately led to two World Wars.

Michael Charlton

The sagacious Italian publicist Luigi Barzini, writing about the present "decadence" of Europe and its chances of renaissance through unification, warns readers that Europe should brace itself for "the dangerous, turbulent, and violent decades ahead, possibly the most treacherous times since the fall of the Roman Empire."[1] In a similar vein, a noted Yugoslav art critic comments that "nobody denies today that this is a time of heavy crises, especially in social and economic plans, a time of the exhaustion of all ideologies, a time of extreme uncertainty for individual lives, and all this could not but have repercussions on the artistic life itself."[2] These individual and collective crises concern every part of the globe and, when combined with the notion of the acceleration of history, assume a distinctly ominous aspect. Every day we are bombarded with the news of turbulence somewhere in the world, and one single event may affect the global picture in a signal but immediately undecipherable way. This point is essential. How in fact should we interpret, without the benefit of hindsight, the importance and the consequences of a recent happening? Did, for example, the second visit of Pope John Paul II to Poland (June 16–23, 1983) lead to a reconciliation between people and government, with the church achieving a victory and the government suffering a "catastrophic" defeat (as an extremely well-written editorial in the *New Republic* of July 18–25 suggested)? Or did the visit benefit the Jaruzelski government, giving it badly needed legitimacy and opening the way to Western economic help, thus relieving the Kremlin's worries about the trip? The awarding to the Polish communist leader of the Order of Lenin, Moscow's highest civilian honor, a few days after the pope's visit indicated that Kremlin displeasure with Jaruzelski, hinted at earlier, had at least temporarily abated, making the general's position stronger than before the pontiff's visit.[3] Finally, how should one treat the element of surprise in international affairs, for example, a sudden invasion of West Germany by the Red Army?[4] Before dismissing such an "adventuristic" Soviet move, we should remember that the "self-invasion" of Poland—General Jaruzelski's coup of December 13, 1981, and the introduction of the martial law—surprised practically everyone.

The preceding observations on the quasi-apocalyptic character of our time (analyzed by John Lukacs in his seminal work, *The Passing of the Modern Age*) make it apparent why it would be foolhardy to predict the outcome of momentous events unfolding at the present moment. We may now return to firmer ground—namely, the fate of Eastern Europe since the end of World War II. The region under investigation comprises six countries (East Germany, Poland, Czechoslovakia, Hungary, Romania, and Bulgaria) that formally belong to the Soviet bloc through their membership in the Warsaw Treaty Organization (WTO) and the Council for Mutual Economic Assistance (CMEA), plus Albania and Yugoslavia, which, though tightly ruled by their communist parties, remain outside of the bloc (Yugoslavia is an associate member of the CMEA).

The statement of Michael Charlton, quoted at the outset, reminds us that the two world wars started in Eastern Europe. The region is again one of the potentially most explosive parts of the world. If Poland is once more the center of a possible conflagration, it is not the result of that country's capriciousness but of the policies of the great powers, which at the end of World War II and during its aftermath imposed on Poland (or failed to prevent the imposition of) a political system that the overwhelming majority of Poles found intolerable.

More precisely, a ruthlessly determined Stalin wanted and succeeded in subjugating Poland; the Western allies, for their part, failed to oppose Stalin, although their leaders were fully aware that Soviet aggrandizement at the expense of Poland flouted the principles for which World War II had been fought. If the sacrifice of Poland had brought lasting peace and cooperation among the wartime allies, it might have been worth it. Instead, Poland has remained a festering wound at the heart of Europe.[5] A left-wing political analyst vividly describes the present situation: "Almost 40 years after the end of World War II, 'Eastern Europe' remains an extremely heterogenous and explosive conglomerate, held together only by the Soviet military presence."[6] A former leader of the Polish anti-nazi resistance suggests in the same context that "*Solidarity* was really in existence in a latent form since the last war."[7] With regard to the Western powers, Professor Adam Ulam, the most systematic and perceptive American analyst of U.S.-Soviet relations, observes that if "Eastern Europe is once more a major cause of international tension [it is] largely because of what the USSR did, and the US failed to do, concerning this area in the 1940s. Had the US, as was then within its power, restrained the Soviet Union from imposing Communism upon Poland . . . the Kremlin would be spared its present dilemma."[8]

With this background in mind, we can now address the key question: What presently are the characteristics of both Soviet and U.S./NATO policies that vitally concern Eastern Europe?

Leninist Determinant of the Soviet Empire

The domestic institutions and foreign policies of every country are the result of factors, among which tradition weighs heavily, even after revolutionary upheavals. In the case of Russia, the tsarist imperial legacy lingered long after the downfall of the Romanov dynasty. Stalin, in particular, adapted the tsars' methods and appeals to the needs of his own rule. In Russia, however, the break with the past was attempted with a greater intensity than in any other revolution, in the aftermath of the Bolshevik seizure of power in November 1917. The surgeon of this clean-cut excision of the past was Lenin, whom Sidney Hook in a masterly historical analysis described as "an event-making individual. . . without whom there would have been no October Revolution."[9] Lenin's historical role went beyond that initial point. He was in fact the most important political personality of our century. He created a political party of a new kind, composed essentially of educated sons and daughters of the propertied classes but alienated from their familial milieus. In Lenin's belief, the working class, if left to itself, would develop only a reformist mentality. Hence the task of the Bolsheviks (and later of the Communists on a worldwide scale) was to assume leadership of workers' organizations and subsequently lead them into revolutionary battles and to ultimate proletarian victory. The new party was organized on the strictest hierarchical principles, with the concept of absolute discipline ("democratic centralism") reigning supreme. This new elitist party was then suffused with Lenin's teaching of a merciless, polarized domestic and international civil war between the bourgeoisie and the proletariat, the final victory of the latter being predetermined by the irreversible laws of history, codified by Marx. Lenin also offered to his disciples an alluring, utopian vision: communist victory to be followed on the domestic level by a simplified, egalitarian, totally new, just, and free social order, and on the international level, "for the first time in hundreds and thousands of years," "the slaves of all nations [defeating] the slave-owners of all nations." But to wage such a war the agents of final proletarian emancipation—the Bolsheviks/Communists—would have to employ *all* means, legal and illegal, peaceful and violent, to defeat the bourgeois-capitalist enemy. The key element in this apocalyptic projection was the phenomenon of *power*. Leninism amounted to a technique of seizing, maintaining, and expanding communist power. The transcendental and traditional God was dead, and his role was replaced by that of the party, the ultimate inspirer, legislator, educator, and punisher. Here are the roots of communist totalitarianism.[10]

Lenin's prescripts were not easy to implement, and communist parties as a consequence achieved victories and suffered defeats. (It certainly was arduous to follow Lenin's rules for being both fanatical and opportunistic in the conduct of super-Machiavellian political battles. And what was true earlier remains true today.) But whatever the destiny of applied Leninism might have been in the past, it is of utmost importance to emphasize and understand its present role in the policies of the Soviet Union. In addition to domestic policy, *all* of Lenin's heirs insisted that his precepts guide their foreign policies. Yuri Andropov today is as apodictic on that score as Brezhnev, Khrushchev, and Stalin before him. Henry Kissinger has vividly described the Leninist continuity of Soviet foreign policy: "The Soviet leaders . . . are tough, ruthless and persistent. But they have originated no profound initiatives; they have usually avoided great risks. They have expanded into vacuums created by irresolution and weakness."[11] In the second volume of his

Memoirs, the former secretary of state made the same point more sharply:

> Like all Soviet postwar leaders, Brezhnev [one could add here Andropov] *sees the US at once as rival, mortal threat, model, source of assistance and partner in physical survival.* These conflicting impulses make the motivations of Brezhnev's policy toward us ambivalent. On the one hand, he no doubt wants *to go down in history as the leader who brought peace and a better life to Russia. This requires conciliatory and cooperative policies toward us. Yet, he remains a convinced Communist who sees politics as a struggle with an ultimate winner*: he intends the Soviet Union to *be that winner*. His recurrent efforts to draw us into condominium-type arrangements—most notably his proposal for a nuclear non-aggression pact—are intended both to safeguard peace and to undermine our alliances and other associations.[12]

This dual and genuine interest in preserving peace and in maintaining and extending communist domination is pure Leninism. According to an authoritative book on the fundamentals of Marxist-Leninist revolutionary theory and the strategy and tactics of the world communist movement, edited by V. V. Zagladin, editor of the *World Marxist Review*, "the Marxist-Leninist theory of the proletarian revolution has scientifically proved that when society's transition from capitalism to socialism has begun the entire world capitalist system has matured for the socialist revolution."[13] As recently as 1981, the prestigious Institute of World Economy and International Relations of the USSR Academy of Sciences confirmed the same theme, while providing a significant explanation of the role of détente in Soviet foreign policy: "The change of quality in interstate relations and the passage from systematic and total confrontation to détente had an objective basis and was stimulated by long-term factors, the most important of which was the shift in the correlation of class forces in Europe and throughout the world in favour of socialism."[14] The multifaceted continuity of Soviet attitudes vis-à-vis the United States and the West in general found the clearest expression in a recent book of interviews with Georgi Arbatov, director of the Institute of U.S.A. and Canada in Moscow, member of the Central Committee of the Communist Party of the Soviet Union, and, most important, chief adviser to the Kremlin on U.S. affairs and a consultant to Yuri Andropov. Considered an accurate purveyor of the official Soviet line, Arbatov explained to his Dutch interviewer that Khrushchev's famous phrase "We will bury you!" still reflected the Soviet attitude in the sense that it conveyed "confidence in socialism's historical advantages over capitalism, which, in our conviction, will make a worldwide triumph of socialism inevitable in the long run."[15]

A final element is the systematically developed cult of Lenin in the Soviet Union and the many purposes it serves. According to the author of a recent book on this subject,[16] "the cult is used to legitimize Soviet policy, and to glorify the fatherland with all its defects. Indeed, the cult is meant to provide the vision of a higher reality that obliterates the need to confront those defects—an intention expressed in the widespread slogan 'Lenin is more alive than all the living.' The cult thus holds that a legendary past will deliver a utopian future."[17]

Leninist Dilemmas of Yuri Andropov

If six decades after Lenin's demise, he is still "more alive than the living," what may one say for his latest successor, Yuri Andropov? The short length of time that the 70-year-old Andropov has wielded supreme power forbids any conclusive statement about his performance and role in Soviet and world history. His reign has been both bustling and fathomless—dazzlingly successful, bitterly disappointing, and above all unpredictable. He maneuvered with extraordinary political skill to assume Brezhnev's mantle, but the meetings of the party's Central Committee and the Supreme Soviet in June 1983 proved that he had to share power with Brezhnev's chief protégé and his own main rival, Konstantin Chernenko. He tried to introduce a new dynamic style in party and state governance, in a marked and deliberate contrast with the immobility of the end of the Brezhnev era. But within nine months, it was obvious that he had failed to break with the Brezhnev style of rule-by-inertia or to carry out a thorough purge or at least a rejuvenation of party ranks. He was initially extremely frank in denouncing the economic shortcomings of the regime, called for greater social and labor discipline, and assigned the highest priority to restructuring the Soviet economy. But when the first industrial reforms were announced at the end of July 1983, they were purely experimental and limited, far less ambitious than expected. And one could predict in advance that the adoption by the Central Committee in the fall of 1983 of a new economic program would disappoint advocates of structural changes—once encouraged by Andropov himself to be bold and innovative.[18]

Andropov's resignation to rule through power-elite consensus did not deprive him of a pre-eminent position at the helm of the party and the state. Unless his health problems incapacitate him irretrievably, he will continue to be, as an American biographer put it, "a man of relentless determination and sharp intelligence, of confidence and self-control, impelled by an ascetic devotion to the Soviet Union."[19] In the top triad of the Soviet hierarchy, Andropov enjoys the support of major party bureaucrats and the military brass and has worked out a *modus vivendi* with the entrenched, Moscow-based central planners and industrial ministers. Out of conviction and political expediency, he has particularly cultivated close relations with the top military leaders. He emphatically stated in his eulogy of Leonid Brezhnev that "we know full well that it is useless to beg peace from imperialists. It can be upheld only by relying on the invincible might of the Soviet Armed Forces."[20] From that time on, he has never neglected to enhance the Red Army's might.

Looking back at his record, I would designate as representing the "essential" Andropov his highly vaunted *soft* and increasingly dreaded *hard* approaches to domestic and international policies, with the occasional changes of line that modify though not necessarily disprove "moderation" and "toughness." Initially he was particularly successful in igniting, in the Soviet Union and abroad, inordinate hopes that his rule would be essentially enlightened and progressive, that deep down he was a "closet liberal," aspiring to a genuine accommodation with the West. He continues to amass propaganda points in the West, by exchanging avuncular correspondence with an American girl on the supreme merits of peace or by favorably impressing Western audiences by loading his major public speeches with antiwar statements and nuclear disarmament proposals. He answers with consummate skill the questions of Western interviewers, leaving them with the impression that Soviet military policies are motivated exclusively by the imperatives of national defense and that the culprits responsible for international tensions are the lawless official centers of American imperialism, headed by the warmongering occupant of the White House.[21]

At the same time, the evidence that, along with an open rehabilitation of Stalin, Stalinist practices are mushrooming in the Soviet Union has become overpowering. The prosecution in May 1983 before the Moscow City Court of a writer accused of "anti-Soviet agitation and propaganda" had all the trappings of a Stalinist show trial. Two leading American Kremlinologists, both men of the Left in the domestic spectrum, denounced the new wave of Soviet repression as "the most vicious crackdown in the Soviet Union since Stalin's death," a phenomenon to be largely explained by "the remarkable comeback of the Soviet political police."[22] The June 1983 plenum of the Central

Committee emphasized the need to heighten the ideological struggle and warned artists, writers, and other intellectuals that the party expected them to act as soldiers in an intensified war of ideas. By-products of the same trend were systematic persecution of dissidents, open manifestations of anti-Semitism, use of psychiatric institutions to silence persistent critics, and banning of rock groups as promoters of anti-Soviet Western influence among impressionable Soviet youth.

The KGBization of Soviet policies at home and abroad had even more sinister aspects, some being supersecret and difficult if not impossible to prove, others surfacing easily and subsequently being covered by the Western media. To the first category belongs the explosive issue of KGB involvement in international terrorism, the most famous case of which was the "Bulgarian connection" with the attempted assassination on May 13, 1981 of Pope John Paul II. Italian police claims, and subsequent judicial evidence, that the would-be assassin was the instrument of the Bulgarian secret police, acting with the knowledge of the KGB (at the time headed by Yuri Andropov) were vehemently denied by the Soviet authorities. Washington refused to get involved in an Italian judicial case, the requirements of diplomacy were paramount, and the "Bulgarian connection" never figured on the agenda of any Soviet-American talks. The KGB's alleged role in global terrorism and infiltration of foreign governments remained, however, on the agenda of investigative scholars and journalists.[23] Persistent Soviet efforts to obtain Western military secrets and advanced technology through espionage led to spectacular expulsions of scores of accused Soviet spies from several countries.[24] The official Soviet reaction and retaliation for these expulsions were uncharacteristically restrained. The most plausible reason for such moderation was that something much more important was preoccupying Soviet leaders.

In the first half of 1983, a series of events signaled a sudden change away from confrontation in Soviet-American relations. The lifting on July 28 of the U.S. grain embargo, and the decision of both sides to sign a new five-year grain agreement, was the centerpiece around which everything else revolved. The prospects for increased industrial trade improved. President Reagan's top trade negotiator, William E. Brock, saw not only a thaw in U.S.-Soviet commerce, but expressed hope of further moves to "improve business relations, political relations, diplomatic relations across the board."[25] Most significantly, the long-stalled negotiations in Geneva on medium-range missiles in Europe were rescheduled to take place between early September and mid-December—the date for the deployment of U.S. Pershing II and cruise missiles unless an arms control agreement had been reached. Official hints of a readiness to compromise by both sides and of a Reagan-Andropov summit meeting during the first half of 1984 were greeted with optimism in the West European and especially the American press.[26] The *Economist* (London) of July 23 called 1983 the Year of the Missiles and offered alternate scenarios of accommodation or dramatic new confrontations between the two superpowers over the issue of deployment.

Behind this issue and the Soviet interest (some commentators call it obsession) in thwarting the deployment lies the Soviet perception of the role of military matters in the world today and their relationship with political plans. The Report of the European Security Study, whose steering group consisted of 27 prominent civilian and military persons from both sides of the Atlantic, people with otherwise very different views on NATO military strategy and particularly nuclear policies, contained the following statement of facts: "First, the Soviet Union has achieved full strategic nuclear parity with the United States. Second, Soviet theater nuclear forces aimed at Europe have rapidly grown far beyond NATO's capability in this category. Third, Soviet conventional capabilities have also continued to expand." Then, a few lines below, followed an obviously carefully worded key formulation:

> We recognize that the Soviet Union seeks to accomplish its purposes through a variety of instruments utilized in a combined and mutually supporting arrangement. It presumably prefers to pursue its aims by means other than a direct military attack. The Soviet Union seeks to use the hard and conspicuous fact of its military power as an instrument of intimidation and political manipulation to sway NATO governmental policies and popular attitudes toward compliance with Soviet aims and interests. Its military power looms as a setting for its diplomacy and arms control negotiations. Indeed, *the Soviet Union's challenge to NATO and its peoples at present is primarily political* [italics added].[27]

Andropov's challenge to the United States and NATO, whose successful aspects are described above, should also be viewed in the light of a series of events that must have deeply worried the Kremlin, among which the prospect of the missile deployment was only the last element. These include the outcome of elections in three of the largest and most powerful industrial democracies, Great Britain, West Germany, and Japan. The elections had three characteristics: the emergence of the strongest anti-Soviet bloc in 30 years; the setback to the antinuclear lobby and mass movement in Europe; and the approval by the electorates of the NATO decision to upgrade European nuclear defenses if no agreement was reached with the Soviets in Geneva. The second set of unwelcome news bore an American stamp: U.S. strategic modernization plans, especially an intensive development of both nuclear and conventional missiles; the concomitant U.S. ideological counteroffensive; support of resilient anticommunist insurgencies in Asia, Africa, and Central America; and the determination, if negotiations failed, to deploy the Pershing II (a particular anathema to the Soviets) and cruise missiles in December 1983. Add to all this the patently anti-Soviet foreign and military policies of socialist France and all the actual and potential trouble the pope of Polish origin was causing wherever he appeared, and one can realize that Andropov was not pleased with many things happening around the globe.[28]

The crux of the matter is the situation in West Germany. During West German chancellor Helmut Kohl's visit to Moscow in early July 1983, the highest Soviet dignitaries did not mince words about the dire consequences for West Germany and the European continent of stationing the new NATO missiles. Premier Nikolai Tikhonov warned that the Soviet Union and its allies would take additional measures without delay to strengthen their security and develop a counterbalance to NATO's new military potential. Yuri Andropov was more precise; he mentioned the possibility of stationing so many Soviet rockets in East Germany that East and West Germany would be forced "to look at each other through dense palisades of missiles."[29] A few weeks before Kohl's visit, the Kremlin had hinted that the NATO arms deployment could lead to the placement of missiles in Hungary—a move (if implemented) without precedent in the Warsaw Pact's history.

Tough words did not mean, however, that tough deeds were the only Soviet policy choice with regard to West Germany. The economic benefits to be obtained from the Federal Republic (imports of modern technology, increases in trade, and West German financing of major East-West projects) as well as the cultivation of improved political ties with Bonn (to which to the astonishment of many the Kohl government proved to be amenable) could have compensatory effects even if the scourge of deployment could not be avoided.

It must be emphasized, however, that Andropov will not passively watch the global balance of power turn in favor of the United States. The spring 1983 decision to place sophisticated air defense missiles manned by Soviet troops in Syria indicates how the Kremlin can retaliate and complicate U.S. efforts in one strategic region of the world. There are other places and situations that could be used as major embarrassments or even serious threats to the West: demonstrations by militant antinuclear groups, especially the West German groups, whose frustration with the slackening of the movement could lead to violence; reopening of the Berlin crisis; deployment of Soviet missiles in the Caribbean; a move into Iran by the Red Army or by surrogate forces; and, of course, a new cold war exploitation of domestic U.S. troubles and even more of anti-American dispositions abroad.[30]

It is impossible to know and idle to guess what Soviet foreign policy will be in view of the aforementioned considerations. It is not idle, however, to conclude this section by invoking some of Lenin's guidelines and statements, the first issued in deepest secrecy and the second made publicly, both stemming from early 1922. They have not lost their topicality and therefore concern Yuri Andropov and his present "Leninist dilemmas." From the end of January to the end of March 1922, in a series of secret memorandums to the highest party organs (published for the first time in the mid-1960s, in the fifth Russian edition of his complete works), Lenin candidly outlined his objectives for the intergovernmental economic and monetary conference convoked by the Allied Supreme Council. The conference opened in Genoa on April 10, 1922, to discuss measures for the economic reconstruction of Central and Eastern Europe. Bolshevik leaders, and above all Lenin, assigned exceptional importance to the Genoa conference. Soviet diplomacy had the task of securing economic and political advantages for the Soviet state by exploiting the contradictions within the capitalist camp. Thus, according to a Lenin letter of January 22, in Genoa, "We protect Germany and Turkey . . . we try to isolate America and in general to divide the powers." In a February 24 draft decision for the Bolshevik Central Committee, Lenin was even more explicit: "Everything possible and even impossible should be done to strengthen the pacifist wing of the bourgeoisie and increase, if only slightly, the chances of success at the elections. This first and foremost. Second, to divide the bourgeois countries united against us in Genoa—such is our dual political task in Genoa, and not at all the development of communist views."[31]

As a by-product of the Genoa conference, Soviet diplomacy achieved a major success in the unanticipated signing, on April 16, of a treaty with Germany in Rapallo, which, in the words of Louis Fischer, won Germany away from the "capitalist united front" against the Soviet Republic to the side of the latter.[32] The basic terms of the Rapallo treaty, namely the granting of equal rights and privileges and the discarding of all mutual claims on the part of the two countries, were unreservedly hailed by Lenin: "True equality of the two property systems—if only as a temporary stage, until such time as the entire world abandons private property, the economic chaos and wars engendered by it for a higher property system—is found only in the Treaty of Rapallo."[33] "Rapallo" in fact became a symbol of sudden Soviet-German rapprochements, and one could hardly blame some present observers of the European scene who, in the spectacle of high-level West German politicians (Franz-Joseph Strauss) conspicuously courting the East, see a specter of what happened over sixty years ago in a small town on the Italian Riviera.

While Lenin's directives remained secret for several decades, he gave an open, essentially economic version of the reasons for Soviet participation in the Genoa conference in a speech delivered at a congress of metalworkers on March 6, 1922: "We are going there as merchants because trade with capitalist countries (as long as they have not entirely collapsed) is absolutely essential to us; we are going to Genoa to bargain for the most appropriate and most advantageous and politically suitable terms for this trade, and nothing more."[34] The merchant theme received systematic support in the Soviet media of that time. Much more could be said about the duality of the Bolshevik (neo-Machiavellian) versus merchant aspects of Soviet foreign policy in history and today. Yuri Andropov is by definition aware of them, and it is up to him to give open preference to one aspect without ever forgetting the other.

In view of the thaw in the spring and summer of 1983, accommodation between the superpowers appears more likely than confrontation. Still, despite optimistic declarations and forecasts, the thaw is more a promise than a reality. It could suddenly turn to a freeze, as has happened so many times in the past. The present Soviet merchant approach may be understood in the light of Soviet economic shortcomings and needs. It is noteworthy that if the USSR is today militarily infinitely stronger than in Lenin's time, its economy is in a systemic crisis whose roots go back to the founding father.[35]

In the coming months, the West will show its ability to cope (or retreat in possible disarray) with the Kremlin's diplomacy. This problem is examined in the next section. As for Eastern Europe, it is fully aware of the exchangeable weaponry of the Leninist diplomatic duality. The region will watch the unfolding of events with passionate interest.

The Crisis in the Atlantic Alliance

That the 35-year-old Atlantic Alliance is in trouble is indisputable; however, what a few years (even a few months) ago seemed to be irreversible symptoms of its demise now appear to be signs of a new lease on life.

A resounding article by Irving Kristol, one of the best-known and most esteemed writers of the neoconservative persuasion, can serve as a perfect example of vehement pessimism with regard to the Atlantic Alliance. In a *Wall Street Journal* column (July 15, 1981), entitled "NATO at a Dead End," Kristol wrote a premature obituary informing readers of "the impending collapse of NATO." His thesis was that while U.S./NATO policymakers were relying on the huge U.S. nuclear superiority over the Soviet Union as a guarantee of Atlantic security and a deterrent to Red Army bellicosity, the situation was changing drastically. By systematic efforts following the Cuban missile crisis, the Soviets reversed the trend of strategic superiority, leaving the once impervious U.S. nuclear umbrella "moth-eaten." NATO, by matching the Soviet buildup on the western borders of the USSR of intermediate-range nuclear missiles, which are capable of hitting any area of Western Europe, with a deployment of its own nuclear weapons on West European and above all West German soil would make the "only *certain* outcome" of "a conflict with the Soviet Union . . . European annihilation." Legitimately frightened by such a prospect, Western Europeans were increasingly receptive to the appeals of the nuclear disarmament movement and, as alternatives to doomsday, to "appeasement" and eventual "Finlandization" as the price of national survival.

Kristol's views merit reconsideration not only because he is one of the most articulate American commentators on domestic and world affairs but also because they are a paradigm of the flood of articles and books that from very divergent viewpoints belabor the "death of NATO" theme. Concepts of neutralism with strongly anti-American undertones flourish in Western Europe, having as their counterpart across the Atlantic an increasingly popular isolationism centered around the desirability of bringing home U.S. troops stationed in Europe.

The course of events has both confirmed and invalidated Kristol's pessimism. The conclusions of a three-day conference organized in Hamburg by *Time* magazine at the end of April 1983 and attended by 45 political leaders, government officials, strategists, and economists from the United States and Western Europe were hardly encouraging. Some participants complained that the continued and rapid Soviet military buildup had intimidated the Europeans, making in particular the so-called successor generation uncertain of U.S. policy and fatalistic about Soviet power. German conferees insisted on the necessity of educating the public about the real nature of the Soviet system and the justifiability of NATO defense policies. The Americans lamented the lack of consensus in Washington and the absence of a bipartisan approach toward foreign affairs in Congress. The conference's consensus was that the deepest split in the alliance was the fundamental difference between U.S. and European perceptions of the Soviet threat. Some opinion surveys confirmed the trend toward the "demise of Atlanticism" on both sides of the ocean. In contrast, a Dutch writer made the distinction between the pro-Americanism of most Europeans and the anti-Americanism of an important minority of those working in the "consciousness industry"—the churches, the schools, the universities, and the mass media.[36]

Kristol's systematic gloom seems invalid today in view of four elements. The electoral outcomes in Great Britain and West Germany, mentioned above, showed that Soviet pre-electoral intimidation reaped the opposite results. Second, reflecting popular nondefeatism, three top-level conferences, beginning with a meeting of the heads of state of the most developed industrial democracies in Williamsburg, Virginia, at the end of May 1983, and followed within days by meetings of NATO defense ministers in Brussels and foreign ministers in Paris, reaffirmed the Western stand on Euromissiles—the deployment of intermediate-range missiles in December unless verifiable agreement on limiting them had been reached in Geneva. During the following weeks, the West German government was particularly anxious to dispel any doubt concerning its support for the U.S. negotiating positions in Geneva. Third, the U.S. economic recovery, stronger than predicted, brightened the prospects of the global economy and may positively affect the West in its overall relations with the East. In the graphic words of Nobel Prize winner Lawrence R. Klein of the University of Pennsylvania, "the U.S. is acting as the locomotive to pull the world out of recession and on to the path of sustained growth." Conflicts of economic interests will continue to mar ties between the United States and the European Economic Community, but here again the strains within the alliance are not forewarnings of its disintegration. A fourth element is the significant progress in the development of a new generation of sophisticated U.S. conventional weapons that can strike deep behind enemy lines to thwart a possible Warsaw Pact attack on Western Europe. In the words of General Bernard W. Rogers, the present supreme commander of NATO, "We depend ultimately on our nuclear strength to deter the most ominous threat to our security, yet building a more capable conventional force posture has become more crucial than at any time in the postwar era."[37] The replacement of existing tactical nuclear weapons with more effective conventional weaponry (which is now partly in existence and whose further development could promptly be completed) would represent a double qualitative breakthrough: militarily, these highly accurate electronically guided weapons would again give to the Western alliance the advantage lost during the systematic Soviet armaments buildup; politically, as well as morally, the receding of the nightmare of nuclear conflagration, which Soviet propaganda has so effectively used to frighten the citizens of the West, would be a great step forward against the psychological paralysis and the unilateral-disarmament temptations that presently haunt so many Westerners.

Western governments are aware of the advantages of the "deep strike" breakthrough. They continue to bicker among themselves on the solution of real but mundane problems caused by the introduction of a totally new weaponry. These quarrels appear philistine, especially in view of Winston Churchill's dictum that "we can afford what we need; what we cannot afford is to say we only need what is easy to provide." Here indeed the mettle of Western civilization is on trial.

A perceptive observer of international affairs, Professor Robert W. Tucker, has well expressed the delicate coexistence of the decay/revival syndrome facing the West: "Unless the Atlantic Alliance breaks apart as a result of the disagreements now wracking it, the Soviet Union faces the prospect of an emerging power balance that will eventually reduce its leverage in Western Europe. That leverage is also likely to be reduced by the weakened Soviet position in Eastern Europe."[38] To paraphrase the last sentence of Professor Tucker's judgment—a Western revival (understanding by this term the re-emergence of self-confidence and the political will to act) will find a profound echo in Eastern Europe.

The Ordeal of Eastern Europe

Reviewing the Soviet Union's foreign policy before the Supreme Soviet on June 16, 1983, Foreign Minister Andrei Gromyko made two statements of central importance to this study. After assailing the West for ideological sabotage and subversive political and economic actions against the Polish People's Republic, he asserted that in the eyes of the Warsaw government and its allies in the WTO, "Poland has been and will remain an integral part of the socialist commonwealth." He thus confirmed the Brezhnev Doctrine, first enunciated in

November 1968. At that time Brezhnev had told a congress of the Polish Communist party (in the aftermath of the invasion of Czechoslovakia) that any threat to socialism by internal or external forces with the aim of restoring a capitalist system concerned not just the socialist country under attack but "the security of the socialist commonwealth as a whole." Nearly fifteen years later, Gromyko echoed Brezhnev and warned the West that it should have no doubts about the Eastern bloc's resolve to "uphold the inviolability of our borders, to ensure the safety of all members of the commonwealth, and to defend socialist gains."[39]

The Brezhnev and Gromyko formulations are clear enough, but they should be viewed within a wider framework. Former U.S. secretary of defense Harold Brown has supplied that framework.

> The retention of Eastern Europe is the next highest priority for the Soviet leaders. It is, aside from the Soviet Union itself, the one area for whose preservation under their dominion they would take high risks of war with the United States. Soviet problems in Eastern Europe are compounded by the practically complete lack of legitimacy of Soviet hegemony among the peoples of Eastern Europe. If Soviet troops were to be withdrawn and the people assured that they could not come back, almost none of the regimes in the area—certainly not the Polish, Czechoslovakian, or Hungarian—would last more than a few days.[40]

Two points should be emphasized here: the illegitimacy of Soviet hegemony in Eastern Europe and the assertion that the communist regimes would promptly collapse without the support or intervention of the Red Army. In regard to the first issue, Soviet theorists have developed a concept of "real" or "actual" socialism, in response to accusations challenging the socialist authenticity of Soviet communism. Their thesis is that the Soviet system is the result of implementing Marxist theories and that with due respect to local conditions, the Soviet model is valid for all communist-ruled countries as well as for nonruling Marxist-Leninist parties. Yuri Andropov is adamant on this issue. In a 1983 article, he postulated that the Soviet Union's "developed" socialist society ("developed" is Andropov's term for "real" or "actual" socialism; he used it three times in this brief, intelligent, and interesting article) was established on the fundamental principles of Marx's and Engels's writings and was complemented and enriched by Marxist-Leninist science. In his view, "our developed socialist society represents a dialectical unity of successes in socialist construction, on the one hand, and unsolved problems." But, Andropov wrote, the solution to these problems must not be found by infusing into Marxism-Leninism ideas drawn from Western sociology, philosophy, or political science. He denounced those theoreticians who call themselves Marxists but are unable to rise to the true stature of Marx, Engels, and Lenin and their "tremendously intellectually powerful" scientific teaching.[41]

The preceding discussion leads to the cornerstone of the Soviet political elite's ideology or, more precisely, of its attempt to legitimize the Leninist party's monopolistic rule. The logic is on the surface convincing: if Marxism-Leninism is indeed a science (a sort of social physics), it is both true and irreversible, and the Marxist-Leninist party is the only objective and historically necessary interpreter of that science. Communist leaders in Eastern Europe, even if they do not like the Soviet model theory, subscribe to Marxist-Leninist ideology as the source of legitimacy for their own rule. But, as argued by one of the most astute students of modern communism, Professor Richard Lowenthal, the question of legitimacy is in fact the party's attempt at self-legitimization. It claims that its task is to coordinate, integrate, and keep society together and rejects the idea that a mature society could exist without a guardian. Lowenthal feels that real legitimacy must be institutional and procedural—that there is no alternative.[42] In reality there was nothing "scientific" (in both the Marxist and non-Marxist senses) in Lenin's extremely voluntaristic, truly adventuristic coup in November 1917 in Petrograd, which was proclaimed a "revolution" following its success.

In Eastern Europe, not a single thread of evidence can be invoked to legitimate the brutal, imperial, hegemonic Soviet rule, imposed through the Red Army and administered by local, minority communist parties. Of course, at the beginning, after the collapse of Nazi Germany, the picture was more nuanced. At first, genuine, then bogus, coalitions with the noncommunists, especially the agrarian parties, were established, and both necessary and popular economic reforms were introduced. But that is beside the point. What followed was the systematic elimination from power of the agrarians, imposed fusion with social democrats, and bloody purges of "heretical" Communists. Stalin did what he wanted, and very few would deny today that the communist rule based on his whims was illegitimate.

The Stalinist period of East European history was essentially passive, but Stalin was barely dead when a huge workers' demonstration in East Berlin, on June 17, 1953, shook Soviet powerholders and prompted a violent suppression of the spontaneous upheaval of East Germans. The full-fledged popular revolution in Hungary in 1956 was crushed after a bloodbath by the Red Army. Military might was used again in Czechoslovakia in August 1968, this time without casualties. Its purpose was to teach Czechoslovakia's reform-minded Communists, who enjoyed broad popular support, that Socialism with a Human Face was not a formula acceptable to the Kremlin. Brezhnev's verbal outburst at a high-level Czechoslovak Communist Party delegation, summoned to Moscow a few days after the invasion, is instructive. Here is how, behind closed doors, the Soviet overlord reviled his terrorized and divided serfs:

> Your country lies on territory where the Soviet soldier trod in the Second World War. We bought that territory at the cost of enormous sacrifices, and we shall never leave it. The borders of that area are our borders as well. Because you do not listen to us, we feel threatened. In the name of the dead in World War Two who laid down their lives for your freedom as well, we are therefore fully justified in sending our soldiers into your country, so that we may feel truly secure within our common borders. It is immaterial whether anyone is actually threatening us or not: it is a matter of principle, independent of external circumstances. And that is how it will be, from the Second World War until "eternity."[43]

Thirteen years after the "normalization" in Czechoslovakia came the "self-invasion" of Poland. On December 13, 1981, a military junta headed by General Wojciech Jaruzelski, a man occupying top positions in the government, the army, and the party, introduced martial law ("state of war" in Polish). There was never any doubt that the coup prepared in absolute secrecy and perpetrated with lightning efficiency, had its inspiration in Moscow and was indeed a feather in the cap of the extremely gifted KGB chief at that time—Yuri Andropov. A Western political scientist commented in connection with the Jaruzelski action that "the regime, bereft of the capacity to govern, still possesses the power to repress."[44]

The foregoing variations on Secretary Brown's theme of the illegitimacy of the Soviet domination of Eastern Europe should be complemented by some observations regarding his cursory statement on the probable collapse—without the backing or the threat of the Red Army—of communist regimes in the area. Here we have to deal with the controversial, but very important topic, from both practical and theoretical standpoints, of "national communism." According to one school of thought, "from its very inception communism has been national and the term 'international communism' has been badly misinterpreted by communists and noncommunists alike."[45] I reject this interpretation. To begin with Marx's basic ideological postulates and formulations, bourgeois patriotism, along with its more virulent nationalist manifestations, is totally incompatible with the economically built-in internationalism of the dispossessed proletariat. Lenin's own vehement antinationalism gave to the concept of proletarian internationalism a radical, revolutionary meaning. As supremely alert political animals, both Marx and Lenin (and all subsequent "Leninists") knew that nationalism was an explosive historical force. If its appeal could be properly channeled, and if the leaders of communist parties could master the neo-Machiavellian art of influencing the masses and maneuvering social leaders, maximum political benefits could be attained. Though difficult to implement, the utilization of noncommunist feelings and movements, along with noncommunist politicians, for the final and exclusive victory of communism has from the beginning been the name of the game.

In Eastern Europe, the initial postwar shock of the Red Army was by definition antinational. Local Communists exercised absolute power as trustees (often untrusted!) of a foreign empire. The momentous changes in the region during the past four decades have not altered two things. First, regional communist leaders would like to obtain greater freedom of action within the Soviet bloc. They can even challenge some of Moscow's bloc policies—up to a point. But they are all aware that in the final analysis their rule would be in jeopardy without the Kremlin's protection. The events in Poland made that crystal clear.

> Pluralistic trends color various social, cultural, and economic policies but they do not extend to questions affecting the determination of the proper relationship between the party and other fundamental institutions. From Romania to East Germany, Solidarity was viewed as a threat to Polish socialism because it operated effectively, with wide popular support, and beyond the party's restraining hand.[46]

The second element to be borne in mind is the utilization, even exacerbation, of the nationalistic dispositions of the masses in order to broaden popular support for communist regimes. The official phrases used in southeast European boundary disputes very often assume absurd propagandistic shrillness, but they allow political leaders to manipulate the masses. To sum up, three interconnected factors, never at ease and occasionally violently antagonistic, characterize the East European situation. The imperial Soviet factor is dominant, but at this time Soviet leaders appear uncertain whether to dominate through greater coercion or measured relaxation. Regional communist elites speak of societal democratization, even pluralism, and are anxious to find means to cope with the calamity of faltering (with few exceptions) economies, but they prevent the third factor—the civic society—from effectively participating in public affairs. The civic society is in irreconcilable conflict—violent or mute—with the Soviet masters. It is inspired by the idea of national self-determination, which Moscow does not want to grant and it refuses to abandon. The civic society is also in conflict with domestic potentates, for it knows that it represents the nation, while the "new class" (in the Milovan Djilas's sense of the term) clings to its privileges. An editorial in the *Economist* (September 12, 1981) defined the boundaries of the civic society: "Solidarity is not just a union. It is the Polish nation." And in a similar sense, *L'Express* of Paris (July 1, 1983) printed on its front page: "John Paul II, King of Poland." Earlier in the year Milovan Djilas wrote about the enormous international importance of the Polish crisis and stated emphatically: "Poland's opposition is the incurable cancer of democratic resistance deep within the body of the Eastern bloc. No Soviet hegemonistic surgery will ever remove it."[47] Such a powerful profession of faith illustrates the dimensions and intensity of the triangular relationship presently characterizing Eastern Europe.

Recession and Socialist Integration

At the beginning of the 1980s, all the East European members of the CMEA faced an economic slowdown unprecedented in the postwar period. While the average growth in the CMEA countries was 6.2 percent between 1971 and 1975, it slipped to 4.1 percent between 1976 and 1980 and to 1.9 percent in 1981 (compared with a 3.5 percent goal). Prospects for the immediate future were not encouraging. The essential factors causing the slowdown were failure to carry out effective economic reforms, huge borrowing from Western banks and governments (between 1970 and 1980 CMEA's collective indebtedness rose to about $80 billion); the Western economic recession, which lowered demand for East European exports; and the dramatic deterioration in the area's terms of trade with the Soviet Union, beginning in 1975.[48]

The main cause of the worsening of USSR-CMEA economic relations was the rapid increase in the price of fuels, especially oil and gas, imported by Eastern Europe relative to the prices of East European–manufactured goods exported to the Soviet Union. The paradox of the situation was that while Eastern Europe's energy needs were growing, it was slated to receive less than before and at increased prices. East European appeals to Moscow to modify the situation failed conspicuously. A working session in Moscow at the end of April 1983, charged with the task of preparing the first CMEA summit meeting since 1971, failed to agree on the agenda, and the summit was postponed indefinitely. The communist Williamsburg conference did not take place.

Given the vital necessity of cutting back on imports and boosting exports to the hard-currency countries, East European planners were forced to reduce domestic growth rates. As a consequence, they lowered living standards, slashed investment rates, and instituted crash conservation programs. An overall belt-tightening has taken place throughout the region. These deep strains in the situation of the CMEA's non-Soviet members reflected to a certain degree the economic difficulties the USSR was facing. Its own need for hard currency led Soviet oil production to be routed to Western markets, bypassing Eastern Europe. But this did not mean that Andropov's Russia had lost interest in Eastern Europe (after assuring that its military control over the region was complete) but rather that the Soviets' own thinking on the problems of socialist economic integration was in flux. One gets the impression of a certain parallelism between Andropov's style in reforming the Soviet economy and the advice Soviet experts were giving Eastern Europeans (first proceed locally and then coordinate economic policies with individual CMEA partners). Real supranational integration, with an abundance of optimistic programs, was left for the 1990s.

Some of the leading U.S. experts on the CMEA believe that at the present time Soviet leaders are inclined to avoid radical solutions in trying to solve the CMEA's problems and handling the worried, impatient, and occasionally even obstreperous junior partners.[49] Despite evidence that there exists a tendency to reimpose policies for integration from the "center," the hard-line approach could cause political complications that should be avoided. The opposite option of comprehensive economic reforms, which has ardent partisans in Eastern Europe, is also not to the Kremlin's liking because of potentially unfavorable political consequences and the increased burden that such reforms could place on the Soviet economy. The choice then would be an intermediate solution, a sort of "muddling through," whose contours one can discern by a careful reading of the articles of an expert on the CMEA, Soviet academician O. Bogomolov. The essence of two of his articles, significantly entitled "CMEA States Can Teach Soviet Economy" and "The CMEA Strategy for the 1980s," may be summarized as follows.[50] There exists an imperative, valid for all CMEA countries, to raise labor productivity through strengthening labor discipline, improving the organization of work, and stepping up moral and material incentives. One way to achieve these goals is a transition from an extensive to an intensive economy. A necessary reduction in the proportion of energy- and materials-intensive production facilities and processes could be compensated by an increased use of computers, the introduction of robots, and the development of fuel- and energy-saving machinery and equipment. Bogomolov complimented in rather lavish terms the work of agricultural cooperatives and enterprises in Hungary and the rationalization of production and conservation of raw materials in East Germany. He then informed his readers that on the basis of "careful experimental testing," significant reforms should be enacted. One would be the expansion of the economic independence of enterprises, and another the strengthening of economic-accountability principles in the planned management of the economy. He criticized the trend toward a lower level of East-West economic cooperation and the West's differentiated policy toward individual socialist states. He endorsed a "united front" of CMEA states in doing business with the West on the basis of mutual advantage and respect for one another's interests.

Dangers and Promises

Eastern Europe is both an asset and a liability to the Soviet Union. Among the institutional assets, and despite the manifold problems within the WTO, I would subscribe to the conclusion of probably the best expert on Soviet and East European military affairs, Professor John Erickson, director of defense studies at the University of Edinburgh, that "for all its faults and faltering, the Pact still has its uses."[51] Another asset is the role played by some Eastern European countries, especially East Germany, in promoting Marxist-Leninist revolutionary goals, as defined by the Soviet Union, in different parts of the Third World.[52] A special asset would be the categorically proclaimed and often iterated determination of Kremlin leaders to preserve the present status of the Soviet bloc. Even if one assumes, with Leszek Kolakowski, that "the empire will crumble," it would be unrealistic to expect its demise as long as the ruling Soviet elite holds together and the central repressive machinery stands ready to stamp out any serious oppositional move, domestic or peripheral. In this sense, Eastern Europe is an unwilling but powerless hostage of the Kremlin.

As for the liabilities of Eastern Europe for the Soviet Union, they are no less numerous. Some of them have been discussed above. The crucial issue is the factors that could suddenly turn the present "order reigning in Eastern Europe" into its opposite. To quote two highly qualified observers of the Eastern European scene, who succinctly describe how and why the oppressiveness of the imperial masters may beget rebelliousness among their non-Soviet subjects:

> Will the combined forces of "the revolution from below"—the "revolution of rising expectations," nationalism and the attraction of Western trade and technology—weaken their dependence on the USSR and lead them toward national independence? This is hardly probable because of Soviet determination to retain control over Eastern Europe. The opposite option of giving up the import of Western technology, dreams of prosperity and independence from the Soviet Union runs contrary to both the economic and political aspirations of the East European people.[53]

Similarly, but even more suggestively, one of the best Western experts on Eastern Europe, Professor Teresa Rakowska-Harmstone, has concluded that "when basic incongruity exists between the political culture and the system, as in Czechoslovakia, Poland, or Hungary, especially if reinforced by modernizing pressures, such a conflict breeds demands for democratization and generates instability leading to revolutionary situations."[54]

There are other elements that may contribute to the emergence of revolutionary situations: most important, East European countries were and are culturally and economically more developed than the Soviet Union; parts of their ruling elites are disaffected with the praxis of the communist exercise of power; large numbers of highly qualified technocrats, aware of their usefulness to the regimes, are pushing for meaningful reforms; most creative intellectuals, in the broadest sense of the term, oppose the official status quo; the workers, above all in Poland, have been forced to disappear as an independent social force and this under a regime that officially speaks in the name of proletarian sovereignty. Last, but certainly not least, East Europeans overwhelmingly identify with Western ideas and realities of representative governments, genuinely free elections, and authentic pluralism of political and social life.

These factors, as previously argued, are presently inoperative and do not represent an immediate threat to the Soviet Union and local communist powerholders. Soviet leaders are, however, fully aware of the flammable potential burning under the surface in Eastern Europe. And here the West faces maximum dangers. It may also be permitted hopes. The dangers are, as soberly argued by former secretary of defense Brown, that in confronting increasing domestic and imperial difficulties, the present or the new Soviet leaders who will assume power during the 1980s may decide to turn to stark repression and foreign adventurism as solutions to the problems that assail them. The main hope is—and here the West should do its persuasive best—to convince the Soviets that the cost of empire is too great to bear and that it would be in their strategic interest to accept a qualitative change in the status of Eastern Europe. How that could be done and what forms an emancipation of Eastern Europe would assume are beyond the scope of this essay.[55] Let me therefore close with a final and more limited observation: if the combustible material of history piles up again, as it did so dramatically in the past, Soviet leaders should realize that it is not in their interest to suppress militarily the ultimately irrepressible democratic aspirations of the East Europeans.

Notes

1. Luigi Barzini, *The Europeans* (New York: Simon & Schuster, 1983), p. 21.

2. *NIN* (Belgrade), June 26, 1983.

3. Three articles with unusually acute and original comments on Poland in the aftermath of the pope's visit are "The Pope and Poland: A Symposium," *New York Times*, July 3, 1983; Abraham Brumberg, "Poland: Planning a Disaster," *New York Times*, August 2, 1983; and A. M. Rosenthal, "The Trees of Warsaw: A Return to Poland," *New York Times Magazine*, August 7, 1983.

4. Cf. Joseph C. Harsch, " 'The Threat,' " *Christian Science Monitor*, May 26, 1983. On the crucially important subject of Soviet military thinking and writing, see Harriet Fast Scott and William F. Scott, eds., *The Soviet Art of War: Doctrine, Strategy and Tactics* (Boulder, Colo.: Westview Press, 1982); and especially Peter H. Vigor, *Soviet Blitzkrieg* (New York: St. Martin's Press, 1983). For the non-nuclear defense of Europe, see the Report of the European Security Study, *Strengthening Conventional Deterrence in Europe: Proposals for the 1980s* (New York: St. Martin's Press, 1983). The widely read books by General Sir John Hackett and other top-ranking NATO generals and advisers are based on the concept of non-nuclear defense of Europe; see *The Third World War, August 1985* (New York: Macmillan, 1978) and *The Third World War: The Untold Story* (New York: Macmillan, 1982).

5. The literature on wartime and postwar Poland is voluminous. Particularly good collections of articles and documents are Abraham Brumberg, ed., *Poland: Genesis of a Revolution* (New York: Vintage Books, 1983); and the two special issues of *Survey* magazine, titled *Poland Under Jaruzelski*, 26, nos. 3 and 4.

6. A. J. Liehm, "Reform in Eastern Europe," *Dissent*, Spring 1983, p. 239.

7. Jan Novak, a courier from Warsaw from the underground army during World War II to the Polish government-in-exile in London, in an interview with Michael Charlton entitled "On the Origins of the Cold War: The Eagle & the Small Birds, 1, The Spectre of Yalta," *Encounter*, June 1983, p. 20. Michael Charlton is one of Britain's leading broadcasters and a veteran foreign correspondent for the BBC. His interviews with prominent British, American, and European personalities on Yalta are of exceptional historical interest. The sequel to the first series of interviews was published in the July/August issue of *Encounter*, with the subtitle "2, The Triumph of the Commissar."

8. Adam B. Ulam, *Dangerous Relations: The Soviet Union in World Politics, 1970–1982* (New York: Oxford University Press, 1983), pp. 21–22.

9. Sidney Hook, *The Hero in History* (Boston: Beacon Press, 1943), pp. 201, 203.

10. As basic bibliographical support for my statement that Lenin was the most important political personality of the twentieth century, see his *What Is to Be Done?* first published as a separate pamphlet in March 1902 (it concerns the creation of the party of a new type); on his utopianism, consult his *State and Revolution*, written during the summer of 1917, as well as his October 14, 1921, article entitled "Fourth Anniversary of the October Revolution"; Lenin's essential pamphlet on techniques for seizing, maintaining, and expanding communist power is his famous *"Left-Wing" Communism, an Infantile Disorder* written in April 1920. The president of the Communist International, Georgi Zinoviev, called this work "the gospel of the proletariat," adding that "for the tactics of Communist parties it is no less important than Karl Marx's *Kapital* for the theory of Marxism." Noted historian Franz Borkenau described the pamphlet as "a handbook of revolutionary tactics and as such can sometimes be compared, for force of arguments, realism, directness, and convincing power, with Machiavelli's *Il Principe*" (*The Communist International* [London: Faber & Faber, 1938], p. 191).

11. "How to Deal with Moscow," *Newsweek*, November 29, 1982, p. 31.

12. Henry Kissinger, *Years of Upheaval* (Boston: Little, Brown, 1982), p. 242. Kissinger wrote these words in a memorandum to Richard Nixon prior to the 1973 summit: the italics in the text represent the former president's underlinings.

13. V. V. Zagladin, ed., *The World Communist Movement: Outline of Strategy and Tactics* (Moscow: Progress Publishers, 1973), p. 30.

14. *Western Europe Today: Economics, Politics, the Class Struggle, International Relations* (Moscow: Progress Publishers, 1981), p. 352.

15. Georgi Arbatov and Willem Oltmans, *The Soviet Viewpoint* (New York: Dodd, Mead & Co., 1983), pp. 17–18. Arbatov's book is very carefully edited and was written to impress U.S. liberal circles positively. Former senator J. William Fulbright in his introduction responded as Arbatov must have expected. For a different reaction, see the review of Malcolm Toon, U.S.

ambassador to the Soviet Union (1976–79) in the *Washington Post* (May 8, 1983). According to Toon, "I have never ceased to be amazed at the man's consummate arrogance and gall; and I have long been disturbed by his one-sided assessment of the world scene and the impact of this on Soviet leaders, with many of whom Arbatov is well-connected." In an earlier book, Arbatov espoused an orthodox Leninist line, writing about "the inevitable struggle between the two world systems" (*The War of Ideas in Contemporary International Relations* [Moscow: Progress Publishers, 1973], pp. 35–36).

16. Nina Tumarkin, *Lenin Lives! The Lenin Cult in Soviet Russia* (Cambridge, Mass.: Harvard University Press, 1983).

17. Nina Tumarkin, "The Remains of Lenin," *New York Times*, April 30, 1983. Two major, recently published books that support Tumarkin's contention of the importance, from the standpoint of the present Soviet regime, of a mythological interpretation of both Lenin's past and his utopian projection of the future are Paul Johnson, *Modern Times: The World from the Twenties to the Eighties* (New York: Harper & Row, 1983); and Michel Heller and Aleksandr Nekrich, *L'Utopie au pouvoir: Histoire de l'U.R.S.S. de 1917 à nos jours* (Paris: Calmann-Lèvy, 1982).

18. Three articles, written by some of the best American correspondents in the Soviet Union, vividly describe this phenomenon: Dusko Doder, "The Reds' Menace—Paper: 800 Billion Documents Choking the Russian Economy," *Washington Post*, June 12, 1983; Serge Schmemann, "The Kremlin Adds Some New Tea Leaves to a Familiar Brew," *New York Times*, June 19, 1983 (the main thesis of this article is that Andropov was overwhelmed by the enormity of his challenge; Schmemann depicted him as "a sick man without a program"); and James Mitchell, "Andropov's Era of Factory Reform Begins with a Whimper," *Christian Science Monitor*, July 29, 1983.

19. Martin Ebon, "The Four Faces of Andropov," *Psychology Today*, May 1983, p. 34. See also idem, *The Andropov File* (New York: McGraw-Hill, 1983).

20. *Information Bulletin* (*World Marxist Review*), January 1983, p. 5.

21. Possibly the best illustration of Andropov's skill as a debater is his conversation with the publisher of the West German weekly *Der Spiegel*. For the text of their April 1983 conversation, see *Pravda* and *Izvestiya*, April 25, 1983. For an English translation, see *Current Digest of the Soviet Press*, May 25, 1983.

22. The first quote is from Dimitri K. Simes, "The New Wave of Soviet Repression," *Christian Science Monitor*, July 13, 1983; the second from Stephen F. Cohen, "Sovieticus," *Nation*, March 12, 1983.

23. Two recent books that deal with the subject are Claire Sterling, *The Terror Network* (New York: Holt, Rinehart & Winston, 1981); and John Barron, *KGB Today: The Hidden Hand* (New York: Reader's Digest Press, 1983). See also Michael Ledeen, "Drugs, Guns, and Terrorists: K.G.B. Connections," *New Republic*, February 28, 1983; and Walter Guzzardi, Jr., "Cut-

ting Russia's Harvest of U.S. Technology," *Fortune*, May 1983. *Time* magazine (February 14, 1983) published a detailed and richly documented article on KGB organizational structures and activities at home and abroad, and the *New York Times* ran a series on KGB activities around the world, July 24–26, 1983.

24. Since January 1983 large numbers of Soviet spies have been arrested and a great many expelled from France, Great Britain, Italy, West Germany, Spain, Switzerland, the Netherlands, Norway, Sweden, Denmark, the United States, Canada, Australia, and Japan. The largest number expelled from any one country was the 47 Soviet diplomats, trade officials, and journalists expelled from France on April 5, 1983 (including the third-ranking official at the Soviet embassy in Paris, believed to be the KGB chief in France). (*San Francisco Examiner and Chronicle*, May 22, 1983.)

25. Quoted in *Christian Science Monitor*, August 4, 1983.

26. Joseph C. Harsch (in his columns in the *Christian Science Monitor*, early August 1983) wrote that under the new circumstances the hostility of the first two years of the Reagan administration would be replaced by a sense of "business as usual" between the two superpowers, with "competitive coexistence" replacing confrontation and possible ultimate war. Joseph Kraft (*San Francisco Chronicle*, August 1, 1983) second-guessed that after scrutinizing all parts of the world from the viewpoint of the USSR's interests, the Soviet leader concluded that the best course of action was a temporary accommodation with the United States, even if he had to overrule Andrei Gromyko and Soviet defense experts.

27. Report of the European Security Study, *Strengthening Conventional Deterrence in Europe*, p. 8.

28. Arnold Beichman's alarming but tightly reasoned article entitled "The Looming Superpower Confrontation" (*Wall Street Journal*, August 5, 1983) merits particular attention.

29. Quoted in *Newsweek*, July, 18, 1983.

30. Beichman, "The Looming Superpower Confrontation."

31. V. I. Lenin, *Polnoe sobranie sochinenii* (Complete Collection of works) (Moscow, 1964), 44:179. The February 24 draft is in *ibid.*, 45:68.

32. Louis Fischer, *The Soviets in World Affairs*, 2d ed. (Princeton, N.J.: Princeton University Press, 1951), p. 240

33. Lenin, *Sochinenii*, 45:193.

34. Ibid., p. 2.

35. See in particular the latest book by one of the most competent and prolific writers on the Soviet economy, Marshall I. Goldman, *USSR in Crisis: The Failure of an Economic System* (New York: W. W. Norton & Co., 1983).

36. *Public Opinion* (February/March 1983) contains important and alarming articles and results of poll surveys on both sides of the Atlantic concerning

the alleged "demise of Atlanticism." For the Dutch writer's article, see Jan van Houten, "Why Intellectuals Abroad Love to Hate America," *Wall Street Journal*, August 3, 1983.

37. Bernard W. Rogers, "The Atlantic Alliance: Prescriptions for a Difficult Decade," *Foreign Affairs*, Summer 1982, p. 1156.

38. Robert W. Tucker, "In Defense of Containment," *Journal of Contemporary Studies*, Spring 1983, p. 48.

39. Gromyko's speech was printed in *Pravda* and *Izvestiya* of June 17. The English translation may be found in *Current Digest of the Soviet Press*, July 20, 1983.

40. Harold Brown, *Thinking About National Security: Defense and Foreign Policy in a Dangerous World* (Boulder, Colo.: Westview Press, 1983), p. 13.

41. Yuri Andropov, "The Teaching of Karl Marx and Certain Questions of Socialist Construction in the U.S.S.R.," *Communist*, no. 3 (February 1983). Abstract in English in *Current Digest of the Soviet Press*, April 6, 1983.

42. Richard Lowenthal, "The Ruling Party in a Mature Society," in Mark G. Field, ed., *Social Consequences of Modernization in Communist Societies* (Baltimore, Md.: Johns Hopkins University Press, 1976).

43. Quoted in Zdeněk Mlynář, *Nightfrost in Prague: The End of Humane Socialism* (New York: Karz Publishers, 1980), p. 240.

44. Walter D. Connor, "Varieties of East European Dissent," *Studies in Comparative Communism*, Winter 1982, p. 412.

45. Peter Zwick, *National Communism* (Boulder, Colo.: Westview Press, 1983), p. 13.

46. Stephen R. Bowers, "An Assessment of the Polish Crisis: The East European View," *Journal of Social, Political and Economic Studies*, Fall 1982, p. 267.

47. Milovan Djilas, "Why Poland Is Lenin's Own Weak Link," *Wall Street Journal*, March 9, 1983.

48. See Jan Vanous, "East European Economic Slowdown," *Problems of Communism*, July–August 1982; Wharton Econometric Forecasting Associates, *Centrally Planned Economies Outlook*, March 1983; and *New York Times*, November 7, 1982, and May 10, 1983.

49. See, for example, Paul Marer and John Michael Montias, "CMEA Integration: Theory and Practice," in *East European Economic Assessment*, Part 2, *Regional Assessments: A Compendium of Papers Submitted to the Joint Economic Committee, Congress of the United States* (Washington, D.C., 1981), pp. 170–71; and Roger Skurski, "Trade and Integration in East Europe," *Current History*, November 1982.

50. The articles were published in *Pravda*, March 14, 1983, and *Kommunist*, no. 7 (May 1983). English translations in *Current Digest of the Soviet Press*, April 14 and July 13, 1983.

51. John Erickson, "Stability in the Warsaw Pact?" *Current History*, November 1982, p. 394.

52. Michael Radu, ed., *Eastern Europe and the Third World* (New York: Praeger, 1981), p. vi.

53. Oleg Zinam, "Economic Dilemma of Eastern Europe: Technology and Progress of Modernization," *Nationalities Papers*, Spring 1983, p. 69.

54. Teresa Rakowska-Harmstone, *Perspectives for Change in Communist Societies* (Boulder, Colo.: Westview Press, 1979), p. 25.

55. From the abundant literature dealing with this and similar subjects, I would recommend Harold Brown, *Thinking About National Security*; the works of the distinguished experts on Eastern Europe Stanislaw Gomulka and Peter Wiles from the London School of Economics, who share similar though not identical views; and the original and thought-provoking articles by Yale Professor Jan Gross, published in various periodicals. Finally, three magazine articles merit particular attention: Walter Laqueur, "What We Know About the Soviet Union," *Commentary*, February 1983; Leszek Kolakowski, "A General Theory of Sovietism," *Encounter*, May 1983; Arch Puddington, "Are Things Getting Better in Eastern Europe?" *Commentary*, August 1983.

———16

U.S. Strategic and
Arms Control Policy

William R. Van Cleave————————

R onald Reagan waged his successful presidential campaign
in no small part on the twin issues of a dangerously de-
teriorating military balance and failed arms control. Reagan assailed the
Carter administration for allowing serious "vulnerabilities and deficiencies" to develop in U.S. nuclear forces, which, he argued, "must be
made survivable as rapidly as possible to close the window of vulnerability before it opens any wider."[1] The arms control process, which was
supposed to enhance U.S. security, particularly by reducing the threat
to deterrent forces, had in fact had the opposite effect. Reagan called
the Carter SALT II agreement "fatally flawed," warned that it would
merely "legitimize the continuation of a one-sided arms buildup" by
the USSR, and recommended that it be withdrawn from the Senate.[2]

As president, Reagan continued to emphasize the need to restore a
military balance and to close the nuclear "window of vulnerability" as
expeditiously as possible.[3] In 1982, he publicly announced that the Soviet Union had attained military superiority:

> The truth of the matter is that on balance the Soviet Union does
> have a definite margin of superiority—enough so there is risk,
> and there is what I have called, as you all know, several times, a
> window of vulnerability.

Today, in virtually every measure of military power, the Soviet
Union enjoys a decided advantage.[4]

At the end of 1983, nearly three years into the Reagan administration, the facts of the situation and the programs and policies of the
Reagan administration were still generating controversy. If anything,
nuclear issues had become even more contentious; and, in general,
public and congressional support for major increases in the U.S. military effort had significantly lessened in comparison with 1980. The administration was on the defensive against a variety of popular and
congressional initiatives for cutting proposed increases in defense
spending and for freezing or reducing nuclear arms immediately. At
the same time, the administration was emphasizing the importance of
nuclear arms control. Surprisingly, the president had pledged that the
United States would not undercut the provisions of SALT II so long as
the Soviets showed similar restraint. Whatever the flaws of that unratified treaty, they were apparently not fatal.

Three years of effort had failed to find a solution to the window of
vulnerability, especially in regard to the vulnerable intercontinental ballistic missile (ICBM) force. At the same time, however, critics were
accusing the Reagan administration of shifting U.S. nuclear policy
from one of deterrence to one of planning to fight nuclear wars.

Nuclear Balance

The fiscal year 1984 *Annual Report to Congress* of the secretary
of defense observes that a sustained Soviet nuclear buildup, coupled
with certain cumulative reductions in U.S. nuclear forces, has produced a profound shift in the nuclear balance. "The Soviets," it concludes, "have acquired a margin of nuclear superiority in most
important categories, while still maintaining superiority in their conventional forces."[5] That statement should surprise no one—Soviet superiority has been anticipated and officially warned against for several
years. If anything, the report's conclusion is an understatement—it
would be difficult to identify a single important category of U.S. superiority.[6] And the shift is qualitative as well as quantitative—it has the
most serious implications for the ability of U.S. forces to fulfill their
intended objectives. In fact, qualitatively, "our strategic programs have
been restrained because of expectations for SALT and détente," according to Defense Secretary Caspar Weinberger.[7]

A study conducted in 1978 identified over forty categories for comparing U.S. and Soviet strategic nuclear forces. In 1962, all favored the United States; by 1982, the study predicted, essentially all would favor the Soviet Union.[8] And this has occurred. In all major indices, the Soviets have seized an advantage that, given the existing programs on the two sides, will continue to grow in the years ahead.[9] In 1982, the Joint Chiefs of Staff presented Congress with a strategic force comparison graph showing U.S. inferiority as far ahead as projected—through 1992, or twelve years after the election of Ronald Reagan.[10]

But, again, this had been anticipated. By 1969, the Soviets were spending twice as much on strategic nuclear forces as the United States, with the gap progressively widening to about three and one-half to one.[11] In 1980, the chairman of the Joint Chiefs of Staff told Congress: "We face an adversary at least our equal in strategic nuclear power and possessing substantial advantages in theater nuclear and conventional forces . . . their momentum will allow them to gain an advantage over the United States in most of the major indicators of strategic force by the early 1980s. Moreover, because of lead times in modern weapons programs, this progressive shift in the strategic balance will continue into the latter part of the 1980s."[12]

Contrary to popular belief, the U.S. nuclear stockpile has been shrinking, not expanding. In 1983, compared with fifteen to twenty years earlier, the United States had about one-third fewer nuclear warheads and total yield had been reduced by a factor of four.[13] At the same time, the Soviet nuclear stockpile has expanded manyfold. In major delivery systems, it is symptomatic that while the United States closed its last ICBM production line in 1977, the Soviets have produced, each and every year for many years, two to three times as many ICBMs as the Reagan administration wishes to produce during this *decade.*[14]

The same trends and situation exist in the theater nuclear balance, where in every category—megatonnage, warheads, delivery systems—the Soviets have advantages over NATO of from three to one to nine to one.[15] One of the many important examples of the continuing Soviet buildup is the mobile SS-20, a MIRVed intermediate-range ballistic missile. When the Department of Defense first issued its report *Soviet Military Power* at the end of 1981, the Soviets had 250 SS-20 launchers; by the time of the second report, March 1983, they had over 350 (*launchers*—each has additional refire missiles, and each missile has three warheads).[16] Secretary Weinberger has described the SS-20s as

having important strategic implications because they "significantly enhance the Soviets' ability to support an unreinforced attack"—a surprise attack—from peacetime deployment.[17]

In addition to a plethora of official statements describing the "vulnerabilities and deficiencies" in the United States' strategic nuclear
forces, including command-control-communications,[18] an analysis released by the prestigious Committee on the Present Danger warned
that these forces are insufficient to meet the deterrence standards officially established for them (see below). It concluded: "In no other area
of military capability is the gap between force objectives, or established
force requirements, and capabilities more pronounced than in the strategic nuclear realm." Specifically, "U.S. strategic nuclear forces fall far
short in survivability, target coverage, and endurance. Their vulnerability increases as Soviet programs expand and mature, and as the U.S.
fails to take the timely measures necessary to improve its own
forces."[19]

There should, then, be little doubt about the danger of the nuclear
balance and of ongoing trends in that balance. Clearly, during the decade and a half of SALT and détente, the trends have moved away from
parity or "essential equivalence" and toward Soviet nuclear superiority;
away from strategic stability and toward critical vulnerabilities in U.S.
nuclear deterrent forces. Those who reject these conclusions base their
objections on a very limited view of strategic nuclear forces and the
nuclear balance, a view that considers only peacetime inventories. They
believe that equivalence with the Soviets is not necessary and insist on
judging adequacy solely in terms of the hypothetical capability to destroy a number of Soviet cities. This is not the place to address my
disagreement with those views; it is enough to point out that they do
not represent official policy and standards. In fact, successive administrations throughout the nuclear age have rejected those views, and over
a period of time—particularly during the past dozen years—policies
and criteria for strategic forces have evolved and been approved by both
Republican and Democratic administrations.

U.S. Strategic Nuclear Policy

The essence of U.S. strategic policy over the years has been deterrence of attacks on the United States and its allies through retaliatory forces that are both capable and credible. This means, in the event
of attacks on the United States, that *surviving* forces must be credibly
capable of carrying out the missions planned for them. Those missions,

which have varied somewhat over the years, are selected (1) for their contribution to deterrence and (2) for their contribution to U.S. and allied political-military objectives. The most important of the latter are limitation of damage and control of escalation in the event that deterrence fails. Successive administrations have judged that these are not alternative objectives; the second not only has intrinsic value of itself, it is also essential to deterrence.

In addition, in assessing strategic nuclear forces and the nuclear balance, it is necessary to be mindful of other important contributions of U.S. strategic forces. They play a critical role in "extending deterrence" to the United States' allies and in providing a "nuclear umbrella" for friendly non-nuclear states. In peacetime, they provide a backdrop for the conduct of U.S. foreign policy, which is one of the reasons that they should, at a minimum, be essentially equivalent to Soviet forces. In the event of regional conflicts, particularly any involving the United States and the Soviet Union directly or indirectly, those forces must provide security against enemy escalation so that other forces can be effective. The strategic nuclear deterrent may be directly applicable only to a fairly narrow range of threats, but the balance of forces at that level is the high ground overshadowing all other uses—or threatened uses—of military force involving the Soviet Union or the United States. With dominance at that level, Soviet leaders may feel freer to use and threaten to use force at lower levels and the United States and its allies may be more fearful of countering such use or resisting such threats.

Because of these considerations, and because of the enormous increase in Soviet nuclear capabilities over the past fifteen years, single massive countercity response capabilities have officially been judged inadequate and inappropriate. Despite the U.S. addiction in the mid-to-late 1960s to "assured destruction" based largely on such capabilities, this has always been the case.[20] It began to be brought into sharp focus, however, when President Nixon asked Congress in 1970: "Should a President be left with only one option, massive attacks on enemy cities in the event that deterrence fails, especially when such a response will be followed by the same attacks on our own cities?"[21]

National Security Decision Memorandum (NSDM)–242, first announced to the public in January 1974 by Secretary of Defense James Schlesinger, provided the official answer. And, through review by successive administrations, from Carter's Presidential Directive (PD)–59 to Reagan's National Security Decision Document (NSDD)–13, the answer, and the policies and criteria based on it, has remained essentially constant. Thus, in his fiscal 1984 *Report to Congress*, Secretary

Weinberger emphatically stated, "We need to be able to use force responsibly and discriminately, in a manner appropriate to the nature of a nuclear attack." The threat to destroy cities and civilians in retaliation "is neither moral nor prudent. The Reagan Administration's policy is that under no circumstances may such weapons be used deliberately for the purpose of destroying populations."[22]

The continuity of U.S. policy regarding the need for flexible responses to failures of deterrence (to assure that if deterrence initially fails, it need not fail entirely) is demonstrated in the 1984 report by an appendix showing the similarity of statements by former secretaries of defense.[23]

Since 1974, U.S. defense policy has explicitly provided that U.S. strategic forces must be able to absorb a "well-executed surprise attack," have a variety of controlled and selective strike options against the full range of enemy targets, including hardened counterforce targets, and still have an assured destruction capability against enemy economic targets, which could be withheld for even an extended period of time.

The Carter administration, in announcing its "countervailing strategy" (and acknowledging at the same time that "the name is newer than the strategy"), said that U.S. forces must be able to "(1) survive a well-executed surprise attack; (2) penetrate any enemy defenses; (3) react with the timing needed, both as to promptness and endurance, to assure the deliberation and control deemed necessary; and (4) destroy their designated targets." At the same time, it rejected any distinction between a "deterrence-only" strategy and one based on a "war-fighting capability" and the ability to control escalation. ("Our surest deterrent is our capability to deny gain from aggression . . . There is no contradiction between this attention to militarily effective targeting . . . and our primary and overriding policy of deterrence.")[24]

A subsequent report to Congress spelled out the targeting and war-fighting implications of this policy:

> PD-59 specifies the development of plans to attack a comprehensive Soviet/Warsaw Pact target system, with the flexibility to employ these plans, should deterrence fail, in a deliberate manner consistent with the needs of the situation and in a way which clearly exceeds his expected gains. This could entail initial retaliation on military and control targets while retaining the capability either to withhold for a relatively prolonged period, or to execute, broad retaliatory attacks on the political control system and on general industrial capacity. These individual target systems, which

we feel the Soviet leaders value most, include leadership and control, military forces both nuclear and conventional, and the industrial/economic base. Highlights of targeting aspects include an increased number of situation-oriented options, and more flexibility for selectively attacking all categories of targets.[25]

Obviously, then, it is erroneous to assert that the nuclear policies of the Reagan administration make a sharp break with deterrence and place a new emphasis on nuclear war-fighting. Rather, any close perusal of official statements, and particularly Weinberger's *Annual Reports*, reveals a marked similarity and continuity of policy. As Secretary Weinberger emphasizes in his fiscal 1984 report, the Reagan administration's policy of "seeking to enhance deterrence and to limit the level of destruction by having flexible and enduring forces is not new. It has been squarely in the mainstream of American strategic thinking for over two decades." Not only does this capability enhance deterrence, but if deterrence fails, "the dividends of a viable war-fighting defense are unquestionable."[26]

Except for such partial and general statements in the *Annual Reports*, the Reagan administration has not been as forthcoming about its strategic nuclear policy as the two preceding administrations. It has seemed reluctant to engage in public discussions of the matter; hence, descriptions of its strategy have come from an apparent series of press leaks; for example, *Washington Post* columnist George C. Wilson allegedly drew on leaked classified Defense Guidance in describing that strategy:

> Forces capable, under all conditions of war initiation, of attacking a wide range of targets, even when retaliating to a massive strike received without strategic warning . . . Employment plans that assure U.S. strategic nuclear forces can render ineffective the total Soviet, and Soviet allied, military and political power structure through attacks on political/military leadership and associated control facilities, nuclear and conventional forces, and industry critical to military power . . . Forces that will maintain throughout a protracted conflict period and afterward the capability to inflict very high levels of damage against the industrial/economic base of the Soviet Union and her allies so that they have a strong incentive to seek conflict termination short of an all-out attack on our cities and economic assets.[27]

If Wilson's report is accurate—and nothing in the *Annual Reports* or other available Defense Department documents refutes it—then it demonstrates the continuity and similarity of Reagan administration policy to PD-59 and NSDM-242. If anything, the administration's policy seems slightly more ambitious; which raises a question discussed at the end of this essay: Is there such a large gap between official plans and objectives and actual and planned strategic forces that, in fact, there is considerable ambiguity within the Reagan administration's strategic policy?

Nuclear Force Programs and Expenditures

Soviet military spending first surpassed that of the United States in 1969, and the gap has widened each year since. Between 1969 and 1979, while Soviet spending increased annually, U.S. spending decreased in nine of the eleven years. For the period 1970–1982, according to the Department of Defense, the cumulative differentials were $700 billion in overall spending, $450 billion in investment, and $150 billion in strategic nuclear forces (fiscal 1983 dollars).[28] Direct U.S. spending on strategic nuclear force programs ran to 6–8 percent of the U.S. defense budget during fiscal years 1980–1983. Even with larger increases for fiscal 1984 to fund the B-1B bomber and the MX missile, among other programs, this spending is still only about 10 percent of the total. At least three conclusions can be drawn from this: (1) despite media depiction of such spending as expensive, if not excessive, it hardly dominates or drives the defense budget; (2) major, affordable increases, necessary to correct the vulnerabilities and deficiencies in U.S. nuclear forces, are possible; and (3) spending on these forces remains inadequate; given their importance, the administration has not assigned them the high priority they deserve.

As of fiscal year 1984, the administration plans (for details, consult the *Annual Reports* for 1982 and 1983):

1. To deploy 100 MX missiles in 100 existing Minuteman silos at Warren Air Force Base and begin a ten-year development program for a small, single-warhead ICBM and basing modes for it. (The administration accepted these recommendations of the President's Commission on Strategic Forces after the release of the 1984 *Annual Report.*)

2. To request funding for an eleventh Trident submarine. (Some twenty are tentatively planned, with deployment proceeding at the rate of one per year. The second of the ten authorized Trident subs was deployed in 1983. Trident I missiles have now been

deployed on twelve Poseidon submarines and will be placed in the first eight Trident subs, while the longer-range and more accurate Trident II missile is under development for deployment by 1990 in the ninth Trident sub. Some 400 land-attack nuclear cruise missiles are planned for attack submarines and a few surface ships.)

3. To have 100 B-1B bombers operational by the late 1980s and to deploy the advanced technology bomber (or Stealth), now under development, in the 1990s. (Air-launched cruise missiles [ALCMs] are being produced for deployment on part of the B-52 force and on the B-1B, but the originally planned number has been cut substantially, presumably because of anticipated earlier success with development of a follow-on cruise missile.)

4. To develop more capable, survivable, and durable command-control-communications-intelligence (C^3I) systems to provide early warning, attack assessment, and communications (apparently with heavy reliance on satellite systems and major improvements in ground-based radar surveillance).

5. To conduct a modest modernization of surveillance and intercept capabilities for air defense. (The administration has made no commitment to any significant air defense capability. The major increase in strategic defensive effort is in research and development for ballistic missile defense. This increase, from under $500 million in fiscal 1982 to $1.5 billion in fiscal 1985, was proposed prior to the president's television address on March 23, 1983, proposing a national commitment over the long run to the development of truly effective defenses.)

These programs may seem substantial, and some of them—C^3I improvements, the B-1B and complementary advanced technology bomber, the Trident submarine and Trident II missile programs, and the ALCM programs—promise significant improvements.[29] However, in view of the problems previously noted, as well as of official strategic force requirements, there are serious inadequacies in the administration's modernization program. For the most part, it lacks a sense of urgency and timeliness, particularly in restoring essential equivalence to the strategic balance and in closing the window of vulnerability. It promises improved capabilities mainly for the 1990s, while leaving severe vulnerabilities and deficiencies throughout the 1980s. Even so, it will not close the gap with Soviet capabilities or even keep pace with current and expected improvements in Soviet forces.

Particularly disappointing has been the administration's handling of the vulnerability problem, especially that of the ICBM force. It rejected not only the specific MX basing plan of the Carter administration, but also the very concept of multiple-shelter deceptive basing. But having accepted the MX missile, the administration wasted valuable time trying to resolve the unresolvable: how to base the MX survivably after precluding the only possibilities (multiple-shelter basing or anti-ballistic missiles [ABMs]). The problem was that the administration rejected a basing plan that was basically sound in concept but accepted an ICBM that was not. The problem in survivable ICBM basing is not the lack of viable basing options *per se*. With the right ICBM, there are a variety of concealment and/or mobility measures available. The problem is with the MX, which is more a product of SALT than of strategic logic. Strategic logic would argue strongly for dispersing ICBM capability among a larger number of smaller missiles (which could be adapted to a variety of survivable basing modes and individually would be less lucrative and less attractive targets) rather than concentrating it on a small number of very large and very heavy missiles (which are difficult to move and difficult to conceal but constitute highly lucrative and attractive targets).

In accepting the report of the Commission on Strategic Forces, chaired by retired Air Force general Brent Scowcroft, the administration decided, in essence, to ignore ICBM vulnerability for the time being and to deploy the MX in admittedly vulnerable fixed silos, while embarking on a long-term development of a small ICBM. It not only rejected recommendations (for example, by its Department of Defense Transition Team in 1980) to redeploy existing Minuteman III missiles in a more survivable multiple-shelter mode at existing deployment areas, but also rejected other "quick fixes" for near-term easing of vulnerabilities and deficiencies in strategic forces.[30]

The Scowcroft Commission emphasized the many benefits of a small, single-warhead ICBM,[31] but still recommended a leisurely development not "burdened" by a crash program, while proceeding with MX deployment. In a May 12, 1983, letter to Senator William Cohen, President Reagan pledged that "we will promptly undertake a major effort to bring the proposal of a small, single-warhead ICBM to fruition on a high-priority basis." Nonetheless, as of the end of 1983, there was no indication of such a priority or effort. The reason is simply that the Pentagon and the Air Force will regard the small ICBM as a competitor to the MX unless its development is deferred. That seems the only reason why, if the value and the strategic and arms control benefits of the small ICBM are as great as the Scowcroft Commission described, the United States has not proceeded with dispatch to develop and begin deploying that missile in four to five years.[32]

The rationale used by the commission, and accepted by the administration, for vulnerable deployment of the MX was partly "strategic" (addressed in the conclusions to this essay) and partly (a large part) arms control. The commission evinced great faith in the United States' ability to reach a "stabilizing and equitable agreement" with the Soviets if it demonstrated its will by deploying the MX, but felt such an agreement "illusory" if it did not. Thus, arms control considerations, which led to the MX in the first place (limiting the numbers of things—launchers, missiles—tends to result in putting more and more capability into the limited number of units), are being used to rationalize deployment of the MX. This is not a new phenomenon. For over a decade, arms control has had an important and adverse impact on the United States' strategic capability.

Arms Control

Justifiably, given the sorry experience of some fifteen years of major effort to achieve meaningful strategic arms limitations agreements with the USSR, candidate Reagan was critical and skeptical of arms control. Both he and the 1980 Republican platform pledged a new realism about arms control, and during its first year the Reagan administration enunciated certain realistic principles and guidelines.[33] These can be summarized as follows:

1. There would be no agreements for the sake of agreement—agreements must be militarily meaningful and promote stability and U.S. security; nor would the United States accept agreements merely to keep the "arms control process" going.

2. There would be no more one-sided arms control, or arms limitation, to set an example in the hope that the USSR would follow. (As the president said: "We have tried time and again to set an example by cutting our forces in the hope that the Soviets will do likewise. The result has always been that they keep building.")[34]

3. The United States has relied too much on arms control at the expense of defense programs, which has been detrimental to national security as well as to the success of arms control. (To quote the president again: "Unless we demonstrate the will to rebuild our strength and restore the military balance, the Soviets . . . have little incentive to negotiate.")[35]

4. The United States must recognize that there is little prospect of agreements that will help solve such basic security problems

as the vulnerability of its land-based deterrent forces until it demonstrates the capacity to solve them itself.

5. The United States has based arms control on limiting the wrong things, such as "launchers," which do not really reflect destructive capacity. It will now emphasize reductions, but in destructive capacity and in the most destabilizing systems. Any such reductions must be both stabilizing and strictly equal.

6. Agreements will be based on strict verification, which will not necessarily be restricted to national technical means, such as radar and satellite surveillance, and the United States will insist on full compliance by the Soviet Union.

7. The arms control process must be placed in the context of Soviet worldwide conduct. As Secretary of State Alexander Haig stated, "Pretending that there is no linkage promotes reverse linkage. It ends up by saying that in order to preserve arms control, we have to tolerate Soviet aggression. This Administration will never accept such an appalling conclusion."[36]

In the absence of agreements, it is premature to attempt to evaluate the administration's consistency with its own principles. However, during 1982 what Eugene Rostow, former director of the Arms Control and Disarmament Agency, has called "arms control fever" (which, he says, "defies the visible lessons of experience")[37] arose in Congress and some states (in the form of votes on nuclear freeze resolutions) and among a vocal part of the public. Senators and representatives, Democrat and Republican alike, began to vie with one another in suggesting arms control proposals, from the simple to the complicated, and insisting on wrapping weapons programs and defense appropriations in the smothering blanket of arms control rationale. In specific legislative terms, this amounted to very little. (On May 4, 1983, after countless hours of debate over an extended period of time, the House passed House Joint Resolution 13, calling for "an immediate, mutual, and verifiable freeze," followed by reductions in nuclear weapons. However, so many qualifications were attached as to render the resolution virtually meaningless.)

The fever, however, did move the administration to begin to adopt some of the rhetoric of the movement, to couch many of its own strategic policies and arms programs in terms of arms control objectives, and to show willingness to adjust its positions in the two major ongoing U.S.-Soviet arms negotiations. In part, at least, this resulted in short-term success: it did undercut some of the freeze momentum; it countered charges in the United States and Europe that the Reagan administration was anti–arms control; and it succeeded in reversing congressional opinion, resulting in approval of funds to develop and test MX.[38]

Some light on the administration's consistency with its principles might be shed by summarizing U.S. positions in the Strategic Arms Reduction Talks (START; formerly SALT). The U.S. position from the beginning and through the spring of 1983 was based on a two-phased approach to reductions in (1) the number of strategic ballistic missile warheads and (2) the number of deployed ballistic missiles, followed in the second phase by limits on missile throw-weight at similarly reduced levels. In more specific terms, the United States proposed a 5,000 ceiling on warheads (no more than half on ICBMs) and a limit of 850 on deployed ICBMs and submarine-launched ballistic missiles (SLBMs), with initial and reduced sub-limits on heavy ICBMs (which, following SALT II, meant only ICBMs of the size and throw-weight of the Soviet SS-18, thereby classifying the SS-17, SS-19, and MX as "medium"). Throw-weight, bomber, and cruise missile limits were to be left to the second phase. Verification would be by "cooperative means" in addition to national technical means.

The Soviet position, in general, was to stick with the SALT II framework and to suggest some reductions in the aggregate number of launchers, but to reject throw-weight limits, as well as significant reductions. The Soviets also warned that their START proposal was tied to nondeployment of ground-launched cruise and Pershing II missiles in Europe.

There clearly were problems in the U.S. position. The most significant limitation—throw-weight—was left to a "second phase." "Deployed missiles" was not defined, but seemed to be equated with SALT-type "launchers" (also never particularly defined), leaving open the question of limits on "nondeployed" missiles, of which the Soviets apparently have an impressive number.[39] A limit of 850 could fairly be said to be contradictory to stability by reducing the number of aim points, by encouraging very large missiles (obviously the intent was to bolster MX), and by precluding small, single-warhead ICBMs. The warhead number, in that context, was both too large and too small: It was too large, coupled with the 850 missile limit, to promote survivability and stability (2,500 ICBM warheads versus some 350–400 ICBM aim points, depending on the number of SLBMs deployed); and—unless survivability were very high, indeed—the number was too low to be consistent with the requirements of U.S. strategic policy and targeting doctrine. Limiting numbers of missiles and warheads *per se* also failed to take into account the enormous differences in their capabilities.

(The bulk of U.S. warheads, for example, consist of 150-pound, soft-target Poseidon warheads, while the bulk of Soviet warheads consist of hard-target ICBM warheads five times that weight.)

Some members of the administration, and others, favored a focus on throw-weight plus warhead limitations rather than low numerical limits on missiles. This view was reinforced by recommendations of the Scowcroft Commission. The administration responded by promising changes and new initiatives in the START round beginning in June 1983. In line with its recommendation to develop, and eventually deploy, a small, single-warhead ICBM, the commission proposed "an evolution for the U.S. ICBM force in which a given number of ballistic missile warheads would, over time, be spread over a larger number of launchers." It concluded:

> Over the long run, stability would be fostered by a dual approach toward arms control and ICBM deployments which moves toward encouraging small, single-warhead ICBMs. This requires that arms control limitations and reductions be couched, not in terms of launchers, but in terms of equal levels of warheads of roughly equivalent yield.[40]

In June 1983, the administration announced a modification of its START position. In the interests of "flexibility," the proposed limits on deployed missiles would be increased from 850 to an unspecified number (rumored at about 1,200); and while the United States still preferred direct limits on throw-weight, indirect limits—through missile limits and sub-ceilings on heavier missiles—would be acceptable. The change seemed more in consonance with the Soviet position than with the recommendations of the Scowcroft Commission, but it apparently did meet congressional pressure for more flexibility.

In the meantime, Soviet activities raised serious questions about noncompliance with existing arms control agreements. For years there had been possible to probable Soviet violations of the SALT I agreements, at least as those agreements were understood by the United States.[41] Unequivocal evidence mounted of Soviet production, stockpile, transfer, and use of lethal biological and chemical agents in Southeast Asia, Afghanistan, and the Middle East. Several Soviet nuclear weapons tests seemed well above the 150-kiloton limit of the Threshold Test Ban (unratified, but observance pledged by both sides). Finally, during 1982 and 1983, there was evidence of noncompliance with SALT II: reports of operational SS-16 missiles; simultaneous development and flight testing of two new ICBMs; testing and apparent preparations to deploy long-range cruise missiles on the Backfire bomber; Backfire production rates increased beyond those stipulated in a codicil to SALT II; and heavy encryption of missile telemetry to impede U.S. verification.

Assessments

A decisive shift in the correlation of forces will be such that come 1985, we will be able to exert our will wherever we need to [Leonid Brezhnev, Prague, 1973].

We are not only facing a period between 1981 to perhaps 1987 in which we are deficient in regional nuclear power, and in conventional power, but for the first time in post–World War II history, we will be vulnerable and deficient in central strategic nuclear power . . . The United States has permitted itself to be exposed in this vital area of first-strike vulnerability . . . I think that is an unacceptable position for us to be in." [Alexander Haig, Washington, D.C., 1981.][42]

The extent to which the Reagan administration's defense program will change this situation has been exaggerated by both the administration and its critics. The administration has valiantly battled congressional attempts to cut spending and programs, but the very fight itself has obscured that both spending and programs were inadequate to begin with. The Committee on the Present Danger concluded: "The Administration's defense program is a minimal one. It will not halt the unfavorable trends in the U.S.-Soviet military balance, let alone reverse them."[43]

An important supplementary problem is that the administration has failed to move with the dispatch and sense of urgency necessary to the situation. Failure to utilize budget and program plans formulated during the campaign and transition resulted in failure to request an extraordinary supplemental appropriation for the fiscal 1981 budget. In fact, it was nearly two years before the administration could put together its own program, for fiscal 1983. The two years were costly not only in time lost to the USSR, but also in support lost for substantial increases in the U.S. defense effort. As noted above, the administration has made little attempt to accelerate programs necessary to close the gap and has not established the proper priorities for closing the strategic window of vulnerability.

The term "window of vulnerability" refers in its most general sense to the overall gap between Soviet and U.S. strategic capabilities—a gap that allows the USSR to enjoy strategic superiority, which it regards as critical to a favorable "correlation of forces," with which it can expect to expand Soviet power and influence. In a more restricted sense, the term refers to the gap between U.S. strategic objectives and its capability to accomplish them, due to the dynamics of that Soviet superiority. And in a more limited sense, the term refers to acute vulnerabilities in U.S. nuclear deterrent forces. The most dramatic of those—and the one to which the Scowcroft Commission limited its attention—is, of course, the essentially total vulnerability of the U.S. ICBM force to hypothetical Soviet attacks. But the C³I network and the bomber force are in equally severe trouble. To this can be added the very questionable penetrability of whatever bombers might survive attack. For the near future, the sea-based force appears more survivable (for boats at sea), but there is an area of uncertainty: the communications link is an Achilles' heel; and current limitations in SLBM targeting capability make it a force on which the United States cannot, or does not wish to, depend for initial retaliation. Certainly, it cannot fulfill the targeting objectives contemplated in the descriptions of U.S. policy summarized above. Rather, it is a force the United States would wish to hold in reserve. An analysis of the situation by the Committee on the Present Danger concluded that in a surprise Soviet attack "80 to 90 percent of U.S. force capabilities could be lost, leaving us with an inadequate and inflexible response capability."[44] In essence, that would leave the United States with a force much closer in capability to Defense Secretary Robert McNamara's minimum "assured destruction" countercity capability than the type of force described by the policy and objectives that have evolved in the past decade.

Thus, while strategic policy has been evolving in one direction, limitations on force capabilities—when compared with Soviet capabilities—have led in the opposite direction. This leads to inevitable ambiguity in U.S. policy. Policy requires survivable and *endurable* forces capable of a considerable range of targeting over a protracted period; yet most U.S. forces could not absorb and survive the attacks the Soviets are capable of, and most of those that might survive are use-or-lose forces of little endurance. This certainly characterizes C³I as well. The situation may be leading the United States to a *de facto* launch-on-warning strategy, something that should be avoided at all costs.

Officials have generally agreed on these problems for a number of years; and Reagan and his supporters certainly emphasized them during the campaign. Now, in the face of inadequate actions to remedy them, the administration appears to be making an effort to rationalize them away—much as the Carter administration was accused in 1979–1980 of rationalizing away real problems. This seems demonstrated by the decision on the MX, by the Scowcroft Commission report, and by the president's acceptance and strong endorsement of that report (including, presumably, its logic).

On the one hand, the commission warned that the Soviets "now probably possess" the means to destroy the U.S. ICBM force with only a portion of their own ICBM force, that ICBM survivability "is today a matter of concern," and that U.S. strategic forces must be modernized to enhance their overall survivability. On the other hand, it deferred resolution of these matters to the 1990s, stating that "the vulnerability of silos, viewed in isolation, is not a sufficiently dominant part of the overall problem to warrant immediate steps." Ignoring the vulnerability of other components of U.S. forces, the commission concluded, in essence, that due to the totality of the TRIAD of ICBMs, SLBMs, and bombers, there is no real window of vulnerability. In other words, the president had been wrong all along, as had all those congressmen and analysts who were worried about the problem.

In fact, the commission suggested that silo vulnerability, which exists, is of so little concern that the United States can safely increase substantially the counterforce capability of missiles in those silos.

The report made a pass at arguing the difficulty of a coordinated attack on the bomber force and the ICBM force,[45] a difficulty that was addressed, examined, and largely dismissed as long ago as the Safeguard ABM debate in 1969. In doing so, it not only ignored other vulnerabilities and deficiencies, it also ignored U.S. strategic policy, the major role of ICBMs in that policy, the key attractiveness of attacking those ICBMs in order to disrupt that policy, and the long-agreed criterion of crisis stability (that is, that the United States must never allow *any* major component of its strategic forces to become so vulnerable as to tempt the Soviets to seize an advantage in a time of crisis by destroying it.)

Without a viable ICBM force, it is impossible to carry out U.S. strategic policy; without that policy, no comprehensive, integrated military strategy is possible. That means that the window of vulnerability, in every sense, will extend through this decade.

One of the arms control principles cited earlier, and supported by both logic and experience, is that there is really little prospect of agreements that will help solve such a basic problem as the survivability of the United States' ICBMs, at least until it has demonstrated the capacity to solve the problem itself. This capacity has not been demonstrated; yet the Scowcroft Commission turned hopefully to arms control to handle the problem. Of the three components it recommended, one was to seek arms control to enhance strategic stability (the other two were MX deployment and small ICBM development). How is this to be done? What evidence is there that the Soviets will help the United States resolve such problems, when it cannot resolve them itself (particularly since the Soviets have put so much effort into creating those problems in the first place)?

This is no argument against the enhanced missile capability represented by the MX; certainly, there are strong strategic, political, and arms control reasons to have that capability. The Soviets have for too long felt free to deploy 10–11 million pounds of ICBM throw-weight, with a one-sided counterforce capability against U.S. ICBMs, in vulnerable silos—simply because the United States has not produced the capability to put them at risk.

It is necessary to do so if the Soviets are ever to become seriously interested in reductions of such destabilizing systems. But to do so without corresponding improvements in the survivability of this increased capability makes little strategic sense; it is destabilizing rather than stabilizing.

That enhanced capability can be had with the small ICBM, without the attendant problem of vulnerability. The determination to produce the MX clearly delays the development of a small ICBM. Moreover, the MX debate is far from over; further opposition to it and further delay in the program are more likely than not, and this is likely to mean even more delay in closing the window of vulnerability. All in all, it seems past time for a major change of course.

Finally, some comments about arms control seem in order in view of the expectations being broadly expressed and the importance being placed on it.

Politicians and arms control enthusiasts are far too careless about the realities and prospects for arms control; they overstate dramatically the benefits of agreement and the risks of nonagreement. They forget that, in the democratic states of the West, arms are always controlled. They are controlled and limited by traditional values, by political and budgeting processes, and by the influence of the media and of public opinion. None of those limiting forces exist in the Soviet Union to any appreciable extent. And Soviet strategic objectives do not encourage any real limitations.

It is often forgotten that arms control was never more than a modest supplementary means of national security, the success of which required that the United States first assure that security through its own means. Arms control agreements simply reflect the reality of the strategic situation and the trends in it; if we are not happy with those, it is unlikely that we will be comfortable with arms agreements based on them. It is necessary first to change the adverse trends and improve the situation. It is illusory to expect "truly meaningful" and helpful agreements with the Soviet Union until that is done. If that logic is correct, the administration has not yet done enough to promote the likelihood of such agreements—in which case it would do a great service to the nation if it would patiently explain and candidly point this out to the public, rather than trying to outdo the optimistic rhetoric of uncautious arms control enthusiasts.

Notes

1. "Strength: Restoring the Margin of Safety," address to the national convention of the American Legion, August 20, 1980.

2. Examples of these statements on arms control and SALT II are "SALT and the Search for Peace," September 17, 1979; "Arms Control and the 1980 Election," May 1980 (answers to questions supplied by the Arms Control Association); "Peace: Restoring the Margin of Safety," address to the national convention of the Veterans of Foreign Wars, August 18, 1980; interview with the Associated Press, *New York Times*, October 2, 1980.

3. For example, in his interview with editors and reporters of the *Washington Star*, August 5, 1981. The term, "window of vulnerability," as discussed below, refers specifically to a period of risky vulnerability in U.S. strategic nuclear forces and broadly to general strategic nuclear inferiority.

4. Quotes respectively from news conference of March 31, 1982, and television address of November 22, 1982 (both contained in *New York Times* of the following day).

5. Secretary of Defense, *Annual Report to the Congress, FY 1984* (February 1, 1983), p. 34.

6. This is so for general categories such as throw-weight, megatonnage or equivalent megatonnage (EMT), hard-target kill capability, and even numbers of launchers, missiles, and warheads; and it applies to theater nuclear as well as intercontinental "strategic" nuclear forces. Possible categories of U.S. advantage include numbers of submarine ballistic missile warheads or weapons on "heavy bombers" as counted in SALT.

7. Secretary of Defense, *Annual Report to the Congress, FY 1983*, p. II–11

8. *Measures and Trends: U.S. and USSR Strategic Force Effectiveness*, Report for the Defense Nuclear Agency, Department of Defense, by the Santa Fe Corporation (Alexandria, Va., 1978). A 1982 review and update of this report by the Defense and Strategic Studies Program, University of Southern California, reinforces its findings and projections.

9. The only major index in which, arguably, the United States may have retained a lead has been in the numbers of strategic (offensive) warheads. This has long been fictitious because the putative lead depended on SALT counting rules, which exaggerate U.S. numbers and artificially depress Soviet numbers by, for example, excluding the Backfire bomber while maximizing U.S. bomber loadings (beyond available inventory, in fact); counting projected U.S. cruise missiles, while ignoring the more numerous existing Soviet cruise missiles and the additional Soviet ICBMs beyond SALT-counted launchers. In any case, Secretary Weinberger announced in March 1983 that this one area of possible U.S. advantage had been lost (press conference of March 9, 1983, reported in *Soviet Aerospace*, 37, no. 10 [March 14, 1983]).

10. In addition to the above sources, see U.S. Department of Defense, *Soviet Military Power, 1983* (Washington, D.C.: Government Printing Office, 1983); and Committee on the Present Danger, *Has America Become Number 2?* (Washington, D.C., 1982).

11. Secretary of Defense, *Annual Report to the Congress, FY 1981*, pp. 73–74; Committee on the Present Danger, *Has America Become Number 2?*, pp. 5, 15; see also Steven Rosefielde, *False Science: Underestimating the Soviet Arms Buildup* (New York: National Strategy Information Center; Rutgers, N.J.: Transaction Books, 1982), for an analysis showing even these estimates to be understated.

12. Chairman, Joint Chiefs of Staff, *U.S. Military Posture for Fiscal Year 1981* (Washington, D.C., 1980).

13. According to State Department official Paul Wolfowitz, the megatonnage of U.S. nuclear forces has been reduced by some 60 percent in the past twenty years, and the numbers of U.S. nuclear weapons by "many thousands" ("The Debate over a Nuclear Freeze," *Wall Street Journal*, October 28, 1982). For corroboration, see Secretary of Defense, *Annual Report, FY 1984*, p. 55.

14. U.S. Department of Defense, *Soviet Military Power, 1981*, pp. 12–13.

15. Donald R. Cotter et al., *The Nuclear Balance in Europe* (Cambridge, Mass.: United States Strategic Institute, 1983).

16. *Soviet Military Power*, 1981 and 1983 eds. The 1983 edition (p. 7) estimates "more than 330 SS-20 missile launchers"; subsequent official statements used the number 351.

17. Secretary of Defense, *Annual Report, FY 1983*, pp. 11–12.

18. All Department of Defense *Annual Reports* have documented these at least back to Secretary Donald Rumsfeld and the FY 1976T–1977 report. For a recent review of command-control-communications vulnerabilities, see "Our Achilles' Heel," *Newsweek*, May 2, 1983.

19. Committee on the Present Danger, *Has America Become Number 2?* pp. 20–21.

20. Successive Department of Defense *Annual Reports* since fiscal 1975 have generally pointed this out; see also, for discussion and documentation, Wil-

liam R. Van Cleave and Roger W. Barnett, "Strategic Adaptability," *Orbis*, Fall 1974; and Van Cleave, "Countervailing Strategy," in Werner Kaltefleiter and Ulrike Schumacher, eds., *Conflicts, Options, Strategies in a Threatened World* (Kiel, West Germany: Christian-Albrechts University, 1983).

21. Richard M. Nixon, *U.S. Foreign Policy for the 1970s*, Report to Congress (February 1970).

22. Secretary of Defense, *Annual Report, FY 1984*, pp. 54–55.

23. Ibid., Appendix A.

24. Secretary of Defense Harold Brown, *Annual Report, FY 1981*, p. 67.

25. Secretary of Defense Harold Brown, *Nuclear War Strategy*, U.S. Senate, Committee on Foreign Relations, 96th Cong., 2d sess., September 16, 1980, p. 29.

26. Secretary of Defense, *Annual Report, FY 1984*, pp. 52, 34.

27. "Preparing for Long Nuclear War Is Waste of Funds, Gen. Jones Says," *Washington Post*, June 12, 1982, p. A3.

28. The data are included in the fiscal 1983 and 1984 *Annual Reports*, as well as in the Committee on the Present Danger report.

29. U.S. Congressional Budget Office, *Modernizing U.S. Strategic Offensive Forces: The Administration's Program* (May 1983).

30. See, for example, William R. Van Cleave and W. Scott Thompson, *Strategic Options for the Early Eighties: What Can Be Done?* (New York: National Strategy Information Center, 1979); Van Cleave, "Quick Fixes to U.S. Strategic Nuclear Forces," in W. S. Thompson, ed., *From Weakness to Strength: National Security in the 1980s* (San Francisco: Institute for Contemporary Studies, 1980); and Van Cleave, "The Trouble Isn't the Basing Mode," *Washington Post*, December 17, 1982.

31. "From the point of view of enhancing stability, the Commission believes that there is considerable merit in moving toward an ICBM force structure in which potential targets are of comparatively low value—missiles containing only one warhead. A single-warhead ICBM, suitably based, inherently denies an attacker the opportunity to destroy more than one warhead with one attacking warhead." (*Report of the President's Commission on Strategic Forces*, p. 27.)

32. The Minuteman system, which required several major technical and operational breakthroughs to complete, went from start of full-scale development to deployment in four years. Four years is also about the time it takes commercial aircraft companies to design, develop, and begin to deliver a new generation of aircraft. The United States went from decision to the placement (and retrieval) of the first man on the moon in eight years, certainly an achievement exceedingly more complicated than a small ICBM program, which, as the Scowcroft Commission observed, would utilize existing technology.

33. These points are drawn from a large collection of statements made by the president, the secretary of state, the secretary of defense, and the director of the Arms Control and Disarmament Agency (ACDA) during 1981 and into 1982. Presidential statements are mostly from press conferences; Haig's remarks were set forth in speeches, which were published by the Department of State (a principal example was "Arms Control for the 1980s: An American Policy," address to the Foreign Policy Association, New York, July 14, 1981, published as *Current Policy*, no. 292); Weinberger's remarks are mostly in his first two *Annual Reports*; and Rostow's remarks are contained in numerous speeches available from ACDA Public Affairs.

34. President Ronald Reagan, televised address to the nation on arms control, Washington, D.C., November 22, 1982; text in *New York Times*, November 23, 1982.

35. Ibid.

36. Haig, "Arms Control for the 1980s." Or, as the 1980 Republican platform said, "Arms control negotiations, once entered, represent an important political and military undertaking that cannot be divorced from the broader political and military behavior of the parties" (p. 62).

37. "Arms Control Fever," Speech, April 7, 1983, New York, mimeo.

38. The House reversed itself on May 24, 1983, voting the funding, and the Senate on May 25. Key members of both Houses pointed to the administration's arms control promises as the reasons for their votes. As Senator Dan Quayle (R., Ind.) said, the reversal "comes down to two words—arms control" (San Francisco *Chronicle*, May 26, 1983, p. 1).

39. "The Soviets have stocked extra missiles, propellants, and warheads throughout the USSR . . . The Soviets have made provisions for the delivery of reserve missiles, warheads, and propellants to ICBM complexes for reload purposes. None of these extra missiles or warheads are counted under SALT agreements." (*Soviet Military Power, 1983*, pp. 17, 21.)

40. Released report, pp. 43, 44.

41. For an analysis of SALT I "violations," see Van Cleave, "SALT on the Eagle's Tail," *Strategic Review*, 4, no. 2 (Spring 1976). Reports of other violations are contained in official documents cited earlier, such as *Soviet Military Power*, and are regularly covered in *Soviet Aerospace*—for example, the issues of February and March 1983. Also available are two letters on Soviet violations from Senator James McClure (R., Id.) to President Reagan, dated March 23 and April 25, 1983.

42. Quotations from Committee on the Present Danger, *Has America Become Number 2?*

43. "Is the Reagan Defense Program Adequate?" (Washington, D.C., 1982), p. 34.

44. Committee on the Present Danger, *Has America Become Number 2?* p. 21.

45. One of the ones who contributed to the report and endorsed it was former

secretary of defense Harold Brown. It might be recalled what he wrote in his last official report on this subject: "It is equally important to acknowledge, however, that the coordination of a successful attack is not impossible, and that the 'rubbish heap of history' is filled with authorities who said something reckless could not or would not be done. Accordingly, we must take the prospective vulnerability of our ICBM force with the utmost seriousness." (*Annual Report, FY 1980*, p. 81.)

17

The U.S. Intelligence Establishment and Its Discontents

Arnold Beichman

F or those of all political persuasions who scoff at the need to safeguard U.S. technological secrets from prying eyes, especially those of the Soviet Union, let me call as a witness for the rebuttal Senator Daniel P. Moynihan (D., N.Y.), vice-chairman of the Senate Intelligence Committee. Senator Moynihan's words should give pause in particular to all those who press for arms control agreements between the United States and the Soviet Union, but at the same time regard a strengthened U.S. intelligence establishment—even one under congressional oversight—as a danger to U.S. democracy.

It is Senator Moynihan's opinion that the sale of secrets about U.S. surveillance satellites by two American traitors during the late 1970s was a major reason why the second U.S.-USSR treaty on limiting nuclear arms failed to win Senate ratification. In 1977 Christopher John Boyce, 29, and Andrew Daulton Lee, 30, were convicted of spying for the Soviet Union, specifically for selling secrets to the Soviet Union that Boyce had obtained while working as a maintenance employee at an intelligence contracting concern. Senator Moynihan said in a television interview:

> Basically with respect to the satellite systems that were compromised, they [Boyce and Lee] made them, temporarily at least, use-

less to us because the Soviets could block them, and the fear that that would happen, had happened, permeated the Senate and, as much as any one thing, was responsible for the failure of the SALT treaty. And if you think as I do that the breakdown of our arms negotiations with the Soviets is an ominous event, then nothing quite so awful has happened to our country as the escapade of these two young men.[1]

Had not Boyce and Lee been apprehended (accidentally, it turned out), the U.S. intelligence establishment might have gone along, as indeed it had before the arrests, for several more years offering as verified fact to U.S. policymakers data on the state of Soviet missile readiness and manufacture. In other words, the confidence of U.S. decision makers in satellite surveillance systems for verification was woefully misplaced; in fact, the compromised satellite systems, like a compromised human agent, had been "turned around" in the service of the Soviet Union and against the U.S. program of satellite data collection.

Today when there is a world consensus on the need for arms control, a secure national intelligence establishment is a necessity for preventing violations of arms control agreements. One of the most important reasons for strengthening the U.S. intelligence system is to prevent the Soviet KGB and its ancillary organizations from stealing U.S. technology secrets. Acquisition of U.S. technology is a major KGB priority.

According to Senator Sam Nunn (D., Ga.), KGB efforts to obtain U.S. microelectric, laser, radar and precision manufacturing technologies are "massive, well-planned and well-managed." In early 1983, the Senate was considering legislation to prevent the USSR from acquiring U.S. technology and to strengthen technology controls. In a speech to the Senate on February 2, 1983, Senator Nunn said that "by relying on American technical development, the Soviets save time, resources and tremendous amounts of research and development costs." Little of this U.S. technology is then devoted to consumer products or used to enhance the lives of the Soviet people. Said Nunn: "Instead, they make military applications of it in virtually every instance. This total emphasis upon their war-making capabilities forces us to upgrade our own military capability . . . *Like a 'Catch-22,' we thereby end up by competing with our own technology.*"[2]

The question for us is how can the United States achieve—if, indeed, it is achievable—a secure intelligence system that can be trusted to supply the data requisite for optimal decision making? Intelligence is required because the risk of surprise to the United States must be averted and because surprise is an integral part of Soviet military and strategic doctrine.[3]

To create a secure intelligence system, we must first understand the intentions of the opponent against whom the system is directed and who, in turn, is directing his system against us. We must understand the operational code of the Soviets as, one hopes, they understand ours. The question of intentions can be applied tactically and strategically as well as politically. For example, Rear Admiral G. W. MacKay in a comparison of the two navies has asked: "Why is the Soviet Union, historically a continental, land-oriented power, so concerned with having a formidable navy when all the strategic raw materials it needs are already available within its borders?" There can be only one answer for their ever-increasing naval superiority, on and under the ocean, says Admiral MacKay: to give the Soviet navy and especially its submarine forces, the ability to destroy the United States' ability to keep the seas open for free passage.[4]

There can also be a political answer regarding the ultimate intentions of the Soviet Union toward the West and, specifically, toward the only equivalent superpower, the United States. It is at this point that real differences in interpreting Soviet intentions begin to appear, that is, between those who take a benign view of the Soviet Union and those who are inclined to pessimism. On the difference between these two assessments will depend the nature of and investment in a national intelligence establishment.

Quite likely there can be no final judgment on Soviet intentions because of the paucity of information from sources inside the Kremlin. As Malcolm Toon, former U.S. ambassador to the USSR, once said, ". . . the only experts on the Soviet Union are those who sit on the Politburo in Moscow. The rest of us have varying degrees of ignorance."[5] Yet interpretations of Soviet actions must be made and accompanied by decisions on national policy in the years ahead. It is important to know Soviet priorities and options so that we can determine politico-military policies and, especially, the thrust of U.S. intelligence. The Soviet Union confronts enormous problems—its economy; relations with Eastern Europe, southwest Asia, China, and the Middle East; the East-West arms balance; the nationalities question; and technological competition with the United States. One can list many more, but which problems enjoy the Politburo's priorities and which are secondary?[6]

U.S. intelligence suffered serious wounds during the late 1960s and 1970s. Tragically, some of these wounds were self-inflicted, although Senator Barry Goldwater (R., Ariz.) argues that "every one of these wounds was inflicted by the President of the United States both Republican and Democrat. They were the ones who ordered the Agency to do things that were not only against the law, but against common sense." These breaches seriously weakened U.S. intelligence and, especially, counterintelligence at a time of crisis over Soviet foreign and military policy moves and the seemingly endless divisions within the Atlantic Alliance.[7]

With the election in 1980 of President Reagan, a full-scale attempt was made to narrow what had become without doubt an "intelligence gap" between the two countries. It was widely recognized by spring 1983 that CIA Director William Casey was "overseeing the biggest peacetime buildup in the American intelligence community since the early 1950s." At a time when retrenchment was the order of the day for other agencies, the CIA and its fellow intelligence organizations were "enjoying boom times . . . [The CIA had] become the fastest growing major agency in the Federal government, according to Administration budget officials." So reported the *New York Times* in an article based on interviews with Director Casey and other intelligence officials.[8]

The Reagan administration was proceeding on what may be regarded as easily verifiable assumptions about Soviet intentions. Détente or no détente, SALT I, II, or III negotiations or not, nuclear freeze or not, deployment of this missile or that missile—Soviet designs against the Western democracies are intended to weaken them, particularly the United States; to transform the Western alliance into a crumbling, dispirited structure of second-class powers whose populations are terrorized by nuclear threats from the Kremlin while Western commercial and banking interests, fearful of their investments in the communist bloc and Third World, are grateful donors to an overburdened Soviet economy.

The basis for this particular belief about Soviet intentions is that the Soviet Union is not like any other conventional power. It is prepared to move militarily whenever its inner dynamics demand and whenever it feels secure that its aggression will meet ineffective resistance. To further its policies, it is prepared to use any tactic, any stratagem, as part of its greater strategy of world conquest, an inevitable concomitant of its Marxist-Leninist-Stalinist heritage.[9] As part of that strategy, the Soviet Union has revealed a tremendous potential to insinuate its agents into the intelligence bodies of the democratic countries and an enormous ability to manipulate democratic public opinion,[10] an ability to cultivate, on the highest levels of democratic culture and politics, understanding and willing dupes supportive of Soviet foreign policy aims and military buildups.[11]

Beyond all this is the Soviet audacity in November 1982 in promoting Yuri Andropov, longtime head of the KGB, to be general secretary of the Soviet communist party, an action that portends even greater peril for the democracies.

These designs and intentions of the Soviet Union can be the only basis for a theory of intelligence. If the Soviet Union is regarded as just another power, as some historians and publicists regarded Nazi Germany before 1939, then the need for intelligence services capable of dealing with domestic as well as overseas infiltration by communist powers is indeed exaggerated and, therefore, to be opposed. That is not the opinion of the present writer.[12] Despite the buildup in early 1983 of Yuri Andropov as a "closet liberal," I see no possibility that he will repeal the Brezhnev Doctrine, which legitimized military intervention into any "socialist" country regardless of geography or popular resistance to the USSR. I can see that under Andropov and his successors, intervention into a nonsocialist country could be justified if it "threatened" a socialist country allied to the Soviet Union.

The most formidable problem that faces the needed rebuilding of U.S. intelligence structure is that leading intellectual-cultural opinion, especially in the media, seems to live by two perceptions. (1) Suspicion about the Soviet Union is dangerous because it can lead to military confrontation; the Pentagon and other military propagandists exaggerate such suspicions in order to increase military appropriations; besides there is little to choose between Soviet and U.S. behavior.[13] (2) Intelligence agencies can too easily become rogue elephants, and, therefore, must continually be exposed in public for the dangers they represent to freedom. Although it is not often stated publicly, there may be a powerful undercurrent of opinion that it is better to have no CIA than one that endangers freedom.

Such perceptions arise from misperceptions about Soviet strategic thinking and actions, actions that are ignored in the media despite a certain amount of initial attention: Afghanistan, Poland, Eritrea, Surinam, Cuba, Nicaragua, Soviet-Bulgarian secret police relations. Soviet aggression becomes routinized, and old misperceptions die hard. As Professor Richard Pipes has written:

> When we deal with Soviet strategic doctrine, we tend to think in terms of contrasts rather than interrelationships. We view, for example, "deterrence" as the opposite of "war fighting." It is not.

> In Soviet thinking, deterrence is an intrinsic part of war fighting. We view defensive weapons as being different from offensive weapons. The Russians do not . . . Our methodology prevents us from understanding that the Russians, in marked contrast to American thought, do not see a real antithesis between war and peace.[14]

As the United States and its allies enter the mid-1980s and while present and future politico-military dangers multiply, those who accept the need of a secure and strong intelligence establishment in the same way that they accept the need for deterrent military force and collective security against the Soviet Union must address certain fundamental questions:[15]

1. Do U.S. intelligence agencies have the proper tools to combat Soviet intelligence?
2. What kind of mix should there be between technological and human methods of intelligence—in intelligence jargon, HUMINT as against ELINT, COMINT, and SIGINT?[16]
3. Have the leaks and revelations in the 1970s about U.S. intelligence activities injured the United States' ability to nurture and keep useful foreign intelligence assets?
4. Is it possible to improve intelligence estimates and analysis, one of the most important aspects of intelligence and yet one that professionals and informed outsiders agree the CIA did rather badly in the past?[17]

It is, of course, easy to say no to the first question, debate endlessly the second, say yes to the third but doubt that a democratic society can ever create an intelligence agency capable of meeting U.S. security requirements. In regard to question 4, it is fairly easy to demonstrate that secret intelligence and an open democratic society are almost mutually exclusive. And if they are mutually exclusive it means that Soviet penetration of the intelligence community may be inevitable.[18]

It is not too well known that during the 1970s and for several years thereafter, covert actions by the CIA had to be reported to eight congressional committees and their staffs, a total of 163 persons. None of them, by the way, were required to take lie-detector tests as are CIA and other intelligence service employees.[19]

Covert action is only one of the four elements of intelligence, the other three being clandestine collection, counterintelligence, and analysis-estimates. Clandestine collection is what is popularly called espionage, which means the use of human sources and technical devices like microphones emplaced by humans.[20] Counterintelligence is the national effort to inhibit foreign intelligence services and foreign-controlled political movements, often supported by intelligence services, from infiltrating U.S. institutions and establishing the "potential to engage in espionage, subversion, terrorism and sabotage."[21] Covert action describes an activity or event, occurring generally in the public domain and observable by those who happen to be at hand. The covertness lies in the relationship between the instigator or sponsor and "some hidden, unacknowledged, authority or source of assistance." The aim of covert action is get something done that is compatible with or directly serves a country's interests. Almost invariably the covert action is believed by those who carry it out to be compatible with their own interests.[22]

Within the intelligence community, analysis-estimates are the most controversial element because the same information can lead to different conclusions and clashing predictions. And the reason for these disparities in conclusions and predictions is that there is never enough "information" and sometimes too much "disinformation." Sherman Kent, a former chief of the CIA's Office of National Estimates, once observed: "Estimating is what you do when you do. not know."[23]

There seems to be little question that the CIA, even before the many exposés about its activities, had made serious errors in its estimates of the Soviet Union's military ambitions and of other areas, like the stability of the Shah's regime in Iran.[24] The debate over why the CIA was so wrong (and it may be an unbalanced attack because we do not know when and where its estimates were on target) is endless, ranging from suspicions about a Soviet mole in the agency to the portentous cry about "politicization" of CIA analysis-estimates. These arguments are probably unresolvable since it may happen that one analyst's "politicization" may be another analyst's "reality."

I think that there should be better analysis-estimates in the CIA, and there seems to be a consensus that the Casey regime is doing much to improve this process, of which his predecessor, Admiral Stansfield Turner, thought very little. Realistically, however, analysis-estimates about the Soviet Union will always be guesstimates. After all, if Lavrenti Beria, onetime head of the Soviet secret police, could not predict his downfall and execution in 1953 and Nikita S. Khrushchev could not predict his own dethronement in October 1964—and, *ex officio,* they had access to the highest sources of information—it becomes difficult to blame the CIA for missing so much about Soviet internal and external policies.

There is an additional problem faced by the CIA analyst. He may be excluded from essential information obtained by the very executives who presumably depend on the validity of his estimates. For example, then Secretary of State Kissinger was criticized for "crippling U.S. intelligence by refusing to keep analysts informed of his intimate conversations with foreign leaders. To do so, however, would have created the possibility of leaks and might thereby have crippled his diplomatic maneuvers."[25] In other words, it was in the interest of the policymaker to keep his intelligence analysts in the dark.

Under President Reagan, there have been some changes, at best marginal, in the intelligence community under CIA Director Casey, the community's statutory head. (On an executive level, there are two new faces in the Casey cabinet, but whether they have any real power is yet to be seen.) These changes are far from the complete reorganization of the agency that some observers have claimed. Whatever changes have been made, it seems doubtful that they will soon improve the operations or effectiveness of the agency, certainly not in regard to national estimates about Soviet intentions, an assignment that the CIA has never really done well, according to competent sources.[26] One problem in this regard is that the CIA has never successfully decided what information the agency wants its collectors to bring in. Collectors who are unsure of what is wanted will either bring too little or too much, which can be as useless as too little.

Of one thing, however, we can be sure: a new approach to recruitment is an essential for U.S. intelligence. By "better," I mean that the system of higher education has fallen woefully behind in training people, not necessarily for intelligence appointments, but in language skills and areas studies. Admiral Inman has decried the fact that "we're far short of the skills and trained manpower that we're going to need for the coming decade."[27] The intelligence gap between the Soviet Union and the United States cannot be bridged without trained U.S. personnel. To recruit people into CIA, standards have been lowered, an obvious obstacle to improving CIA performance. The recruitment itself could also be improved if those in charge went outside the normal "intelligence culture" milieu, which means recruitment outside middle and upper middle-class individuals. CIA recruiters have traditionally ignored other sectors of the population.

The agency problem is compounded by the fact that the lead time needed to train the analyst or the collector is anywhere from five to ten years; yet the shortage of educated young people grows annually, not only in the humanities and the social sciences but also in the natural sciences and engineering.

A second concern is that it is not enough to have an oversight function in the Congress. I would urge that trusted outside specialists be brought into the CIA for particular assignments focused on CIA estimates. The outside experts would be given access to the same CIA material on which CIA estimates were based, and they would be asked to confirm or disallow them. Such a practice was used in 1976 under President Ford, and it should be institutionalized.[28]

Dangerous years lie ahead for the United States and its allies in Europe and Asia. The facts, the ideology, the aspirations, the designs of the Soviet Union are no mystery to anyone who reads and sees. What it takes is will. The first test is whether the United States is prepared to create—anew—an effective intelligence service and whether the Congress will allow this service to function without niggling hindrance.

Intelligence is important in the nuclear age because it can preclude confrontation and eye-blinking tests. An overwhelmingly capable Soviet KGB unmatched by an equally capable U.S. intelligence community could raise doubts that the United States will be able to defend its allies, even if it has the will. Those doubts have already been raised by those, and not only Soviet leaders, who believe that the laws of history point in the direction of a Marxist-Leninist-Stalinist victory.

A turnaround in U.S. policies about intelligence has begun. Will that turnaround last? Intelligence rearmament—ever-flowing and dependable information about Soviet intentions and activities—must be regarded just as much a priority for foreign policy in the 1980s as military rearmament and missile deployment are now. Thrashing about in quagmires may be an inevitable and dramatic end for the uninformed dinosaur. Such a fate would not be seemly for a democratic superpower on whom the free world depends for its ultimate safety.

Notes

1. The CIA's intelligence-gathering system included the Rhyolite and Argus satellites, among other systems. These were used to intercept telemetry signals transmitted by Soviet missiles during test launchings. It must be assumed that as soon as the Soviets knew the inner workings and signals of the Rhyolite and Argus, they took countermeasures—physical camouflage of defense sites during transit of these satellites or transmission of false data. Some six months after the arrest of Boyce and Lee, the Soviets began encoding telemetry signals, thus making satellite verification impossible. Senator Moynihan appeared on the CBS news program, "60 Minutes"; see report in *New York Times*, November 22, 1982, p. 8. SALT II was signed by Carter and Brezhnev in June 1979, but the treaty failed to win Senate approval after

the Soviet invasion of Afghanistan. For a detailed chronicle of the Boyce-Lee penetration and how they were caught, see Robert Lindsey, *The Falcon and the Snowman* (New York: Simon & Schuster, 1979).

2. *New York Times*, February 23, 1983, p. 12.

3. John G. Hines and Philip A. Petersen, "Strategies of Soviet Warfare," *Wall Street Journal*, January 7, 1983, p. 26; see also John Erickson, "The Soviet Military Potential for Surprise Attack: Surprise, Superiority and Time," in Robert L. Pfaltzgraff, Uri Ra'anan, and Warren Milberg, eds., *Intelligence Policy and National Security* (Hamden, Conn.: Archon, 1981), pp. 49–73.

4. Quoted in Paul Ciotti, "The Enemy Offshore," *California*, August 1982, p. 53; see also Drew Middleton, "Soviet in Asia: Navy Buildup in the Pacific," *New York Times*, December 30, 1982; and idem, "War Against Subs: West Hones Skills," *New York Times*, January 16, 1983.

5. Quoted in *Proceedings, U.S. Naval Institute* 108/10/956 (October 1982): 107.

6. John P. Roche has asked: "How do you decide, for example, the question, 'What are they planning?' Well, that is an interesting question; maybe they are not planning anything. Maybe sometimes they are just as confused as we are. Maybe they are playing by ear. You have to be leery of the notion that there is *a* plan, what I call the reification of uncertainty. It is easy, too easy, to discern a massive master plan when, in fact, they may have a general purpose, but they have not yet figured out the fine print." ("Intelligence Problems as Viewed from the White House," in Pfaltzgraff, Ra'anan, and Milberg, *Intelligence Policy*, p. 270.)

7. Personal letter to the author from Senator Goldwater, chairman, Senate Intelligence Committee. See also Arnold Beichman, "Can Counterintelligence Come in from the Cold?" *Policy Review*, Winter 1981, pp. 93–102; and "Gentlemanly Spooks," *American Spectator*, April 1981, p. 32, in which I wrote: "I do not exonerate the CIA and the FBI from blame for the follies and excesses which were uncovered in this campaign against the CIA. Nor do I believe that these follies and excesses could have occurred without resolute 'blind eye' encouragement by Presidents Eisenhower, Kennedy, Johnson and Nixon." For a self-inflicted wound, see Thomas Braden, "I'm Glad the CIA Is Immoral," *Saturday Evening Post*, May 20, 1967, pp. 10–14. Braden was a top CIA executive who, on leaving the agency, told a great deal about the covert actions he had inspired and supervised.

8. Philip Taubman, "Casey and His C.I.A. On the Rebound: The Director Is Presiding over the Biggest Peacetime Buildup in the Intelligence Community in 30 Years, Even as the Agency Faces Continuing Questions from Critics About Its Intentions, Integrity and Capabilities," *New York Times Sunday Magazine*, January 16, 1983, pp. 20–21. The use of the word "peacetime" in the *Times* subtitle to the article is ambiguous when one thinks of the Soviet invasion of Afghanistan, events in Poland, the "monstrous" militarization of the Soviet Union and the threat to Western Eu-

rope, and the tremendous Soviet naval presence in the North Atlantic and the Pacific (see Leon Wieseltier, "The Great Nuclear Debate," *New Republic* 188:1–2 [January 10, 17, 1983]: 18ff).

9. Alexander Solzhenitsyn has written that "we would understand nothing about Communism if we tried to comprehend it on the principles of normal human reason. The driving force of Communism, as it was devised by Marx, is political power, power at any cost and without regard to human losses or a people's physical deterioration." ("The USSR at the Moment of Brezhnev's Death," *National Review*, January 21, 1983, p. 28; see also Leszek Kolakowski, "A General Theory of Sovietism," *Encounter* 60, no. 5 [May 1983]: 19–21.)

10. "Public resistance to deploying the new missiles in general and the 'peace' movement in particular are being fanned by a Russian 'peace' offensive which is being conducted with the skill and sophistication of Madison Ave." (*The Economist*, January 15, 1983, p. 57). See also Ronald Radosh, "The 'Peace Council' and Peace," *New Republic*, January 31, 1983, pp. 14–18.

11. Former U.S. ambassador to the Soviet Union Joseph Davies said that "Russia in self-defense has every moral right to seek atomic-bomb secrets through military espionage if excluded from such information by her former fighting allies." He made his statement coincident with the Canadian atomic spy scandal. (*New York Times*, February 19, 1946, p. 10.) Davies's book, *Mission to Moscow*, was a whitewash of the Stalinist regime and the purge trials.

12. Robert Conquest has written that "the error at the heart of most misapprehensions about international politics, and in particular the issue of disarmament, is misunderstanding of the attitudes and motives of the Soviet leadership . . . that the Politburo are unlikeable people, addicted to misleading doctrine, but nevertheless, 'rational' and willing to draw 'sensible' conclusions from the facts of the world situation . . . We must get these respectable stereotypes out of our minds." (*London Daily Telegraph,* November 13, 1982, p. 12.)

13. "A document describing the Russian system of exile and forced labor has been produced by the British Government and is to be placed before the United Nations," began a *New Yorker* commentary, which then discussed the growth of "a group of American political prisoners (who) are being marched steadily, imperceptibly, toward the queer Siberia of our temperate zone." The commentary, which equated the horrors of the Soviet Gulag with the U.S. political system, concluded that a report should be "placed before the UN reminding [us] that no country has a monopoly on political terror." (*New Yorker*, August 6, 1949.) A *New York Times* editorial (December 18, 1982) equated the Soviet KGB and the CIA while exculpating Yuri Andropov from any connection with the attempted assassination of the pope. "In a world of murderous bureaucracies," said the *Times*, "crimes of state are not so much ordered as implied. That Yuri Andropov willed an attack on John Paul II is possible but hardly proven. That his people became mired in a sleazy conspiracy on imagined authority is a likelihood Americans

should be the first to understand." See also Michael Ledeen, "The Bulgarian Connection and the Media," *Commentary*, 75, no. 6 (June 1983): 45–50. In the Never-Never-Land inhabited by *Times* editorial writers, there is a dream that one day a runaway Soviet Council of Ministers, defying the Politburo, will investigate Andropov and the shooting of the pope, just as the U.S. Senate did in its investigation of the CIA, and the Soviet investigation findings will be publicly printed and distributed in some ten volumes. Then we will know all we want to know about Andropov's "plot" against the pope.

14. Pfaltzgraff, Ra'anan, and Milberg, *Intelligence Policy*, pp. 78–79.

15. The intelligence establishment or community comprises the CIA, FBI, Defense Intelligence Agency (DIA), National Security Agency (NSA), the intelligence branches of the Army, Navy, Air Force, and Marines, intelligence units of the Treasury and Energy Departments, and the State Department Bureau of Intelligence and Research. The DIA was created in 1961 to unify Pentagon intelligence activities and to reduce the duplicative activities of the three service intelligence agencies. Instead, and in keeping with the laws of bureaucracy, these service agencies regenerated themselves. By 1971, they were larger than they had been before the DIA's inception. (See Richard K. Betts, "Analysis, War and Decision: Why Intelligence Failures Are Inevitable," *World Politics* 31, no. 1 [October 1978]: 79.)

16. Electronic intelligence (ELINT) is derived from the collection or interception and processing of foreign electromagnetic radiations such as radar. Communications intelligence (COMINT) is intelligence information derived from foreign communications, not including the foreign press, propaganda, or public broadcasts. Signals intelligence (SIGINT) involves the interception, processing, analysis, and dissemination of information derived from electrical communications and other signals. (Tyrus G. Fain, Katharine C. Plant, and Ross Milloy, eds., *The Intelligence Community* [New York: Bowker, 1977], p. 967.) Human intelligence (HUMINT), the preoccupation of the clandestine services, "is the process of extracting from others information or national assets they would not willingly part with under normal circumstances" (E. Drexel Godfrey, Jr., "Ethics and Intelligence," *Foreign Affairs*, April 1978, p. 629).

17. This paradigm is based on a paper presented by Dr. Michael M. Uhlmann, a former assistant attorney general in the Ford administration, at the Consortium for the Study of Intelligence (CSI), which was organized in 1979 by a group of scholars interested in national security policy, law, and values of an open society. Their primary interest, as professors of international relations and international law, was, among other things, to determine what steps might be taken to improve U.S. intelligence performance in the future. The CSI, under the auspices of the National Strategy Information Center, has brought together, in addition to scholars, intelligence specialists and other groups and individuals interested in this hitherto little studied subject. None of the CSI's meetings are classified, and all papers and subsequent discussions are publicly available through Transaction Books (New Brunswick,

N.J.). The Uhlmann paradigm is taken from the first CSI volume, Roy Godson, ed., *Intelligence Requirements for the 1980s: Elements of Intelligence*, p. 12.

18. William J. Casey, CIA director under President Reagan, has said: "I question very seriously whether a secret intelligence agency and a Freedom of Information Act can co-exist for very long. The willingness of foreign intelligence agencies and their services to share their information and to rely on us fully, and of individuals to risk their lives and reputations to help us, will continue to dwindle unless we get rid of the Freedom of Information Act . . . Secrecy is essential to any intelligence organization. Ironically, secrecy is accepted without protest in many areas of our society. Physicians, lawyers, clergymen, grand juries, journalists, income tax returns, crop futures—all have confidential aspects protected by law. Why should national security information be entitled to any less protection?" (*American Bar Association Intelligence Report*, October 1982, p. 6.)

19. Godson, *Elements*, p. 80. The House and Senate committees engaged in intelligence oversight were Select Committee on Intelligence, Foreign Relations, Appropriations, and Armed Services. Even though only two committees, one in the House and the other in the Senate, are now empowered to oversee the CIA, leaks still occur. Admiral Bobby R. Inman, (USN, Ret.), former director of the NSA and former deputy director of CIA, has said that there have been staff leaks from the Senate Intelligence Committee and offered to name names of the leakers. He criticized a House Intelligence Committee staff report on Central America and the CIA, which, he said, had been leaked several days before it was officially released. (*American Bar Association Committee on Law and National Security Intelligence Report* 4, no. 11 [November 1982]: 4.)

20. Not only is clandestine collection difficult in Eastern Europe and in the Soviet Union (technically called "denied areas"), but even the Third World countries "have been erecting their own barriers to outside inquiry of all types and thus hampering the activity of foreigners, especially Westerners, whether from the press, academic institutions or diplomatic representatives" (Henry Kamm, "The Third World Rapidly Turning into a Closed World for the Foreign Correspondent," *New York Times*, January 14, 1976, p. 12). See also Godson, *Elements*, p. 37, and Godson, *Clandestine Collection*, pp. 1–14. Godson is a professor of political science at Georgetown University and has been coordinator of the Consortium for the Study of Intelligence from its inception.

21. Newton S. Miller, "Counterintelligence," in Godson, *Elements*, p. 49. See also *Counterintelligence*, volume 5 in the series Intelligence Requirements for the 1980s (New Brunswick, N.J.: Transaction Books, 1982).

22. Hugh Tovar, "Covert Action," in Godson, *Elements*, p. 69. See also *Covert Action*, volume 4 in the series Intelligence Requirements (1981).

23. Quoted in *New Republic*, November 22, 1982, p. 36. See also Sherman Kent,

"Estimates and Influence: Some Reflections on What Should Make Intelligence Persuasive in Policy Deliberations," *Foreign Service Journal*, April 1969, pp. 16–18, 45. "Disinformation" (the Russian word is *maskirovka*) "is a well-designed message containing both true and false information, leaked to an opponent to deceive him. Disinformation is intended to dupe decisionmakers: politicians, intelligence and foreign policy experts, military strategists or scientists, rather than the public at large." (Ladislav Bittman, "Soviet *Bloc* 'Disinformation' and other 'Active Measures,' " in Pflatzgraff, Ra'anan, and Milberg, *Intelligence Policy*, p. 219.) Bittman spent fourteen years in the Czech intelligence service and left Czechoslovakia in August 1968 following the Soviet invasion.

24. "The CIA managed for more than a decade, to underestimate, significantly and systematically, the growth of Soviet military power" (Uhlmann, in Godson, *Elements*, p. 12). One reason, perhaps, for CIA misestimates could be the widely known "hostility of large numbers of senior intelligence analysts in CIA toward counterintelligence and sometimes toward the clandestine services" (ibid., p. 17). Without a properly functioning counterintelligence section, *maskirovka* by Soviet agents becomes fairly easy. See also Robert Wohlstetter, "Slow Pearl Harbors and the Pleasures of Deception," in Pfaltzgraff, Ra'anan, and Milberg, *Intelligence Policy*, p. 27; and, the important article by Abul Kasim Mansur, pseud., "The Crisis in Iran: Why the U.S. Ignored a Quarter Century of Warning," *Armed Forces International*, January 1979, pp. 26–33 (the author is a former State Department official with intimate experience in Iran). This article, written before the Khomeini revolution, makes fascinating reading. A change in U.S. policy about covert action, a practice heavily downgraded during the Carter administration, seemed to be in the offing in 1983 since Secretary of State George Shultz said he had no qualms about such operations if they were necessary (Bernard Gwertzman, "The Shultz Method," *New York Times Magazine*, January 2, 1983, p. 28).

25. Betts, "Analysis," p. 77.

26. For a devastating attack on CIA "misestimates," see Steven Rosefielde, *False Science: Underestimating the Soviet Arms Buildup* (New Brunswick, N.J.: Transaction Books, 1982), especially the "research summary," pp. 9–12. See also Arnold Beichman, "Does the CIA Know What It's Talking About?" *Washington Times*, March 1983, p. 10.

27. Inman, *Christian Science Monitor*, October 29, 1982, p. 13.

28. President Ford appointed a so-called Team B, headed by Professor Richard Pipes of Harvard University, a recognized expert on Soviet affairs. (He was from 1981 to 1982, senior adviser on Soviet affairs at the National Security Agency.) Team B used CIA data on the USSR to see if it arrived at the same conclusions as the agency. Team B disagreed strongly with the CIA findings, even though it used the same data. (Tom Ricks, "The Intelligence Gap," *New Republic*, November 22, 1982, p. 36.)

DATE DUE

MAY 03 1986			
~~MAY 05 1987~~			

DEMCO